FINDING EDEN

A PERILOUS QUEST FOR A SAFE MIGRANT HOMELAND

A Novel by Brad Dude

Publishing Services provided by Paper Raven Books LLC
Printed in the United States of America
First Printing, 2022

Paperback ISBN= 978-0-9964470-4-1

DEDICATION

To the brave and daring migrants and asylum-seekers who put themselves and their families in mortal danger to find a safe place to live.

ACKNOWLEDGEMENTS

A big thanks to Dr. D. Jones, B. Hosea, L. Dupuy at RumbleBrand Marketing & Design, and the many editors and readers of the first few drafts. An even bigger thanks to my wife, Sue, for her patience and support throughout the writing and publishing process.

FREE BONUS

Would you like an audio companion story to
"FINDING EDEN" narrated by the author? It's entitled,
"The Betrayal Aboard the Ralik-Ratak"

Available for FREE here:
https://braddude.com/findingeden/bonus

FINDING EDEN

CHARACTERS

MV RALIK-RATAK (Shipwrecked)
Captain Tareq Kara
First Mate Aroche
Amman Boulas
Akila Samar
Issa Blaise
Fariji Sarr
Imam Ashraf Agha
Hassan Alwan
Mohamed Aboud

MV YAP ISLANDER (Arrived one year later)
Captain Hassan Al Bourké
Desta Kado
Awa Niame
Ada Niame
Chiké Niame
Jay Rawal
Balla Mendy
Ahmed

MV MILITOBI (Present day)

Captain Anna Kruger
First Officer Jorge Estrada
Navigator Gabby Fernandez
Helmsman
Radio Operator
Chief Engineer
Okeke Ka
Mohammed Kassab
Ashé Gaye
Lulu Gaye
Dr. Arun Rao
Esha Rao

SANTA INEZ ISLAND PIRATES

Commandant Rafael Delgado
Lucia Santos
Alonso Rivera
Bartolo Molina

TABLE OF CONTENTS

FINDING EDEN

"Wherever my travels may lead, paradise is where I am."

-Voltaire

PROLOGUE

Cruising at twenty knots per hour, the speedboats should have taken just over five hours to reach the anticipated location of the large freighter, however dense fog required a slowdown that added another hour to the trip. Rafael Delgado, the pirate leader, ordered all boats lashed together as they waited in the damp fog. Lucia Santos, second-in-command, checked the radar constantly for nearly an hour before reporting that the ship was now heading their way. Delgado's lead boat pushed slowly ahead with the others close behind, not wanting to get lost in the ever-thickening soup of gray fog.

They heard it seconds before they saw it. The MV *Ralik-Ratak*, a 3,000-ton freighter, appeared not fifty yards away as it swept through the dark choppy waters at slow speed. Delgado triggered his stolen police siren and flashing blue light. A spotlight from the ship bathed the three Bayline speed boats and *Luhrs Tournament 350* fishing boat in a diffused yellow aura made all the more eerie by the swirling fog. Delgado shouted a *heave to* order through an electronic megaphone. Within minutes an accommodation ladder was winched down the port side and all four of Delgado's boats tied up at its lowest rung. The pirates scurried aboard as the obese pirate leader struggled to climb the ladder's steps.

The top deck of the *Ralik-Ratak* was jammed with hundreds of migrants, yet all were oddly serene and motionless as they stared blankly at Delgado and his motley crew of cutthroats. Many sat together on the deck and remained unnaturally silent, as if awaiting a judge's final pronouncement of guilt or innocence. Lucia immediately sensed danger and motioned for the rest of the pirates to spread out over the ship. Delgado scanned the deck. Tarps obviously erected for protection from the rain and wind were ripped and torn, some completely shredded and sprayed with bullet holes. The men and women sitting on the deck appeared to be in shock. A thirty-year-old Libyan, Amman Boulas, who had been sitting beside a young Arab woman stepped forward, almost in a state of semi-consciousness.

"You are police? You will rescue us?"

Boulas was dressed in torn and bloodstained pants and a ripped white shirt with blood splattered across his chest.

"Yes, of course," Delgado lied, continuing to survey the deck and the glassy-eyed passengers. "What happened here? Where is the Captain?"

Boulas bowed his head and spoke in slow English, "Sorry, he is dead. They are dead."

The pirates returned from scouring the vessel and gestured to Lucia that they found no other ship's crewmen. She rejoined Delgado and just caught the Libyan's last word.

"Dead? Who is dead?" Lucia asked.

Boulas took a deep breath before answering, "The Captain... the crew, everybody is dead. They were very evil. They killed us."

Delgado and Lucia exchanged a questioning glance.

"They *all* tried to kill you? Where are they? Who is left?" Delgado asked, glancing around the deck.

Boulas shook his head in a matter-of-fact manner. "We... they are over the side."

"Who is in command of this ship?" Delgado demanded.

"No one; the ship is autopilot, sir. One passenger was military and up in your bridge."

Lucia immediately headed aft.

"No wonder you are so far off course," Delgado said. "We almost missed you in this fog. Thank God we found you!"

Akila Samar, the young Arab woman who sat with Boulas, joined the Libyan carpenter and reminded him in Arabic of their mission.

"Oh, yes," Boulas explained to Delgado. "We are going Canary Islands. We are asylum there. Can you help us?" Regaining his senses, Boulas scanned the men and women of Delgado's pirate gang. "You are police, right? Military?"

Delgado nodded. "Of course, my friend. I am Commandant Rafael Delgado. You are now under my command and protection." He turned to three of his pirates and whispered orders.

"Search all the cabins. There must be drugs or cash around here. And check for weapons." Delgado gestured at all the passengers who continued to stare out blankly from their seated positions on the main deck. The fog now shrouded them like living corpses and sent a chill down the pirate's spine. "Where are all these people from and what's wrong with them?"

Boulas responded in a calm voice, "We are Libya, Egypt, Burkina, Morocco, and we are Pakistanis and many, many Africans. We are very quiet because—"

He was interrupted by Akila Samar who was now fully in control of herself. "Because we are afraid we will all be in trouble for what we have done. But sir, these were bad men who attacked us. They killed many. Women...even children."

Boulas stood closer to Akila, as if protecting her from additional danger. "We fought them, Commandant," she explained. "Many of them were ex-military. The Captain said he was an officer. They had knives and there were guns, many guns. They shot at us but we fought back."

Amman Boulas took over the story, "We knew they are smugglers, sir. But even wounded they shot. They are shooting and shooting. We...we pushed them over the side."

"There was nothing more we could do," added Akila. "They would have killed everyone."

Delgado sighed and considered the situation. "I see. I see. No matter, they were smugglers. They deserved to die! They deserved what they got. Terrible business," he said. "Just terrible but you are all safe now. You are...you are under my protection, er, stand-by." Relieved, Boulas and Akila returned to sit with the other passengers.

On the bridge, Lucia Santos pushed aside the Nigerian migrant who now captained the ship and found the radar unit smashed beyond repair. It looked as if the entire navigational console had been sprayed repeatedly with machine gun fire. Wedged between two tables she found an empty weapon and held it up to the migrant captain.

"Any more ammunition for this?" she asked.

He shrugged in response. "I do not know."

"What about the radio?" Before the Nigerian could respond, Lucia donned a pair of headphones and listened. She twisted a dial to pick up VHF chatter and leaned forward when she heard the dissonant crackle of static. Tuning the radio dials again, she listened closely until her eyes widened in surprise. Lucia slammed down the headphones and faced the migrant. "Did you send a signal to the authorities? Did you call for help?"

He nodded. "I tried. I did not know how to work this type of radio, so I made a distress call after I put the ship on autopilot."

Clutching the empty machine gun, Lucia raced from the bridge and scampered down the stairs leading to the main deck.

"It's the Spanish!" Lucia shouted at Delgado, who was talking with several other pirates near the port railing. "It's the Maritime Rescue Service. They are about an hour away. We should go." Several more pirates rejoined Delgado who turned to face them.

"Have you found anything? Drugs, weapons, money? We need money!" Delgado fumed.

The men bowed their heads indicating failure, but Lucia held up her weapon. "I found this, but we must get going! Let's get to our boats."

Delgado stopped for a moment and held up his hand. He had an idea. He pointed to individual pirates. "Wait! You two get to the bridge and try to get this ship underway. Head northwest at full speed and disengage any tracking devices."

Lucia was puzzled. "North takes us away from the Canaries. Away from home."

"That's the idea," said Delgado. "Let's use this fog and go where no one expects us to go. Get some men down in the engine room. Leave our boats tied up where they are. We can drag them along with us. This is our ship now."

Lucia was shocked. "We're taking the *whole* ship?"

"The whole ship!"

The MV *Ralik-Ratak* got underway and within fifteen minutes was heading into open ocean under the cover of an impenetrable fog. Many of Delgado's pirates had never been farther away from the Canaries than fifteen miles, and that was when they had hijacked their first freighter a year earlier. The fog had now gotten even thicker, and Lucia tried to persuade Delgado to reduce speed, but he wouldn't hear of it. The farther away from the Spanish authorities the better, he had told her with his usual air of superiority that was increasingly gnawing at her soul. "Don't worry, Lucia. I will keep my promise to you."

From the bridge, Lucia monitored the VHF channel while Delgado announced to the passengers they were being temporarily taken to shelter in a safer place than the Canary Islands. He explained to both Boulas and Akila, truthfully for a change, that asylum-seekers were no longer allowed in the Canaries. He told them not to worry and that he, Commandant Delgado, would take full responsibility for their care and safety.

In the wee morning hours, still surrounded by a moist blanket of fog, the ship smashed into an uncharted reef and shuddered to a noisy, grinding stop. The violent collision threw sleeping passengers and dozing pirates hard to the deck. Delgado banged his right knee into a railing and was momentarily paralyzed with severe pain. On the bridge, Lucia and two other pirates were slammed into each other but shielded themselves from falling debris and shattering glass with an overturned chart table.

Listing to port, and water flooding below decks, the ship's rudder and engine suffered catastrophic damage. Ocean swells repeatedly lifted the ship then dropped it ferociously across the sharp coral immobilizing it forever. Passengers slowly regained their footing in the dark. The crying and wailing of women and children echoed throughout the dying ship.

Over the next few terrifying hours, passengers and pirates alike steadied themselves against the ship's crumpled superstructure. They trudged through ankle-deep water flooding the main passageway to the top deck where they huddled together and waited for daylight.

As dawn broke, the shipwreck survivors were amazed to find one of the most beautiful sights imaginable. Not five hundred yards away, and bathed in bright morning sunlight, stood Santa Inez Island. The lush emerald green isle luxuriated in tall palms, thick banyan trees and succulent vegetation. White, fluffy clouds swirled around the verdant mountain peaks. The soothing sounds of waterfalls could just barely be heard in the far distance.

The island was surrounded by a wide coral reef with a moat-like blue lagoon caressing its sandy shore. A wide pass through the reef to the lagoon lay some twenty-five yards to starboard from the wreck of the *Ralik-Ratak*. They had just missed it.

CHAPTER 1

TWO YEARS LATER, WELCOME TO SEA-SWEEP

It was an online newspaper article that first intrigued Anna Kruger about the private search and rescue group called Sea-Sweep, out of Regensburg, Germany. Her subsequent research revealed they owned a converted cargo runner that she suspected was under 4,000 tons. The MV *Militobi* had a mission to rescue as many migrants as possible from smugglers at sea or through arranged pickups at secret ports all across North Africa. They would then cross the Mediterranean to seek asylum in various European countries. Crews risked years of imprisonment and fines of up to a million Euros, if caught by local Coast Guards, while the migrants themselves could be arrested and held in detention camps for up to eighteen months to await deportation back to their home countries.

For many asylum-seekers, deportation meant a death sentence. For Anna Kruger, such missions reminded her of Grandfather Dirk's advice to help those in need, if it was within your power. Anyway, she was bored with the way her life had become. Over the years she had signed on as a First Officer and then eventually made Captain on a number of tramp steamers and freighters all over the world. Sea-Sweep was an opportunity she could not pass up.

Responding immediately by email to the non-profit's job opening for an experienced sea captain, Anna arrived in

Regensburg within a month. Two weeks later she was named Captain of the MV *Militobi*. Her crew consisted of Spanish, German, and Italian sailors, all committed to risking their lives to help those fleeing poverty and persecution. She felt she had finally found a place worthy enough to call home.

Soccer and sailing had been the two most important aspects of Anna Kruger's life growing up in the German village of Freiburg, two miles from the rocky shores of the frigid North Sea. She remembered with special fondness those wonderful weekends with her grandfather on his sailboat, *Gitane*. Four times each year they would sail down the nearby Jade River. Each voyage provided her with more opportunity, and responsibility, for guiding the sleek forty-two foot ketch along the fourteen-mile channel.

Orphaned when she was twelve, Dirk Kruger had become both her mother and father following the passing of his wife, Brigitte. Besides sailing, Dirk had taught Anna three important rules for living a life with strong values. First, he would say, you needed an education, second, you needed to be bi-lingual in English at a minimum, and finally, you needed to help those who were either unable to help themselves or did not have an opportunity to do so. For those you could not help, he said you just say a simple prayer.

At college in the picturesque town of Elsfleth, Anna studied nautical science at Jade University's School of Applied Sciences where she minored in English. It was in her advanced English class that she met Hans, a Dutch engineering student, and had her first full-blown love affair. They would stroll the quaint, 700-student campus hand-in-hand and often ended up downtown at a café or restaurant where Hans would teach her dirty words in Dutch. Their relationship, and love, lasted but a single school year, which shattered Hans, yet Anna took in stride. She doubled down on her studies and focused on obtaining practical sea experience. As part of her program, Anna interned on a container ship during the summer while Hans headed back to Holland to care for his aging parents. She loved being back at sea. As her nostrils filled with the North Atlantic's tangy salt sea air, she immediately recalled the *Gitane* and visualized her grandfather's wiry frame and tanned skin, nearly wizened from years in the sun. Hard work and long sea hours kept Anna's mind off Hans, although during some of the more lonely times, a few of the tall, young seamen reminded her of him. Her skipper, Captain Herman Koch, felt it his duty to watch out for the pretty German intern and assigned her a variety of duties aboard ship that gave her a wide variety of practical experiences and, most importantly, kept her protected from some of his more worldly crew members.

Sometimes Anna's duties required her bringing coffee to the bridge or submitting updated reports to the Second Officer during his eight-hour watch. Other times, she worked with the Chief Safety Officer sorting through forgotten storage containers of old fire prevention equipment. What she liked most, however, was when she was assigned duty on the bridge. That was where Captain Koch showed her how to *drive* the ship. There were actually only three ways. The first was to take the wheel in your own hands and steer it. The second was to put the ship on autopilot then correct for wind and current, as necessary. The third was to use the computer. The Voyage Management System, or VMS as it was called, was an ultra-modern navigational tool that scanned paper charts like one would an applicant's resume on a computer. The VMS, like a glorified desktop printer, would then reproduce a direct course and add a fine red line from point A to point B. You just followed the red line. Captain Koch laughed when Anna admitted to him one night that she preferred the first method. He preferred it too.

During her senior year, Anna became a successful intramural girls soccer team coach. Although she found coaching young girls extraordinarily stimulating and satisfying, especially when they won the school championship, Anna felt most happy aboard ship. *Well,* she thought, *Grandfather always said to explore as many opportunities and interests as possible.* On the field of play, whether designing a surprise counterattacking strategy or playing midfielder herself, Anna experienced wins, losses, and sometimes complete failures. Each afforded her an opportunity to develop the discipline, self-awareness, and courage she and her girls needed at that stage of their lives—the stage when personal character was formed.

Anna coached her team the way her grandfather had coached her aboard the *Gitane*: she stressed the need to learn the rules of the game, she stressed the need to learn and practice English and other languages beside German, and, most importantly, she stressed the need for teamwork and for helping those who could not help themselves. She also urged her players to be proactive and to develop confidence in their own abilities. Teamwork, she believed, would always be an essential ingredient to any success—whether in the world of business, the military, government service, or even volunteer work. She also believed that while Germany continued to be a male-dominated society,

German women were strong, intelligent, and could do anything that a man could do—usually better!

Anna graduated with a bachelor's degree in Nautical Science Studies and immediately earned her third mate's license. Armed with Captain Koch's recommendation and top marks in celestial navigation, advanced firefighting, hands-on engineering, and four successful summer training cruise internships, she qualified for her first job on the container ship MV *Fairwood Atlantic* out of Hamburg. Her job was ensuring that 1,000-ton containers were balanced and securely moored to the deck. Twelve weeks on and twelve weeks off kept Anna extremely busy, but she was able to visit her ailing grandfather a few days before he passed away at the age of seventy-eight. Anna was grateful that before assuming duties aboard the *Fairwood* she had been able to get him back aboard the *Gitane* one last time and had entertained him with her own sea stories, just as he had regaled her as a young girl with epic tales of great storms, dangerous sea rescues, and sunken treasure.

Anna Kruger spent the next five years learning the practical lessons that only long hours of actual experience aboard a ship could teach, including an understanding of the importance of crew morale. Her onboard successes resulted in rapid promotions. By the age of twenty-six, Anna had risen to Second Officer where she stood her own eight-hour watches and once, during a summer voyage, was pleased that coffee had been served *to her* by another female intern from Jade University.

At thirty-two, Anna was promoted to a Deputy Captain position that enabled her to hone navigation and charting skills while developing an ability to communicate and work more effectively with international crews. She was beloved by all of them, especially the Spanish and Filipino sailors who teased her when she bought several rounds of drinks for them after returning late to port one evening. Anna laughed when they joked about her strict disciplinary approach to managing ship operations and wisecracked that it was because of her German heritage. She teased them right back.

Alessandro Garono, her Captain, had never sailed with a female deputy before but was won over by Anna's professionalism and navigation skills. She overheard him once speaking in his halting English and strong Italian accent to his First Officer about how strange it was sailing with a woman, but he *believed* in Anna, he had said. She had proven herself to be an effective leader. Captain Garono added that he was *proud* to have sailed with her. Anna was more than thrilled.

At thirty-seven, Anna Kruger was promoted to full Captain. She had now served on all seven classes of cargo and container ships and had even spent six months as First Officer on a luxury cruise line. However, attending cocktail parties and speaking at Captain's Table dinners while pretending to enjoy herself among the very rich, got old very quickly for Anna. She could not help but compare the lifestyles of wealthy European and American tourists with the poor and desperate of India, Pakistan, Egypt, and East Africa, whom she had met during her travels.

With the passing of her grandfather, Anna had very little reason for returning to Frieburg. Her cousin now lived in the old house with his own family. He had Anna's contact numbers and could always reach her if he ever needed to, but somehow Anna believed he never would. They were not all that close anyway, and she expected nothing more than a card at Christmas with a family photo that usually included their chihuahua, Heidi. An enclosed form letter summarizing the family's activities for the year would be the only contact Anna would ever have with her remaining family. It suited her. She was content to lead a solitary life at sea. The drama of family entanglements was to be avoided at all costs, in her mind. Anyway, she was too busy with the rigors of managing 85,000-ton ships laden with nearly 14,000 twenty-foot long containers, often in rough seas with howling winds and torrential rain.

Over the following years, Anna Kruger captained several cargo vessels for Euro-Maritime Shipping between Rotterdam and Frederikstad, Norway. Her favorite route was the two-week Norwegian run from Rotterdam to Bodo, with stops in Bergen, Flore, and Trondheim. The long trip enabled Anna to reflect upon her career, her future, and her entire life, especially her non-existent love life. She had dated occasionally while living in her Rotterdam studio apartment in the Feijenoord neighborhood near the port, but there was never anyone serious. At sea most of the year, it was nearly impossible to maintain a healthy relationship, or any relationship.

Once starting at Sea-Sweep, Anna was surrounded by eligible men. Tall and very blond Germans, short and swarthy Italians, thin sailors from the Philippines, and distinguished Spaniards. This included a muscled and extremely handsome First Officer from Barcelona named Jorge Estrada. The Catalan had learned his seafaring skills after graduating from the

Educacíon Secundaria Obligatoria at sixteen. He immediately entered the *Ciclos Formativos de Grado Superior* secondary school and his academic success entitled him to automatic acceptance at the Barcelona School of Nautical Studies. His life was changed forever the moment he realized that a seafarer's career would take him all over the world and, happily, away from the troubled streets of Barcelona.

Estrada earned a degree in Nautical Science and Maritime Transport, focusing on ship systems, power plants, and the design and construction of vessels. He was a hands-on student and opted for on-board internships to learn first-hand about navigational maneuvers, ship safety, and the handling of special cargos. Many summer internships were available since Barcelona's harbor was the world's ninth largest container port and a regular cruise ship destination. Estrada took advantage of these opportunities and decided he would one day become a ship's captain.

Jorge Estrada's teenage years of street fighting and avoiding Barcelona's neighborhood gangs piqued his interest in on-board safety methods, defensive ship tactics, and various types of protective equipment. He often wondered how a ship at sea could ward off terrorists, hijackers, disorderly crew members, or for that matter, unruly passengers. A Chief Safety Officer on one of his summer internship voyages taught him that each ship was permitted a number of weapons, tactics, and techniques, depending on their size and budget, to protect crew, passengers, and cargo from danger. He learned that most vessels kept a loaded rifle locked up in the bridge, and that water cannon, rolls of barbed wire, cargo netting, and even sound waves could be used as deterrents to unauthorized boarders.

At sea, Jorge found the peace and quiet he never found in his Olympic Harbor Marina neighborhood just east of the Port of Barcelona. After graduation, he earned his third mate's license and was hired by the last cargo ship on which he had served as a summer intern. The MV *San Miguel* provided a pathway to promotion, yet it took five more years and two additional ship assignments to become a Second Officer. Two years after that and yet another ship later, he was finally promoted to First Officer. However, he had grown tired of the boring duties and late night watches aboard reeking cargo ships that were requirements for further promotions and a successful nautical career. Frustrated at still not qualifying as a line captain, Jorge had decided to search for a new position with more excitement. He pored over want ads and online job listings for opportunities until reading about Sea-Sweep and how they risked seizure and imprisonment to rescue migrants from the Mediterranean. Often the underdog himself in his own youthful street battles with toughs from Ecuador and Columbia, Jorge Estrada immediately made his way to Germany and signed on to the MV *Militobi* as its First Officer.

* * * * *

Anna Kruger and Jorge Estrada's initial mission was to rescue 122 migrants in the dead of night a mile off the coast of Benghazi, Libya, and to transport them to Malta and Italy where Sea-Sweep officials would assist them in applying for asylum. Jorge was impressed with the *Militobi's* new female captain. Anna Kruger was only a few years older than he was and appeared quite professional and extremely competent, just the way he believed he would someday be perceived when he made captain. Jorge noted however that Captain Kruger did not have much of a sense of humor. Her orders were precise and detailed, and she expected the crew to respond immediately when ordered.

On their initial rescue voyage, Jorge's chief concern was that the ship was virtually unprotected and completely exposed to any and all types of external attack. There were no weapons or other defensive procedures in place to use as deterrents against local government forces who might frown on having citizens leave their country. He did not mention this concern to Captain Kruger but thought he might bring it to her attention before the next rescue mission. As Jorge's appreciation grew for Anna Kruger's commanding presence on the bridge, he found himself continually eager to please her and to demonstrate his own competence and expertise. After all, he was new to Sea-Sweep as well and wanted to present a positive impression that he could handle any situation with confidence and effectiveness.

"Mr. Estrada?" called Anna Kruger, as she peered into the darkness through binoculars. Almost midnight, the bridge was quiet as they awaited two fishing boats that were to deliver the smuggled migrants.

"Captain?" he responded.

"The two transports should be here soon. Is everything ready?" Jorge nodded, noticing how the ship's lights created a bright aura around her.

"Yes, Ma'am," he said, nearly standing at attention. "Sleeping accommodations are prepared for the women and children below, and the top deck is ready for the men and boys. Tarps are in place for protection from the elements. Food and water are standing-by."

"Very well, Mr. Estrada," responded Anna. "Stand-by." She fingered the binoculars dangling around her neck and stared into the First Officer's soft brown eyes as if for the first time. "Mr. Estrada...er, Jorge, would you mind doing me a personal favor?"

"Just name it, Captain."

"Would you be so kind as to take one more tour of the ship yourself to insure we are fully prepared for all passengers? Since this is my first rescue mission, I am *determined* to make it a success. No..." she corrected herself, "I *will* make it a success." She smiled at him.

Pleased at her sudden openness and implied vulnerability, Estrada wondered, *was that smile for me?*

"My pleasure, Captain, you know it is my first rescue mission too. I will be happy to make a final check." Estrada darted down the bridge stairwell to the main deck. Days later, he would realize that it was that sudden glimpse of Anna Kruger's compassion and candidness when he began to fall in love with her, although he lacked the self-confidence in communicating such personal feelings to her.

The main deck was lined with sleeping mats and pillows in anticipation of its new occupants. Orange and blue plastic tarps were fashioned into makeshift tents. Jorge nodded to crew members who stood awaiting their orders then made his way to the lower deck that ran halfway across the hold. Designated for women, young girls, and smaller children, rolled sleeping mats were wedged into all available spaces. Large yellow water coolers with red lids were full. Tins of ship biscuits were stacked and ready for distribution. Armed with a walkie-talkie, Jorge reported to Anna that the *Militobi* was indeed fully prepared to receive its cadre of new migrant passengers. Impressed with her handsome First Officer, Anna had a good feeling about him. *He is an up and comer*, she thought.

The successful midnight off-loading of all 122 migrants from the two fishing vessels went without a hitch, and over the course of a week the tired migrants were off-loaded in two batches: the first in Malta and the second in Lampedusa, Italy. At both locations the passengers were met by Sea-Sweep staff who registered and aided them in the excruciatingly long bureaucratic process of applying for asylum.

Keenly aware of the importance of maintaining positive shipboard morale, Captain Kruger had complimented Estrada and the crew to Sea-Sweep headquarters after the success of their first mission. Her supportive letter and oral report on their behalf was somehow leaked to the crew, and they had invited their beautiful new German Captain to join them for several rounds of Eisbock Bavarian beer at the Sausage Kitchen, one of the oldest public restaurants in the world, in downtown Regensburg. The crew was even happier when Anna bought the first round.

The *Militobi* was speedily readied for its second mission which was to patrol the sea lanes between Libya and Egypt searching for overcrowded rafts and/or unseaworthy vessels that could not survive the long and dangerous voyage to European ports. Jorge Estrada debated whether or not to mention the ship's lack of defensive capabilities to Anna and finally decided to wait for a more opportune time. They had been at sea for two days and nights when Sea-Sweep radioed that a riot had broken out at a refugee camp on the Egyptian coast and at least eighty asylum-seekers had escaped and were being hunted by the authorities. Sea-Sweep reported that the migrants were headed for an abandoned port near the town of Salûm, less than five miles from the Libyan border. They were expected to reach it by midnight. Anna was reminded that if she volunteered to mount a *land* rescue, the authorities could label her a smuggler and severe penalties should be expected if she and the crew of the *Militobi* were captured. If the mission was successful, the migrants were to be transported to Malta.

Captain Kruger did not hesitate in calling her senior officers together on the bridge where she explained the situation. Given their current location, according to the ship's lanky Spanish navigator, Gabby Fernandez, the *Militobi* could easily rendezvous with the migrants by midnight. There was immediate acceptance of both the timetable and Anna's plan to make a quick pick up at the old dock and return to Mediterranean waters. They estimated a one-hour timeframe once they entered the narrow channel leading to the Salûm pier. Food, water, tarps, sleeping mats, and pillows were standing-by and eighty passengers could be boarded and processed quickly and efficiently. Anna asked her officers to speak up if they had any other concerns with the plan. Jorge finally dredged up enough courage to ask about the defense of the ship.

"Captain, there is one thing."

"Mr. Estrada?"

"I wanted to mention that..." He hesitated, and Anna could sense something was bothering the handsome Catalan.

"*Ja*, let us hear it, Mr. Estrada, no secrets here."

Biting his lip, Estrada blurted out his concern, "Captain, we are going into unknown waters and tying up at a potentially dangerous location with no protection at all."

Anna was puzzled. "Protection?"

"I have a rifle and some ammunition locked up in the bridge closet, and I think we should have an armed guard at the ready, perhaps in the crow's nest, when we tie up tonight."

Anna frowned, thinking this was a rather bizarre suggestion. "Mr. Estrada, we are a *rescue* ship, not a *war* ship. Our mission is to *save* lives, not take them. I am uneasy with having an armed guard looking over our shoulder while we are helping women and children who are running for their lives from the Egyptian authorities."

"But Captain, that is exactly why we need protection! There *are* women and children. We must provide some level of security."

Gabby Fernandez interjected his own opinion. "Captain, we have never picked up migrants on land before. We have always rescued them at sea. You never know what may happen and— "

Jorge interrupted, "And you said the authorities are tracking them. What if they...what if they think *we* are smugglers and come after us?"

Anna cut him off, "Thank you for your suggestion, Mr. Estrada, and your comment, Mr. Fernandez. *I* know we are not smugglers. *You* know we are not smugglers. But I believe those eighty asylum-seekers do not care *what* we are as long as we can get them off that dock tonight at midnight. I am committed to helping these people find a safe haven. This is what we all signed up for and that is what I aim to do! Please be sure the crew is ready and call me if there's a problem. I will return at twenty-two hundred hours." Anna turned and exited the bridge.

"Yes, Captain," Estrada said to himself as he watched Kruger leave. Slightly embarrassed, Jorge and Gabby exchanged resigned glances and shrugged.

"It is not quite like the *Caine Mutiny*," offered Gabby. "But it could be."

"No talk of mutiny, my movie-loving friend," said Jorge. "Let's just get back to our duties." Disheartened, Jorge regretted bringing up his idea. In his mind, for the first time, he had failed his Captain. He had displayed weakness to her.

Just before midnight, under a full moon, the *Militobi* slowly edged into the narrow channel leading to the ancient Salûm wharf. On the bridge, Anna Kruger peered through her binoculars and spoke quietly into her walkie-talkie. "Chief Engineer? Slow to one-third." She turned to the rest of her bridge crew. "Sharp lookout, gentlemen, full moon tonight. We should see them coming up on our starboard."

Estrada, Gabby Fernandez, and the Radio Operator all aimed their binoculars dead ahead. The moonlight bathed the abandoned dock in soft white light revealing a startling and unexpected sight.

"Captain?" said Jorge, staring straight ahead.

"Captain!" shouted Fernandez, looking over at Anna Kruger.

"Captain!" said the Radio Operator at almost the same time as the others.

Captain Kruger nodded at the crewmen without looking. "I see them."

Two hundred yards ahead and just coming into full view, several hundred migrant men, women, and children squatted along the Salûm pier. As the *Militobi's* lights appeared from the darkness, the migrants began standing up and cheering. Anna grabbed her walkie-talkie and gave orders to the engine room.

"Chief Engineer? Slow ahead." She turned to Estrada. "Rig for docking. Man the stern and forward breast lines. Ready the accommodation ladder!"

"Aye, Captain," responded the First Officer. He shot out of the bridge and shouted orders into his own walkie-talkie. On deck, the crew scrambled both forward and aft to ready the mooring lines as the *Militobi* edged closer to its destination.

"All stop." Kruger bellowed into her walkie-talkie. "Slow astern." The mass of anxious asylum-seekers pushed closer to the wooden dock's concrete-rimmed edge. Mooring lines were thrown and caught then looped securely over rusted metal cleats. Anna stepped outside the bridge and stared down at the sea of migrants awaiting the order to board. The *Militobi's* crew pushed its large boarding net over the side of the ship and slowly winched down the accommodation ladder.

"Mr. Estrada?" Anna called calmly into her walkie-talkie. "Let us get them aboard as fast as possible." Hearing his garbled reply she returned inside the bridge, picked up an electronic megaphone and stepped back outside to the bridge railing to address the impatient crowd. "This is the Captain. Please! Please! Let us have some order here! Wait your turn. We will take all of you. Please wait your turn!" She watched as several migrants jumped prematurely for the descending ladder while others leaped for the boarding net. This triggered a massive surge by the crowd toward the ship. As the ladder reached the pier, a rush of passengers pushed forward, trampling each other to climb aboard. *God help us*, thought Anna.

As the first of the migrants reached the main deck, they saw the rows of sleeping mats then dropped to their knees to give thanks to their God, blocking access to others who were forced to leap or stumble over them, which created even more panic and obstructed access along the railing. Jorge and other crew members struggled to help women and children off the boarding net then directed them to find space on deck. Thirty minutes later, there still remained over a hundred migrants waiting on the dock to board.

High above the mass of humanity on the pier below, a lookout in the crow's nest saw headlights from a line of trucks in the far distance speeding toward the port.

He spoke frantically into his walkie-talkie, "Captain, look due south! We have some uninvited guests."

Kruger immediately aimed her binoculars as directed then shouted orders into her walkie-talkie, "Mr. Estrada, cast off all lines. It is the Egyptian authorities."

"Are you sure, Captain?" asked Jorge, carrying a young Sudanese boy to a sleeping mat. "We are not yet fully..."

"That's an order, Mr. Estrada! Cast off all lines. Board as many as you can! We can't endanger any of the passengers we have aboard."

"Aye, aye, Captain, casting-off all lines." Within moments Jorge ordered crewmen over the side to release the mooring lines. Winches growled noisily as the ropes retracted into the ship and the accommodation ladder slowly rose, still jammed with frightened migrants. Afraid of falling, several pushed and punched at each other, protecting their place on the ladder. On the pier, the remaining migrants, panic-stricken and fearful of being left behind, hurled themselves onto the boarding net. As the ship edged further away, several fell into the water.

Captain Kruger shouted into her walkie-talkie, "Full-astern! Full-astern! Take us out of here." The *Militobi's* engines raced in reverse, and the ship backed away with forty men, women and children clinging to the boarding net on the starboard side of the ship like flies caught in a spider's web. Migrants ashore pleaded in Arabic for the ship to return. Crewmen lined the railing to assist those who agonizingly reached the top of the net, pulling them aboard grateful but exhausted. Jorge Estrada entered the bridge.

"Are you all right, Mr. Estrada?" Anna asked, relieved to see him.

Jorge picked up his binoculars and peered back at the moonlit dock. "Yes, Captain, but we have a problem, a big problem."

Filled with Salûm municipal constabulary and a local unit of the Egyptian National Police (ENP), four camouflage-covered trucks screeched to a halt at the wharf, kicking up clouds of dust. Headlights streamed bright rays of light into the moonlit night as the remaining migrants ran for their lives. Uniformed officers from the first truck, all armed with rifles, scurried to the platform's edge and aimed their weapons at the retreating *Militobi,* while the other trucks were rapidly unloaded of soldiers who chased after the fleeing migrants. The Officer-in-Charge grunted out an order in Arabic and the riflemen opened fire at the ship. Bullets whined high overhead as frightened passengers dropped to the deck for cover. Several migrants clinging to the boarding net were hit and fell backwards into the water.

Anna shouted into her megaphone, "Stay down! Stay down!" She turned calmly to Jorge. "Douse all lights, Mr. Estrada. On-the-double!"

"Aye, aye, Captain," responded Jorge. "Dousing all lights!"

On deck, children shrieked and clung to their parents as the now darkened ship, bathed only in moonbeams, picked up speed at *full-astern*. Arab and African migrants shouted at each other not to move as the ship made its turn forward. Two crewmen were wounded, and three migrants were nicked with gunfire, their flesh wounds immediately wrapped in bandages.

On the bridge, Captain Kruger spoke to the engine room again, her voice calm and collected, "Flank-speed, Chief Engineer." She glanced at her worried First Officer. "I believe we are nearly out of range now, Mr. Estrada."

"Just barely, Captain."

"In five minutes, rig the lights."

"Aye, Captain."

Before Jorge could exit, Captain Kruger felt a pang of guilt about disregarding his earlier advice and called out to him, "Oh, Mr. Estrada?"

"Captain?" replied Jorge, stopping at the bridge entryway.

"Jorge," Anna said softly. "I apologize for not listening to you before. When we get back to Germany, I want you to conduct a complete assessment of our defense systems and make some specific recommendations."

"I will be happy to do so, Captain."

"*Gut.* This was a disaster, wasn't it? And do not be afraid to make any other recommendations you may have."

"I will, Captain. It could have been much worse."

Kruger nodded and smiled ruefully at the Catalan officer. "So now we have to feed about a hundred more passengers than we planned?"

"I'm afraid so, Captain," Jorge responded. *Was she smiling at me again*, he wondered. "We will have to make do until Malta."

"*Ja*, Malta, I hope that will go smoother than this part of our journey." Anna turned to Gabby Fernandez. "Navigator?"

"Captain?"

"Course set?"

"Aye, aye, Captain, Malta it is."

* * * * *

Hours later Jorge watched Anna check the navigation charts and then make eye contact with him as she exited the bridge. It was then that he realized he was absolutely in love with her. He was sure of it now. It was a feeling that had escaped him up to this point in his life. Why did he feel this way? He knew the answer. She was everything he wanted in a woman and life partner. She was a great leader. She was loved and respected by the crew. She could be a regular shipmate at the bar having a beer but was also a stern disciplinarian aboard ship. He had heard her upbraid sailors arriving late for a duty watch but had also seen a tender side when she was interacting with the migrants she had rescued, especially the children and young girls. *That had to be it*, Jorge thought. That was the key to his love. That was the key to Captain Anna Kruger. Competent and disciplined, yet tender and caring. Perfect. Just perfect.

Four nights later, off the southwestern coast of Malta, the *Militobi* neared its drop off point when Sea-Sweep informed them by radio that both Malta and Italy had officially closed their borders to all asylum-seeking migrants, and they were to hold their position to await instructions from the Italian Coast Guard.

Anna was incensed and shouted into her headphones, "I cannot believe it! These people have come so far and now you are telling me we cannot land? That is unacceptable!" She listened impatiently as the Sea-Sweep official tried to explain the organization's official response to the new ruling. Anna frowned.

"I understand perfectly what you are saying, but it isn't fair and it's not right." She listened once more but finally had to interrupt. "Ja? So you are telling me that it is actually *my* decision as Captain after all." She waited what seemed like an eternity for a response before nodding her head. "Understood. Then we are off-loading everyone in Malta as originally planned. Make sure there are Sea-Sweep people there to meet us. Thank you. I will see you soon, *Militobi* out."

Under cloud cover and running once again without ship's lights, the *Militobi* dropped anchor near Gozo, Malta's northern-most island. *It was not my passengers' fault there is no legal place to land, and they have nowhere else to turn*, Anna thought.

Jorge was nervous and approached her on the bridge. "Captain, if we are captured by the Italians it will mean detention camp for the passengers and their deportation back to Egypt."

"*Ja*, Mr. Estrada, and I am told there could be prison for us too, but as soon as all are ashore, we will head back to Regensburg."

"Captain, you are sure? We don't have permission to—"

"When *all* are ashore, Jorge, *ja*? I need your support on this. *Do* I have your support on this?"

"*Si*, Captain, you have it," responded Jorge, stiffening. He was learning that his Captain had a mind that was not easily changed. Anna and Jorge looked down from the bridge on the main deck as the passengers lined up in a surprisingly orderly fashion to board the ship's two lifeboats and be ferried to the shoreline. She knew that she had been somewhat abrupt with him before and now struggled to find a way of making conversation. She rather liked him.

"Mr. Estrada, you are from Barcelona, correct?"

"Yes, Captain, the Olympic Harbor district."

"Tough neighborhood, if I remember my short time around the port there."

"Sometimes it was, lots of fighting with the Columbian migrants."

"Why was that?"

"I am a Catalan. Our language is different. I can speak both Catalan and Spanish, but other kids couldn't, especially the migrants from South America and that led to trouble."

"They thought you were talking about them?"

"Precisely."

"And they were right sometimes, I suspect?"

"Precisely."

"I'll give you this, First Officer, our rescues so far have been a lot more dangerous than I thought they would be."

Estrada nodded. "I agree, Captain." He headed for the bridge ladder but stopped when Anna placed her hand on his shoulder.

"Jorge?"

"Captain?" Estrada turned back to face her.

Anna stared directly at the handsome Spaniard with a look of gratitude. "Thank you for your help on this mission. When you finish the off-loading, let us get back home to Germany and work on the defensive plans for the ship that you mentioned."

"I look forward to it, Captain."

"I appreciate your thoughtfulness and professionalism. I think we make a good team."

Jorge returned Anna's broad grin. "I do too, Captain." He hurried down the bridge stairwell, leaping onto the main deck to assist the crew direct the remaining passengers into the lifeboats to begin their perilous journeys to find new, safer, and hopefully more peaceful, lives in Europe.

Anna had learned a hard lesson. From that moment on she always assigned an armed crewman to the crow's nest during each rescue. Jorge had also persuaded her to advocate to Sea-Sweep officials for additional ship protection and armament. Four water cannons were installed, two to starboard and two to port, along with some other unique weaponry.

CHAPTER 2

A HUMANITARIAN RESCUE AT SEA

A stinging rain bounced high off the deck of the crowded MV *Militobi* a month later as it rolled in twenty-foot swells three miles off the coast of Libya with 500 migrants and asylum-seekers aboard. They had been at sea for nearly three weeks and had made four sea rescues already. Some thirty yards to starboard, and overflowing with fifty smuggled migrants each, bobbed two forty-foot rubber dinghies. This was not a scheduled rescue but another chance encounter in the middle of a violent storm. It was Anna's navigator, Gabby Fernandez, who had spotted the flickering flashlights in the darkness as the ship was battening down for the night on a northeast heading for France. Bracing herself on the railing just outside the bridge, Anna cupped her eyes and peered into the darkness at the overcrowded inflatables.

Her wet slicker glistened in the ship's lights as she shouted back at the bridge, "All stop!"

Jorge Estrada, his shock of long black hair slicked back from the rain, repeated the order, "All stop, Ma'am!" He shouted the order again into his walkie-talkie to engineering then turned to the fat Helmsman who acknowledged the directive and squinted into the stormy night, his grip tightening on the ship's wheel. Anna focused on the two dinghies, now only ten yards apart. Standing in the prow of each rubber craft stood a Libyan smuggler armed with a machine gun in one hand and a rope wrapped tightly around the other to keep from falling overboard. Each smuggler gestured repeatedly at the rescue ship to turn away, batting at the air as if swatting flies. They shouted at the migrants to stay down as the *Militobi's* spotlight swept over them.

Anna shouted into her electronic megaphone in English, "Heave to! Heave to! We are a German rescue ship. We will take your passengers aboard!"

The smugglers shook their heads and continued to wave their machine guns until one fired into the air, creating panic aboard both rafts. Terrorized, passengers bolted in fear, jumping overboard to swim toward the *Militobi*. Ducking reflexively at the sound of the gunfire, Anna moved along the starboard railing and stared down in frustration at the people flailing in the dark water. Rain pounded across her shoulders as she clicked the megaphone on once more.

"No! No! No! Go back. Stay in your boat! Stay there!"

More women and children hurled themselves into the deadly sea and struggled to swim toward the ship. The smugglers cursed at the people in the water then aimed their guns at them and fired. Many were killed, disappearing immediately beneath the waves. Anna gestured for Jorge to hurry below. Built like a prize fighter, he rushed down the bridge stairs and helped crewmen shove the heavy boarding net over the side. Anna peered up to the crow's nest and hesitated, but only for a moment, before motioning to a crewman armed with a rifle who had just reached the top. She knew there was only one course of action now. The crewman fired two deadly shots. Wiping her eyes and nose, Kruger focused her binoculars on the dinghies and watched the two lead smugglers fall dead into the roiling sea.

In the water, a teenaged Libyan girl, clinging to a soccer ball for dear life, dog paddled with one hand toward the ship. Anna followed the girl's progress and looked below where rain-drenched crewmen waited at the railing for survivors to climb up the laddered webbing. Horror-stricken, the remaining migrants in both dinghies jumped into the water and swam toward the boarding net that reached some three feet above the surface of the sea. For every two migrants that reached the net, one vanished beneath the waves never to return. The young Arab girl, squeezing her soccer ball, grasped for the net before losing her grip and succumbing to the depths, her ball floating away in the heavy swells. Anna saw the ball drift into the darkness and cursed, frustrated, in German.

Ashé Gaye and his older sister, Lulu, treading water, moved as close to the ship as they dared without being smashed against its rusty orange and white steel hull. Lining themselves up twenty yards directly across from the boarding net, the teens waited for several moments anticipating the next sea swell.

"Now!" Ashé cried, and they swam hard until the wave lifted them nearly eight feet up the side of the ship where they each grabbed at the boarding net and wrapped their arms through its thick latticework.

On the main deck, Estrada directed the crew to assist the cold, wet, and shivering survivors as they reached the top of the net and clambered over the railing to safety. Scrambling up the unwieldy web ladder, parents urged older children ahead of them while pulling smaller ones up from behind. Ashé guided his sister over the top railing and into the arms of waiting crew members who swiftly wrapped the two Senegalese teenagers in a large sheet and escorted them out of the rain to one of the many tarps erected on the top deck. Weakened and drained, Ashé faced his sister and sighed.

"We made it."

The unelected leader of the African migrants aboard ship was Okeke Ka, a short and chubby Ghanaian Christian who pleaded with his fellow passengers to shelter the new arrivals on deck. "Please! Watch over them. They are cold and frightened. God has given us this challenge and we must respond." Okeke placed a folded towel beneath the head of a child nestled in the lap of his sobbing mother who nodded her thanks at the Ghanaian, who could neither speak nor understand her native Arabic tongue. The African continued to help as many others as he could until he reached Ashé and Lulu, bundled together along with several other wet but very thankful migrants under an orange tarp with another Ghanaian family.

"And you two? You are uninjured?"

Ashé nodded, sensing this smiling man would be their friend. "Thank you so much," he said in English.

"You are from..."

"We are Serer from Senegal," Ashé responded. "My sister and I are going to France to meet our uncle."

The Serer, representing fifteen percent of Senegal's population, lived in the Saloum River Delta twenty-two miles inland from the Atlantic. Many lived on two hundred tiny islands surrounded by mudflats and mangrove swamps. They fished, raised goats, and grew rice. Ashé and Lulu, now fifteen and seventeen respectively, grew up on the island of Bitenti, not far from the bustling town of N'Dangane, in southern Senegal. By the time Ashé was eight, he could catch enough fish to feed his parents, sister, grandmother, and grandfather, Pap, while his father, Moussa, spent time in the rice fields and his mother, Khady, tended to their small herd of goats. Ashé enjoyed the company of his grandfather, old Pap Gaye, who was once an avid fisherman himself. He was also a life-long skeptic of his fellow man, politicians, and all religions.

Pap was especially skeptical of how the delta had become *touristy*, at the expense of many arable acres of traditional planting fields. Tourist lodges were springing up everywhere and Pap chided his grandson who informed him that someday he wanted to work at one of them, the *Bazouk du Saloum* to be precise, a lovely island resort, accessible only by canoe, with a garden and private beach with fifteen cabins, catering mainly to rich Europeans.

"I too am going to France," exclaimed Okeke. "Thanks be to God you are both safe. Rest. Sleep. I will check on you in the morning." He emerged from under the tarp as the rain ebbed and he again gave thanks to his God. Within minutes the rest of the asylum-seekers were sheltered either on the main or sub-decks, and Okeke said a prayer alone at the ship's railing. Joining him moments later was Mohammed Kassab, a thin Libyan with a grey goatee, the unelected ship's leader of the several hundred Arab migrants aboard the *Militobi*.

"Peace to you, my brother," Kassab offered in English.

"And to you, Mohammed," responded Okeke. "How is it?"

"Almost three weeks aboard this crowded ship and now we have added another hundred or so to our living spaces? Incredible! And a few of them are injured. Many are Africans and there is a Bangladeshi couple with a young child. Dr. Arun is with them now. He will be coming to this end of the ship soon."

"Those poor souls were very lucky tonight," reflected Okeke. "Things could have been much worse for them."

"*Inshallah*," Kassab responded. "We are still far from being safe."

"Things will get better. I can feel it," replied Okeke.

Kassab snorted. "I can't feel anything. I am too wet and cold."

Okeke grinned at his friend. "I can assure you that you will feel better. Do not worry. There is always someone watching over you."

They stared pensively at the pitch dark sea. The rain had all but stopped, yet the wind continued to shower the men in a salty mist. Wistful, they peered up at the spotlights glaring out from the bridge that bathed the sea of tarps in a harsh white glare.

"It's almost time for the Captain to close those lights so everyone can sleep," observed Okeke.

Mohammed Kassab nodded. "How many of us are there now?"

The rotund African glanced across the twenty-two-foot wide deck at the fluttering tarps. "We must be more than six hundred. I believe you could say we are at full capacity."

Kassab chuckled at his friend. "We were at full capacity yesterday, my brother! Yes, we have become truly a floating village searching for a safe place to raise our tents."

Ashé drifted off to sleep beside his sister and had a vision of his West African homeland along the Saloum River delta. His pirogue, carved painstakingly by his grandfather, took him to his favorite fishing spot near the backwater mangroves, where snapper and bass always jumped at his line. Sometimes his sister would go out with him. Armed with her bow, Lulu would stand in the prow and stare down into the shallows for the distorted shape of a fish. She had the annoying habit of hitting her target with uncanny accuracy.

"You will not be successful standing up like that!" Ashé would tease her.

"How should I be standing then, Mr. Fisherman?" Lulu asked, peering at the water and not letting her younger brother disrupt her concentration.

"You should be standing back closer to me. The fish will see your shadow."

"Just you throw your line in the water and we shall see who is the most successful fisherman today." Ashé flung his long line as far as he could and flinched when Lulu immediately shot an arrow striking a three-pound bass. She leaned over the side to pull the fish into the pirogue.

"And that," she said, beaming with delight. "...is how you catch a fish with a bow and arrow. It is quicker. It is safer. And you will stay drier as well."

Frowning, Ashé pulled on his empty line. "Why do you want to be a teacher when you could so easily become a good fisherman?"

Lulu removed the arrow from the fish and grew serious. "Mother and Father do not even speak to me about becoming a teacher anymore. I am afraid they will not support my effort."

Ashé pulled at his line a few times. "Did you not know Grandfather wants us to go to school in Paris?"

Astounded at the news, Lulu stared at her brother. "Both of us? Paris?"

"He says you are to become a teacher while I am to become a businessman." Stunned, Lulu sat down in the canoe.

"A teacher! I *will* become a teacher. It has always been my dream, Ashé! Imagine? The Eiffel Tower? The Left Bank? The Arc de Triomphe? But why do you want to become a businessman? You are a fisherman."

"I do not want to be a businessman! I will always be a fisherman," Ashé said, anger in his voice. "This delta will always be home to me! I will accompany you for protection but if I am to become a businessman, it will be for my...my fishing business."

Lulu laughed. "Protection? *You* will protect *me*? I think you have it backwards. Anyway, what does Father say about it?" Ashé shrugged and then flinched when a two-pound Koba hit his line. He turned his back on his sister and pulled it in, hand-over-hand. Lulu watched him bring the tiny black salmon in the boat and carefully remove the hook from its mouth before throwing the line back out.

"Maybe Uncle Dallah will help us. He has a good job in Paris. Perhaps he will want us to stay with him."

* * * * *

Dr. Arun Rao, a middle-aged Pakistani medical doctor, was able to stitch up four migrants wounded by the Libyan smugglers as best he could, considering there were few medical supplies aboard the *Militobi* for him to utilize. His wife Esha, a trained nurse, comforted the patients while checking their vitals with a stethoscope, blood pressure gauge, and a thermometer—the only tools her husband had been able to stuff into their luggage as they left Karachi in the middle of the night for their long journey to escape the Taliban.

Below on the ship's sub-deck, migrant women and children were crammed together in close quarters. Hot, humid, and musty, the sleeping area was at least better than being windblown on the main deck beneath the thin tarps with the great likelihood of being drenched by rain or sea spray. Women fanned their sleeping children until they fell asleep. A few spoke to each other in hushed tones of several African and Middle Eastern languages and dialects.

"Rig for night lights in five minutes, Mr. Estrada," ordered Captain Kruger. "By the way Jorge, you, Gabby, and the rest of the crew did an outstanding job of rescuing those people tonight under very difficult circumstances. I am proud of all of you." Estrada and Fernandez nodded their thanks with somewhat sheepish grins.

"Thank you, Ma'am," they said in unison.

"Having a rifle in the crow's nest saved many lives tonight," Anna added. "I thought you should know that, Mr. Estrada."

"Thank you, Captain," Jorge responded. Anna exited the bridge, warmly touching his shoulder as she passed him.

The next morning Anna Kruger adjusted her radio headset several times to insure what she was hearing was accurate. *It just cannot be true*, she thought. Mohammed Kassab and Okeke Ka stood watching her from the bridge entryway as she shouted back into the headset.

"You are *positive* they will not let us into a French port either? None of them?" The Ghanaian and Libyan exchanged worried looks as they listened, their hearts full of hope for good news. "Water and food for a few more days, copy that," Kruger said, repeating the message. She sighed in frustration. "If those are your orders, I understand. Chopper in two days, copy that. Of course we will be ready!" She listened again for a final response. "Will do. *Danke*! Over and out." Disgusted, she tossed her headset to the Radio Operator then shook out her thick hair and sighed.

Kassab spoke first. "France won't take us, Captain?"

"There is more food and water coming?" asked Okeke, still a sliver of hope in his voice.

Kruger nodded at them both. "Two days and a chopper will bring more supplies."

"What did they say about France?" asked Kassab again.

"Libyan Coast Guard ordered us to hold our position. Said all French ports are now closed to asylum-seekers," explained Kruger.

Astonished, the Ghanaian shook his head in bewilderment. "This is unbelievable! France has always been the friend of West Africa. We have a long history. God must be angry."

Anna leaned back against the chart table. "The French Interior Minister told the press the closing of the country to migrants would stop the, quote, *filthy* business of illegal migration, unquote. They are making an example of us."

"Captain, what will we do?" questioned Kassab, his voice pleading.

"First, we will wait at this position for more food and water, but I believe France was the last European country that would take us. We are to proceed to the nearest port by the end of the week."

Ever the pessimist, Kassab grimaced. "We will be sent to a camp and then deported!"

"Is that true, Captain?" Okeke asked, hoping his friend's logic was not accurate.

"I am afraid so," Anna replied. "Unless we can find another place to go. A safe place."

"But there *is* no other place," responded Kassab. "And we can't return home. Many of us will be put to death."

"And there must be a hundred children on this ship. Many without parents," noted Okeke.

"And a number of pregnant women," added Kassab.

"But where else *can* we go?" Okeke asked his friend. "This is the third country that has turned us away over the last two weeks: Greece, Spain, and now France. Now no one will take us. What have we done to incur God's wrath?"

Anna thought of the overcrowded detention camps in Lampedusa, Italy and the more than 14,000 migrants being housed in tents with poor health facilities on five of Greece's Aegean Sea Islands. Although the European Union was building bigger and better migrant facilities, Sea-Sweep officials had reported the camps were more like jails topped with rolls of barbed wire to prevent escape. Migrants were still being held up to eighteen months before deportation. *What was happening to these poor people*, she wondered.

Struck with an idea, Anna opened a drawer and pulled out a sheaf of old maps. "I was looking at charts the other night, and I want to show you something. It is no doubt a risk, but it could possibly be a temporary solution." She rifled through the maps and pulled out an old, wrinkled chart, yellow with age. "Yes, this is it." She stared up at the two men to ensure they were both watching and listening, as she spread it out across the table. "If we decide to do this, we will be at sea for at least another week, maybe longer. You understand that? And I am not sure we will have enough supplies to last that long."

The two migrants crowded closer to the table as Kruger ran her finger to one spot and stopped. "*This* is approximately our current position." Staring intently, the two men watched as Kruger ran her finger across the map of the Mediterranean Sea, through the Straits of Gibraltar, and out to a tiny dot somewhere between the coast of Morocco and the Canary Islands. "Here is where we might go," suggested Kruger.

"Santa Inez Island?" asked Okeke, reading the map's tiny print.

Kassab looked closely at the speck on the map then straightened up. "Santa Inez Island? I never heard of it."

Anna pulled a newer map from beneath the table and placed it atop the older one. "Now, look at *this*." She pointed again to the Mediterranean Sea near Libya. "Here again is our current position." She ran her finger across the map as before but where the tiny dot was located on the old map, there was nothing but open ocean on the newer one. Puzzled, the two men looked quizzically at each other then back at Kruger.

"It is not there!" Kassab said, confused.

"Was it volcanic? Perhaps an eruption?" asked Okeke. "Did it sink?"

Anna shrugged. "Perhaps, but it is no longer on the new maps."

"Why not, Captain?" Mohammed Kassab asked.

"Yes, why not?" Okeke repeated, as the two men stared closely at the map again.

"It appears now to be uncharted," said Anna. "An actual uncharted island! I do not know why it has been eliminated. I researched it on the computer as well and there seems to be no information on it other than it was named after a Saint Agnes."

"An uncharted island!" Kassab exclaimed. He turned to his friend. "A mystery appears before us in the middle of the sea."

"Perhaps God has saved us after all with this mysterious island," agreed Okeke.

"It may be our only choice given the current political climate toward asylum-seekers," said Anna.

"And, we cannot remain on this ship forever wandering aimlessly and being denied entry from port to port," said Okeke.

"We would soon be the target of every Coast Guard in the Mediterranean," Anna added. "Both of you think about it for a few days until we receive our supplies. It will be our last shipment. The passengers must understand what they are facing, if we choose to do this."

The two migrant leaders agreed. "We will discuss it with the others," said Kassab. "But our fate must be decided soon."

"Our fate will be decided by God," Okeke offered.

"Yes, *Inshallah,* He will be merciful," agreed Mohammed Kassab. The two migrants left the bridge, and Anna stared down at the two charts once again. Jorge Estrada joined her.

"Mr. Estrada, call a meeting with the ship's crew for 0800 tomorrow morning."

"Yes, Captain."

"Navigator? Can you chart a course to an uncharted island that may or may not even exist?"

Gabby Fernandez compared the two charts, glancing from one to the other and back again. "I can only try, Captain. I can get you to where there *was* an island. Just give me the word."

* * * * *

The crew met in the mess the next morning and Anna Kruger decided to get straight to the point. "We are in a bind, gentlemen.

We are no longer able to take our rescued migrants to France, and there appears to be no other country willing to take them. All Mediterranean borders are now closed to asylum-seekers." The crew mumbled and stirred, feeling uneasy about the news. "I have a plan that I would like to discuss with you then I want to hear any objections you might have to it, are we clear?" The crew nodded and mumbled to themselves once more. "The plan is that there is an uncharted island in the Atlantic about a week's sail away. It is called Santa Inez Island. Has anyone ever heard of such a place?" The crew shook their heads and glanced around the room at each other before turning back to the Captain. "Nor have I, and I have no idea what is on this island, whether it can support human life, or whether or not it even exists. I have asked the passengers to discuss if they want us to take them there."

The crewmen muttered to each other again. Several shook their heads while others shrugged their indifference to the plan.

"If Santa Inez Island does not exist or if there is no food or water, we will be forced to sail on to the Canary Islands and turn our passengers over to the authorities in Tenerife. We will have no choice. You should also know that we have been ordered by the Libyan Coast Guard to take our passengers to the nearest port for detention and deportation."

One of the crew members shouted, "That's not right!" Other crew members agreed and shook their heads at the injustice of it all. Anna held up her hands.

"We are a search and rescue ship, but if we are boarded by the Coast Guard, whether it's Libyan or Spanish or even Moroccan, we could all be arrested and fined."

Jorge Estrada stood up. "What the Captain is asking you is whether or not you are willing to go to this Santa Inez Island and help our passengers. What will it be?"

Gabby Fernandez stood and faced the crew that now began to grumble more loudly. "Captain once told me that rescuing people is what we signed up to do. We all know that it can be an dangerous job. I, for one, think we should take a chance on this Santa Inez Island. I don't like the idea of turning our passengers over to the Libyans." As Fernandez sat down, several of the crew applauded.

"Thank you, Mr. Fernandez," Kruger said. "Gentlemen, I ask are you willing to risk arrest by the Libyan Coast Guard and take the chance that our passengers can find a safe haven on Santa Inez Island, or shall we put in to the nearest port?"

* * * * *

The next morning, Ashé and Lulu sat together beneath the orange tarp, where they had slept through the night, eating ship biscuits and drinking lukewarm tea. They were joined by Okeke Ka who, as he had promised, was checking on them.

"Good morning, my young friends, how did you sleep? You know God saved your lives last night. You should be thankful." Lulu nodded but the mention of God reminded Ashé of his old grandfather's warning. Particularly skeptical when it came to local religious practices whether they be Islamic or Christian, Pap Gaye had told Ashé to be wary of the priests and Imams who put one hand on their Bible or Quran while the other reached for your *nafa* or cloth bag.

"We are most thankful," Lulu replied. "And thank *you* for helping us."

"And how did you two end up on that raft with so many other poor souls?"

The siblings exchanged glances. "It is a long story," began Ashé. "We came through the Sahara in a truck caravan from Niger and ended up in Zuwara in a house with many other migrants. We were there for almost two days. All we could take was a backpack. Then, at midnight, we were driven to the port and told to wade out to the rubber boats. But the wind was getting stronger, and the water was very deep."

"That's when we saw the machine guns but by then it was too late," interjected Lulu.

Ashé nodded. "The smugglers told us to stay quiet. They said we were waiting for a different ship to take us to France. We were scared."

"They shot many people," said Okeke. "Many drowned. It was horrible. You were so blessed to have escaped."

Ashé nodded. "We have come a long way from home. Nothing will stop us from reaching Paris. My sister will become a teacher."

"And my brother a businessman," added Lulu.

"For my fishing business!" Ashé quickly corrected her.

Later that morning the doctor looked in on the Senegalese siblings. The Ghanaian family with whom they shared a tarp-covered sleeping space greeted the refined, yet down-to-earth Pakistani as he entered. He briefly exchanged pleasantries with them then turned to the newest ship's passengers.

"Hello, I am Dr. Arun Rao. You were on one of the rafts last night...frightening."

"I am Ashé Gaye and this is my sister Lulu. We are from Senegal."

"Nice to meet you. How are you feeling today? Were you injured last night?"

"No, doctor," replied Lulu. "We are very well, thank you."

"You received food and were warm enough? I am sorry I could not get to see you until now."

"We were well taken care of, doctor," said Ashé. "This family was nice enough to let us stay here." The siblings looked over at the African couple and their two children, still covered with sheets, who returned their smiles.

"We are all in this together," said Dr. Arun. "Although we are many on this ship and come from many places and speak many different languages, we have become family."

"How long have you been on this ship, doctor?"

Dr. Arun shook his head as he backed out from under the

orange tarp. "Too long. Much too long."

CHAPTER 3

ESCAPING GIBRALTAR

Anna Kruger and Jorge Estrada awaited the two migrant representatives in Anna's stateroom. Jorge arranged the chairs while Anna set cups for tea.

"Jorge, I never asked you before, but were you always interested in driving a ship?"

The Catalan stopped, appreciative of the question. "I mentioned before I had a bit of trouble growing up in Barcelona."

"You did."

"I promised my mother I would get away somehow, so I found a spot up at Lookout Point at the *Parc de Montjuïc*. Do you know it?" Anna shook her head. "You take a cable car nearly three hundred feet above the city and you can look right down on the port."

"Sounds like a beautiful view."

"It was. I saw all the yachts and cruise ships come in and a few times I borrowed a pair of binoculars from my father and focused in on the crews. They would wear these wonderful uniforms, and I just knew that I wanted to be like them."

"So, you went to school and then joined Sea-Sweep after a few years?"

"*Sí*, school with some summer shipboard internships and then a number of positions on too many tankers and freighters to think about. Sea-Sweep was something that, I don't know, rescuing people at sea captured my imagination."

Anna's eyes met Jorge's and for some reason she almost blushed. "That is about the same with me. It caught my imagination too. Rescuing people does seem like a worthwhile career, does it not?"

Jorge perused several family photographs on Kruger's tidy desk. One showed Coach Kruger, whistle around her neck, standing beside an all-girl soccer team wearing championship ribbons. One showed Anna holding a trophy, her face beaming with pride and achievement. Another showed a twelve-year-old Anna with her arm around her grandfather aboard the *Gitane*.

Okeke Ka and Mohammed Kassab knocked before entering. Jorge poured tea and Anna motioned for them to take a seat.

"Captain, we have been discussing this uncharted island with the other passengers, as you asked," said Okeke.

Mohammed Kassab leaned forward. "Captain, can there *really* be an uncharted island today? It seems impossible what with radar, satellites, and other technology."

Anna shrugged. "I know historically that Spanish galleons came out in that direction to catch the prevailing trade winds to take them to America. And there was an evacuation of the Canary Islands hundreds of years ago when the Dutch were attacking Spain. Who knows if anyone ever ended up on that island?"

Anna now spoke carefully to avoid any misunderstanding. "You both must realize we have no other place to take you. No country is letting us in, so we must make other plans or do as the Libyan Coast Guard says: put into the nearest port and face the detention camps. Mr. Estrada and I believe this remote island was left off current navigational charts because there were no permanent settlements. Since there was no reason for ships to land, it was left off newer charts. But let me tell you the truth, if you choose to go there, it will take a minimum of one additional week at sea, depending on the weather. And if the island is uninhabitable, you will not be able to stay. Perhaps there was a good reason why there were no permanent settlements."

The two guests sat back and reflected on what they had just heard. Still gazing at several old photos of Anna, Jorge sipped from one of her German Weimer teacups.

"If the island is uninhabitable, we would have to go on to Tenerife. We would be completely out of food and water by then," Anna explained.

"The Canary Islands?" Okeke looked up from the black, red, and gold oval rug on the cabin's floor. "They would send us to a Spanish detention camp, wouldn't they? And then we would be forced to stay there until they decided to deport us. That is unacceptable!"

"We would have no other choice," Anna responded. "The welfare of our passengers is of paramount importance. You absolutely need a safe place. But time is also critical. You know about our pregnant women and the many children on board."

"But if it *was* habitable?" Kassab asked. "If there *was* food and water, and perhaps even shelter. What would you do? What *could* you do?"

Anna sipped her tea as she thought about his question. "There is a good chance there may be food and water, if there were early settlements. Perhaps they planted crops or raised animals. If we could be assured that there was enough food, water, and shelter for everyone, we would return to Germany and work with Sea-Sweep to advocate asylum for you in one of the European countries," she said.

"You would return for us?" Okeke asked, worried.

Anna acknowledged his concern with a nod. "Of course, and hopefully your stay on the island would be a short one. With approval we would take you all back to Italy or Greece or France or whichever country allowed you to stay. Possibly even the Canary Islands, who knows?"

Estrada exchanged a brief glance with Anna before speaking. "But you also must realize for that short period you would be all alone. Probably no other ships would call unless they came across the island by accident. You would be on your own until we returned."

Okeke sat back, considering what such a situation would actually mean. "We would be like castaways!"

"Castaways, yes, but safe from deportation, safe from the camps," countered Kassab.

"But how long could we survive there?" replied Okeke.

Mohammed Kassab shook his head. "Only God knows. We would have to take care of ourselves, my brother! There are too many of us to live on this ship any longer."

"We are now more than six hundred passengers plus fourteen crew," said Anna. "If we did take a chance and tried to go to France or Italy, perhaps under the cover of nightfall, maybe we could find a spot and..." Anna shook her head, answering her own question. "No, there are too many passengers. Too many children and too many elderly to just turn them loose on some beach somewhere."

"We know it is a difficult decision, but it is still your choice," said Estrada.

The African and Arab leaders stared at each other.

"We have no *real* choice," said Okeke, now resigned to the decision he knew he must make. "We are in God's hands."

Anna stood and the men followed her to the door. "We will have just enough food and water to make it to the island, I believe, but as Mr. Estrada said, it is ultimately your choice. Those who do not want to stay can come back with us to Germany, but they should know they will be placed in a camp and then deported, without a doubt." Anna paused, one hand on the door's latch, waiting for a decision.

Kassab clapped Okeke's shoulder. "I am sure all of the passengers will want to stay together on the island, if it is at all possible. What do you think, my friend? Shall we become castaways together?"

Okeke nodded. "It is our only choice, Mohammed. Together it is."

* * * * *

Anna Kruger felt the downdraft of warm air on her face from the whirling helicopter blades as she stood at the bridge railing two days later and watched two huge pallets of food cartons and supply boxes lowered through the *Militobi's* half-opened top deck. Jammed full of water bottles, rice bags, tins of ship biscuits, and other supplies, the wooden pallets were guided by the strong hands of the crew into the near-empty hold. The cables were unhitched, and crewmen scrambled to unload and distribute the cargo to maintain equilibrium to the ship's center mass. Anna watched Jorge Estrada supervise the unloading, approving of the way he handled the crew. *Definitely captain material*, she thought.

Summoned by the Radio Operator, Anna re-entered the bridge and donned a headset. She listened for several moments to the helicopter pilot and frowned.

"*Ja,* report back that we will do so. *Danke!*" It was as she expected. Explicit orders to put into the nearest port where passengers would be temporarily sheltered in a detention camp for processing back to their home countries.

Unloading completed, the chopper edged away from the ship and then sped off through cotton candy-shaped blankets of pink clouds. Anna watched until it disappeared over the horizon, wondering for a moment where it was headed. *Tripoli? Benghazi? Alexandria?* Within an hour the main deck was battened down, and the crew worked with the passengers to reattach their protective tarps. Estrada climbed the steps to the bridge and entered.

"Anna...er, Captain? We are prepared for departure."

Anna Kruger grinned at her First Officer and reached for her walkie-talkie. "Chief Engineer? Let's get underway; all ahead full." Gabby Fernandez looked up from a sheaf of maps.

"Where to, Captain? The mystery island?" Anna glanced at the maps in front of her tall Spanish navigator then clapped him on the shoulder. "Get us out of the Med first, Mr. Fernandez. Set a course for Gibraltar."

"Aye, Captain," he quickly responded.

Anna scanned the horizon with her binoculars for any traces of a Libyan Coast Guard cutter in the immediate vicinity. She was pleased with the speed of the crew in clearing the deck, opening the hold, unloading the supplies, reassembling the passenger tarps and covering the deck in under three hours. She was also pleased by the decisions made by Okeke Ka and Mohammed Kassab in her cabin the night before to take a chance on Santa Inez Island. She knew there really was no other choice for them.

Putting in to a Libyan or Algerian port, or even heading back to Europe, would have resulted in chaos and a revolt by the passengers, most of whom had narrowly escaped death's door in their own countries.

Anna climbed down the last few steps of the bridge's stairwell to the main deck and wended her way through the sea of tarps flapping in the light sea breeze and bright sunlight.

She found the blue tarp she was looking for and called out, "Arun? Dr. Arun?" Dr. Arun Rao and his wife, Esha, were part of a small group of South Asians aboard the *Militobi*, rescued at sea nearly two weeks earlier.

"Captain?" The doctor joined Anna outside, shading his eyes from the sun.

"Hope I didn't disturb you, doctor."

The Pakistani shook his head. "No, Captain, we are just tired and hot, like everyone else. Rice, biscuits, and tea for weeks on end will do that to you. We're so glad for the supplies today."

"*Ja,* we are all happy about that. You should know we are now heading to an uncharted island not too far from the Canaries. The voyage will take at least another week."

"Yes, we heard, but uncharted?"

"It is called Santa Inez Island. The choice was there or a Libyan detention camp."

"So, France refused us as well. It looks like none of these foolish politicians are willing to step up for migrants today."

Anna nodded wistfully. "I know. I know. Politics, I'm afraid. But we are not the only ship being turned away, just the latest one. I am thinking the situation will get worse before it is better though."

Resigned to an uncertain fate and unhappy about it, Dr. Arun sighed. "Most of these governments will not even discuss asylum anymore. It's all about *illegal migration* in their minds. Do you know the United Nations reported that twelve thousand migrants drowned in the Mediterranean between 2014 and 2018 and were never found? I read an article about it! It's outrageous! That is eight people a day!"

"Doctor, I cannot worry about the politics now. We have at least seven pregnant women on board that I know about, and I am certain there are more than that, and we have nearly a hundred children of all ages, most without parents. I am afraid another week and we will have our own deaths to worry about. Can you help us set up an infirmary? We just received some more medical supplies today. I am sure we will need all of it."

"Of course I'll help, Captain. And my wife can assist. She is a nurse."

"*Danke*, doctor, I know it has been a long ride for both of you."

"These last few weeks aboard have been a lot easier than the two months it took us to escape the Taliban. We will start immediately."

Anna paused for a moment, remembering back years earlier to a young couple she met on her trip to Lahore and how they wanted to escape even the *threat* of the Taliban. She had stayed at the Pearl Continental Hotel. It was filled with tourists in loud shirts, oversized purses, and cheap sunglasses, but one of her Pakistani shipmates had recommended it and promised her it was a safe place to vacation, especially since she was traveling alone. Anna had immediately begun to question her choice of Pakistan as a suitable destination while waiting at the airport baggage claim when three male security guards eyed her a bit too appreciatively for her liking. The Continental's hotel staff, however, could not have been friendlier, and she finally dismissed her first impression as silly, if not naïve.

Armed with a Lahore guidebook, Anna headed for the New Anarkali Bazaar to wander the busy marketplace and do some shopping. The 200-year-old market teemed with hawkers, pickpockets, beggars, street musicians, noisy Vespas, and Ravi motorcycles. Side streets overflowed with flower stalls, kiosks with mounds of colorful spices, and quaint six-table cafes. Anna bought a *saluar kameez*, a long shirt and pant combination worn by many Pakistani women, then made her way along a busy alleyway until she found a rooftop cafe with a view of the bazaar below. A young couple sat within earshot at the next table, and Anna could immediately sense something was wrong when their voices quieted as she took her seat. Anna coughed politely and the couple turned to see the German tourist watching them.

"Pardon," the young man said to Anna in slow English. "I am sorry if we are too loud."

"It is quite all right. No bother at all," replied Anna, pouring tea from a four-cup metal teapot.

"Are you English?" the young woman asked.

"German."

"Ah, German? Very good," said the woman. "We would very much like to visit there." She turned to her partner who nodded in agreement, all indications of an argument disappearing. Anna stared for a moment at the young woman, wondering if she would say anything else.

Meeting Anna's gaze, the woman finally reassured her. "We are fine," she said, turning her chair to face Anna. "We were just talking about our——"

"About our next trip," the young man interjected, completing her sentence. "Perhaps to Europe, even to Germany. We have not yet decided." Anna sipped her tea not knowing exactly what to say. The young woman, after waiting for a moment, lowered her voice to speak to Anna.

"Is it difficult to come to Germany?"

Puzzled by the question, Anna found it hard to answer. "Well, I do not really know. It depends on a number of things, I think, like a visa, transportation, and...why do you want to come to Germany?"

"Vacation!" the young man said, too loudly. The woman frowned at her husband in frustration before turning back to Anna.

"We are Sardar. It is a small tribe of Hazara people from Quetta. Do you know it?" Anna indicated she did not. "Our tribe was originally from Afghanistan even though we are Pakistani.

But the Pakistanis do not like us. Our parents were killed in Quetta in 2015." Anna stifled her emotional reaction to such horror and remained calm.

"Killed? How terrible!"

"The Taliban," he said. "You know them?"

Anna nodded. "Of course, I have heard of them, but I have never—"

"They execute people for nothing! My father was killed for shaving his beard just to spite them." The young husband scanned the restaurant as if expecting someone to be listening. "And they would arrest you even for dancing," he added. Anna set her cup down on the table.

"That *is* terrible. Very hard to believe in this day and age."

"It is better now," the young woman explained. "The Taliban is gone from the valley, but many people are still scared. There are some who want the old ways back, the ways of the Taliban. We are in danger by staying there. We have to leave. We *must* leave the country."

Anna was puzzled. "Could you not move here to Lahore or Karachi where there are more people? It might be safer in a city." The young woman shook her head.

"We want to have a family. Even putting a child in school here can be dangerous. They do not want girls to be educated and many are taken as child brides. And, what if our child had a disability? She would be shunned. It is very difficult to live here. We cannot live in Pakistan anymore."

"But where will you go?" Anna asked. She was sympathetic but had no clue how to help them. She imagined they would have a very difficult time trying to emigrate to Germany. She just knew there would be mountains of red tape to cut through and a massive bureaucracy to overcome.

"We will try to find a country that will take us," replied the young man. "We will seek asylum."

"We will find a place," the woman added. "A safe place. There must be a country willing to help us." Her voice had a ring of hope in it. Anna had always wondered later if that young couple, fearing like they did for their future children, ever made it out of Pakistan. She also wondered what such a predicament said about the plight of other Pakistani parents, or *any* parents for that matter? What *was* the obligation of parents to make a better life for their children? Should responsible parents remain and fight for a better life where they were, knowing that their struggle would be long and hard and probably pointless? Or, should they start anew in another place, another country, and break any rules or regulations or laws necessary to achieve that better life? What was the obligation of other individuals, or even other countries, to help them? Were these the people her grandfather was talking about?

* * * * *

Anna walked aft where migrant boys and girls, crushed together shoulder-to-shoulder, held long fishing lines over the stern. Ashé and Lulu stood in the middle of the crowd of youngsters who cheered when Ashé caught a fish and began pulling it up hand-over-hand. Several other children crammed in closer to watch as the youth hoisted it with a final tug over the railing.

"An anchovy!" Ashé exclaimed in English.

Lulu snorted and shook her head. "It's a sardine," she teased with deep sarcasm. In Senegal, such teasing was called *kal,* or friendly mocking. Ashé scowled at his sister then expertly removed the hook and plopped the fish into a borrowed plastic pail. "You are too lucky, Ashé," said Lulu. Her brother made a face then tossed his line back overboard as Captain Kruger joined them, wading through the crowd, careful to avoid stepping on tiny, and mostly bare, feet. She was pleased to see the children smiling and happy.

"How are all of you doing today? Who is the lucky fisherman?"

"My brother Ashé, Captain," responded Lulu in English, grudgingly proud of her brother's skill.

Kruger grinned. "And why is he so lucky, er..."

"My name is Lulu, Captain, Lulu Gaye. He is very lucky, but he is also an *expert* fisherman. And he has survived a long trip to get here." Kruger eyed the young girl. Strikingly beautiful, Lulu was tall, almost reaching Anna's chin. She possessed a gleam in her eyes filled with determination and strength that immediately reminded Anna of a few of the freshmen girls on her soccer team that won the intramural championship her senior year at Jade. Lulu had the same athletic build and lithe physical stature so reminiscent of her best players.

"Survived? Yes, I am sure everyone here is a survivor. Where did you come from?"

"From Senegal, Captain, we came through the Sahara to Libya. We are going to France." Anna stared back at Lulu and her brother, who continued to fish, teasing his line up and down to attract a strike.

"France?"

Lulu nodded. "We have an uncle in Paris. We are going to go to school. I will become a teacher and my brother will become a businessman." Ashé quickly frowned at his sister who corrected herself, "I mean, a businessman in the fishing business."

Anna did not feel it the right time to inform the children of the change in the ship's destination. "You said you came through the Sahara?" she asked.

"It took us nearly a whole week, Captain," responded Ashé, his eyes still focused on his fishing line. "It was cold and it was hot and it was dirty, and I have never been so cold, so hot, or so dirty in my whole life." Lulu and Anna laughed at his description.

"And then we took a rubber boat from Libya, from Zuwara," Lulu said. "That is when you found us. Actually, we found you. We were looking for a different ship, we were told."

"Yes, the two rubber dinghies, quite a dreadful experience," said Anna. Lulu frowned as she pulled up her empty line. Her brother and the rest of the youngsters laughed. Anna tried to hold back but joined in the laughter. "I cannot tell you how happy I am that we found you. That you found us, I should say."

Scowling as the laughing children gathered around her, Lulu stared over the side. "Wish I had my bow."

Ashé turned to the Captain. "My sister is *deadly* with a bow."

Heading back to the bridge, Anna made a stop at the new makeshift infirmary where a delighted Dr. Arun handed a crying newborn to Esha, who swaddled the baby in a towel.

He turned back to the young Nigerien mother and spoke in English, "It's a boy. Congratulations!" The mother wept with joy as Anna peered inside the infirmary.

"Perfect timing, doctor?"

"It's a boy, Captain. Her first child."

Anna grinned. "I'll make a note we have another passenger."

"Another passenger seeking asylum!" Dr. Arun corrected her.

"And the father?" asked the Captain.

Esha moved closer and whispered, "He didn't make it through the desert."

Frowning, Anna cleared her throat. "Sorry!" She patted the nurse on the shoulder. "I am very happy you are with us, Esha. Thank you for your help." Dr. Arun stood beside the new mother as his wife presented her with the newborn.

"I know you'll be very proud of…"

"Dimka," she told Esha, with a big smile.

"Dimka?" repeated Dr. Arun.

"What a lovely name for a boy," exclaimed Esha.

"It was his father's name."

* * * * *

A warm Mediterranean sirocco blew at the protective tarps covering the men, boys, and the few women sound asleep on the crowded main deck under the dark night's sky. Ashé and Lulu, snuggled together for warmth, still shared the tarp with the Ghanaians who now looked at the siblings as part of their extended family. Ashé was in the grips of a slight fever, his body wracked with shivering that woke Lulu several times during the night. It was the second coldest night Ashé could remember. The coldest night, actually it was early morning, was in the Sahara outside of Madama. Huddled among a truck full of migrants, a rear tire blew out. It was 6:20 a.m. and still dark. Several Muslim passengers began their morning prayers while waiting for the drivers to fix the flat. Sitting on the side of the rutted road, Ashé remembered trembling as the desert wind picked up and the sand began blowing, stinging exposed skin like tiny flea bites. He had never been so cold in his entire life, even surpassing his frigid dive in the river during wet season to recover a hook wedged between two mangrove logs. Soaked to the skin, he had walked two miles to reach home well after dark, his lips a dark shade of blue. Khady had scrubbed him down with a dry towel. Six cups of hot tea later Ashé felt well enough to go off to bed. *Always keep extra hooks*, he had learned. *Pay the extra. It is worth it.*

Below deck on the *Militobi*, women and children slept pressed tightly into every conceivable nook and cranny. Elderly women, pieces of cardboard in hand, took up their nightly duties of fanning away the nauseating smell of diesel fuel from the eyes and noses of the babies.

On the bridge, Anna Kruger peered across the eight-mile wide Straits of Gibraltar. Lights blinked in the distance from buildings on each side of the dark undulating sea. Passing tankers and freighters dotted the blackness with white stern lights, red port sidelights, and green starboard sidelights. Kruger spoke calmly into her walkie-talkie to the engine room.

"Chief Engineer? Give me flank speed." She turned to the Helmsman. "Stay abreast of those freighters until we get all the way through. We will be running without lights, and we are not stopping for anyone."

"Aye, Captain," he responded, steering the ship a few degrees to starboard.

Uneasy, Jorge Estrada peered through his binoculars and scanned both sides of the strait. "If the *Guardia Civil* picks us up, we will be escorted to a Spanish detention camp. And we will not like how they treat us."

"*Ja,* my friend, I know. Douse all lights. We have to stay away from their radar and infrared detection systems." She motioned to Fernandez. "Disengage transponder and all radio beacons."

"Aye, Captain," responded Fernandez.

"And Mr. Fernandez? Watch the radar for me, will you? We do not want to bump into anything. This is an active shipping lane."

"Aye, Captain."

Okeke Ka and Mohammed Kassab entered the bridge. The ship lifted and rolled in the wind-driven swells. The men were worried and braced themselves against the bulkhead.

"Captain, the lights on the shore! Many people are frightened," Okeke said.

"They see the lights on both sides of the water," added Kassab. "Some want to swim to shore and strike out on their own. They think they can make it." Controlling her emotions, Anna glanced at the two migrant leaders and pointed into the darkness.

"These straits have strong currents and high winds. Any swimmer will drown. However if, by some miracle, they do manage to survive, they would be immediately arrested." She stared straight into the eyes of the two men. "And, if anybody even *tries* to jump overboard, I am holding you two responsible." The men gasped at the sudden intensity in her eyes and gasped yet again as the ship's lights gradually dimmed then flickered once before completely extinguishing.

Wide-eyed, Mohammed and Okeke, their faces questioning the abrupt change in the normal evening's operation, watched as Kruger pointed to both sides of the narrow straits.

"Over there is Spain. They have a joint military and civilian Coast Guard that finds ships like ours with their radar and infrared cameras." Next, she pointed over to the south side of the straits. "See *those* lights? Moroccan Coast Guard! They don't have those detection systems, so we're staying closer to their side and staying even closer to these other ships to cover our movement on radar." She motioned for the two men to gather closer. "If we get caught, we *all* get arrested. They send *you* to a camp, and *we* go to prison and get fined a million Euros. I do not think that is what you want, is it? It is not what I want." Not completely understanding her, the two migrants shook their heads then nodded. "*Ja,* you go back and tell your people to stay calm and hang on! The weather is always rough through here."

The wind grew even more forceful, and the waves strengthened in size as cold ocean spray burst over the rusty prow and showered the tarps with seawater and salt mist. Below deck, many suffered from nausea and vomited violently into blue plastic buckets. Elderly migrant women now rubbed the backs of crying infants.

* * * * *

Blinking lights on the northern shore outlined the Spanish *Guardia Civil* station. Inside, the young Radio Operator stared intently at her wide computer screen before turning to the Duty Officer standing nearby.

"Sir, I have an unidentified ship," she reported in Spanish. The Duty Officer glanced casually over her shoulder at the screen.

"I'll report it," he said. "Make contact."

On the *Militobi's* bridge, the radio burst into life. The Radio Operator, an Italian father of four, listened through his headphones for a moment and gestured to Anna Kruger.

"Captain, it's the Spanish. You were right that they would make first contact."

A civilian Commander now stood shoulder-to-shoulder with the Duty Officer at the Coast Guard station, both peering over the head of the Radio Operator as she attempted to contact the mysterious blip on her screen.

"Unidentified ship; this is *Servicio Maritimo de la Guardia Civil*. Please identify yourself."

Anna Kruger contacted the engine room and spoke briefly into her walkie-talkie.

"Chief Engineer? Keep us at flank speed, *danke*." Anna turned rapidly to her own Radio Operator and took the headphones. She listened after motioning for everyone to stay quiet. "Yes, this is Captain..." She intentionally garbled her name. "...of the MV..." She intentionally garbled the name of the ship. The Spanish Commander, Duty Officer, and Radio Operator exchanged quizzical looks.

"Please repeat," the Spanish Radio Operator said in English. "Please repeat your last transmission. Your transponder is off. We are having trouble tracking you. Unidentified ship, do you have illegal migrants aboard? Are you transporting migrants?"

Anna shrugged at Estrada and Fernandez then shouted into the microphone. "Guardia Civil we are carrying tons of...and we are heading to the port of..." She garbled her transmission again.

Frustrated, the Commander snatched the headphones from the Duty Officer and listened intently as the Spanish Radio Operator made another attempt to communicate with the unidentified ship. "Captain, your transmission is not clear. Please repeat. Please repeat. Are you transporting illegal migrants?"

Anna grinned at her Radio Operator and dropped the headset on the console as the dark ship, now just a ghostly electronic presence on a computer screen, pulled away from a nearby freighter, still at *flank speed*.

"The safety of our passengers and crew are the most important goal of any search and rescue captain," she said to Estrada, who nodded his agreement, bewildered somewhat at the timing of this teachable moment. "In my opinion, neither a Spanish or Moroccan detention camp is considered a safe place. Agreed?" Estrada grinned as Anna stopped and made eye contact with everyone on the bridge.

"We are with you, Captain," he said, scanning the reaction of the others who were also nodding their heads.

"Sometimes we have to do things that we normally would not do," added Anna. The bridge crew was in agreement once again. "*Ja*, I know I can count on all of you to support me. Wake me at 0600."

The *Militobi* cut through rolling white caps and exited the straits. Ten minutes later and heading west by northwest into open ocean, white, red, and green masthead, port, and starboard lights reappeared as if by magic in the pitch blackness.

In her neatly kept and spotlessly clean cabin, Anna unbuttoned her blouse then hesitated as she glanced at the framed photos on her desk. Smiling, she picked up the one of her holding a trophy. That was when the freshman team won the intramural title. Brushing the fine dust from the top of the wooden frame with a wetted finger, she set it back down on her desk and picked up the photo of her and her grandfather aboard the *Gitane*. She loved that sailboat. Funny, she pondered, how sailing had been so important to her growing up in Freiburg. She recalled with special fondness those wonderful summer days with her grandfather. Anna wetted her finger again and dusted off the frame, thinking about her grandfather's love of the sea. There was no doubt in her mind that it had influenced her career and her life in ways she could hardly fathom.

* * * * *

It was Okeke Ka that gave the bad news to Ashé and Lulu that their journey to France would be delayed and that it was anyone's guess for how long. Bewildered by the decision, Ashé could only mumble that he understood what the overly pious Ghanaian was telling him.

"I'm so sorry for you both, but hopefully God will make our delay a temporary one."

Upset, Ashé brushed past his worried sister and made his way through the billowing sea of tarps and sprawling passengers to the ship's stern where he and many migrant children and teens continued to fish and hang out each afternoon. For many, it was a place to cool off in the fresh air. The wind was always blowing, and it felt good not to be sweaty all the time. For others it was a place to escape the watchful eyes of parents, grandparents, and even the adult strangers who seemed to assume a parental role over those unaccompanied by a guardian or relative.

Ashé, obviously the best fisherman among the teenagers and many of the adults as well, held daily court at the stern with tales of his adventures journeying through the Sahara and fishing from his pirogue on the Saloum River.

At his usual spot on the railing, Ashé tempted the many children and adults fishing or playing cards on the fantail by shouting, "Are you ready to hear another story?"

Children gathered closer and sat cross-legged in the warm sun. "I told you before that my sister and I are going to France. At least that is what we planned," Ashé's sarcasm bled through as his voice cracked. "As all good brothers know without being told, our job is to protect our sisters, mothers, aunts, and grandmothers from danger." The male children nodded in agreement. Most of the female teenagers scoffed at the old school opinions of traditional male and female roles that somehow never changed or disappeared no matter how much education males received. "Let me tell you how I protected my sister as we traveled through the great and very dangerous Sahara desert." Lulu joined the crowd and rolled her eyes as she anticipated her brother's embellishment of the truth. *Here he goes again,* she thought, still concerned about his unsettling reaction to the news of the delay. "My Uncle Dallah works for the Air France in Paris and sent us tickets to fly to Agadez, in Niger. It is the doorway to the Sahara."

One of the younger boys nodded. "Yes, I have also visited Agadez. It is very hot there."

Frowning at the interruption, Ashé continued, "That is where we met the Toubou, a tribe of people that live in the desert, but they are not really Arabs."

Lulu cleared her throat, drawing her brother's attention. In Wolof, she said, "Ashé, you must explain this better. The children do not understand what a Toubou is." Scowling at his sister's interruption, Ashé continued in English.

"Yes, there are two tribes in North Africa: the Tuareg and the Toubou. They used to fight each other but now they each take people to the Mediterranean and there are only two ways to go. The Tuareg will take you through the desert to Algeria. The Toubou will take you through the desert to Libya. Either way you must travel across the great ocean of sand called...the

Sahara!" Ashé paused, waiting dramatically for a reaction from his young listeners and was disappointed when there was none.

A young boy asked, "Which way did you go? With the Tuareg or the Toubou?"

"With the Toubou, we stayed in Agadez for a few days with hundreds of people waiting for the trucks to enter the desert to take us all the way to Tripoli, that's the capital of Libya. It was hot, and people waited in the Toubou ghetto for weeks since the caravan only left Agadez each Monday and there was not enough room for everyone. The ghetto is like a big walled-in waiting area with a few one-room houses for cooking and sleeping. People played checkers and once we saw them playing soccer. There was nothing else to do."

"Did you play soccer?" Scowling, Ashé could not see who interrupted him this time.

"How long did you wait?" Another question rang out from the back, frustrating him even more.

Ashé grimaced. "No, I did not play soccer, and no, we did not have to wait too long. When it was our turn, we were loaded into the back of a truck and given a long stick to put between our legs." The youngsters exploded in laughter.

"Why did you have to put it between your legs?" a young boy sitting close to Ashé asked with a wide grin.

Ashé tried to explain, "It gave you something to hold onto. It reached all the way down to the truck bed and was maybe three feet long. The stick keeps you from falling out because, if you *did* fall out at night in the cold dark desert, the caravan would not stop to help you. You would die a *horrible* death all alone. You would curl up in a ball and the sand would cover you up and the tarantulas and snakes would eat you alive!"

Shocked, the young audience grew silent, and Ashé felt a little better for finally generating a reaction. Lulu however was becoming more and more concerned with her brother's growing anger and darker demeanor.

Ashé continued, "If you were lucky, they might find your dried bones someday, maybe years later. But only if you were lucky."

Another question was shouted from a youngster sitting further back. "Did you ever fall out?"

"Fall off the truck? No, we were very careful."

"What did you eat?" asked another young boy.

"When the caravan stopped at a village or larger town we would buy some supplies. Did any of you hear of Dirkou or Seguédine or Madama or Tummo Crossing?" No one responded. "Well, when we stopped at these places the hawkers swarmed all over us like bees." Many of the smaller children gasped as he continued. "We bought water, sodas, and boxes of couscous and rice."

"Where did you sleep?" another youngster asked, and several others nodded, thinking it was a good question.

"Right in the truck."

"But you could have fallen out."

"We were packed together like fish in a bucket. We could hardly move at all. There were at least twenty-four people in each truck. I stayed awake the whole trip." Ashé glanced over at his sister who shook her head at his lie. "I kept one eye on my sister and one eye on the other passengers all the time. That was my job."

In Wolof, Lulu suggested that Ashé talk about meeting their friend, Mashoul.

"Oh yes," Ashé said, turning to the crowd that now included several adults with nothing better to do than listen to his story. "Do you want to hear about a friend we met on the trip?" The young audience shouted that they did. "His name was Mashoul, and he was from Agadez. It was his third time trying to get to Libya. You know why he failed his first two tries?" The youngsters shook their heads, spellbound. "Because he was caught and put in prison by the police the first two times." His young audience shuddered at the very thought of it.

A question was shouted from an adult in the back. "Was it the *Abu Salim* prison in Tripoli? What did he do?"

"No, it was the prison in Sebha. There are laws against people coming to Libya without the right sort of papers. He told us he did not have such papers. He was arrested and taken away."

"What happened to Mashoul? Is he with you now on this ship?"

Ashé glanced over at Lulu who was watching the reactions of the children, captivated by their rapt attention to her brother's story. "No, but Mashoul helped us throughout our journey. Because he had made the trip to Libya before, he told us things about the desert. Has anyone heard of the Arbré du Ténéré, the tree of the desert?" No one responded. "It was a very old tree and the only one for two hundred and fifty miles until a truck hit it. The driver was drunk. They put what was left in a museum. It's true. Mashoul told us that."

The youngsters laughed and nodded their appreciation for the Mashoul story. Imagine, they put a tree in a museum!

"Once we were in the town of Dirkou," Ashé continued. "We could hear a buzzing sound high up in the sky. You could not see it, but you could hear it far above the trees, hidden in the clouds. It was a CIA drone!" The youngsters were astonished and many repeated the statement to each other, their whispers somewhat annoying Ashé. "The drones watch for *Daesh*, or Isis, as the Americans call them. But maybe you are tired of my story now. Perhaps later I can return and..." He moved slowly away from the railing, but the youngsters pleaded for him to continue.

"No, wait! You did not tell us what happened to your friend," one youngster yelled.

"Yes, what happened to Mashoul?" asked another young boy.

Ashé returned to his spot, the sun making the top rail behind him almost too hot to touch. "As I told you, Mashoul related many things to us about the desert. Have any of you heard of the cave art on the Kaouar Cliffs? Do you know that many thousands of years ago ancient people drew elephants and giraffes and birds on the walls of caves in the desert? Those animals do not live in the Sahara anymore, do they?" The youngsters shook their heads. "But they did once!" The onlookers oohed and laughed, and Ashé realized he was actually enjoying the young audience's reactions. He could almost understand, in a small way, why his sister wanted to be a teacher. "Okay here's the end of the story. Are you ready for it?" The youngsters shouted back that they were. "When we arrived in Libya, our friend Mashoul told us about the Magarhas Arabs, the second largest tribe in Libya."

"Who is the largest?" a tiny voice shouted.

"I am not sure. I think they are called the Warfalla or something like that. Anyway, the Magarhas are the friends of the Toubou. They were driving our trucks and—"

"I thought the Toubou were driving the trucks," another tiny voice called out.

Ashé took a deep breath. *Let my sister be the teacher then,* he decided, *fish do not ask stupid questions.* "We had to change drivers in Sebha because it was too dangerous for the Toubou drivers."

"Why?" squeaked another innocent voice.

"I don't know why. That is what they told us. So, we arrived in Sebha late at night and were stopped by the *Yafars.* They are the ones fighting against the Libyan government."

Lulu realized her brother's story was going in a direction not exactly suitable for his young audience. "Ashé, we should go," she warned in Wolof, before turning to the youngsters and finishing the story herself in English. "So, Mashoul was so scared of being taken by the police that he ran away, and we never saw him again."

All eyes turned back to Ashé. Miffed at his sister's interruption, he could only affirm her story with a nod to the young audience and then headed back amidships.

As he passed his sister, he snapped at her in Wolof, "It was my story!"

Lulu immediately shouted back at him, "You should not tell about nearly getting shot with machine guns! It will scare them to death. They are only children, Ashé."

"They should know the truth. For all we know Mashoul *was* killed."

"We do not know that for sure," retorted Lulu, continuing in Wolof. "And I suppose you were next going to tell them about the taxi driver who tried to rob us too?"

"Perhaps! And perhaps I should tell them how you nearly cut the man's throat."

"What's wrong with you, brother? Why are you acting like this?"

"I should not be here, Lulu. I should be home...fishing."

"But Grandfather said that you wanted to learn about—"

"Perhaps I listened to Grandfather too much! I will never learn to be a better fisherman by studying business in Paris, if we ever get to Paris."

"But Ashé, how can you—"

"I will stay with you until we get to France but then I will go back home. Where I belong!" Ashé turned his back on his sister and continued his way through the dense crowd before sliding under the orange tarp and wrapping himself in his damp sheet. *Why did I ever agree to come on this trip*, he asked himself.

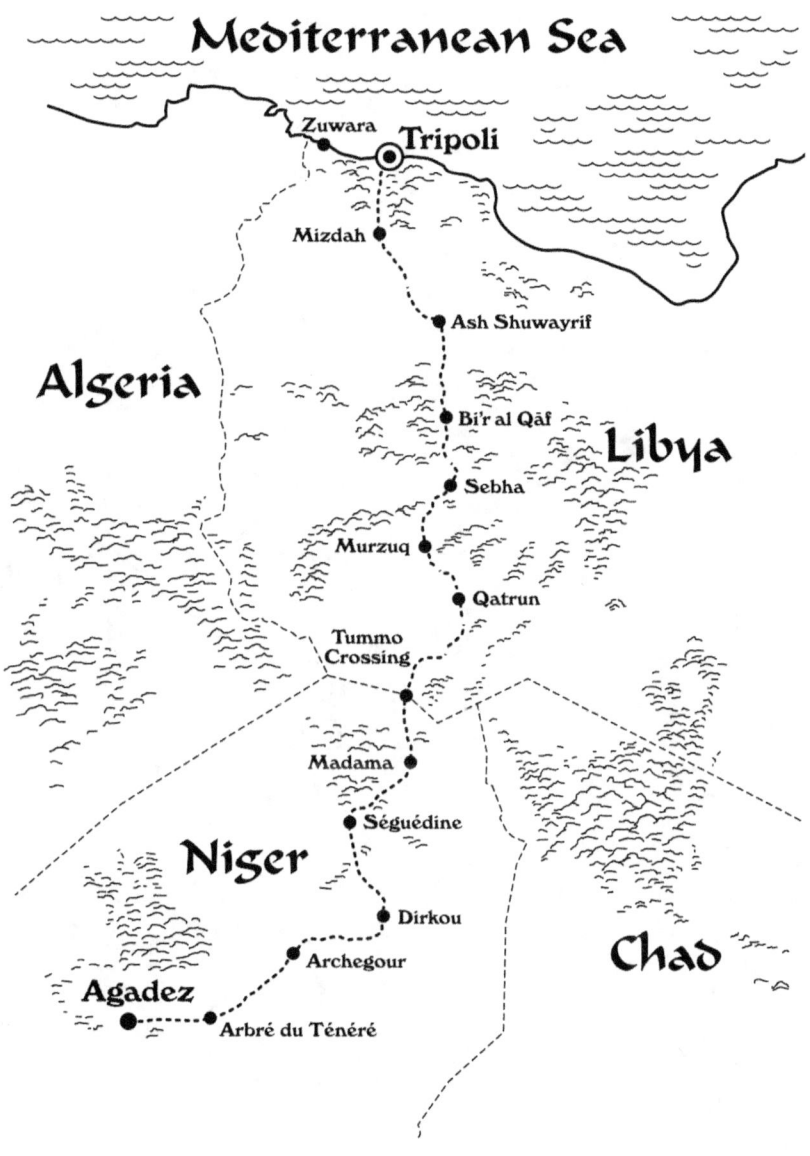

CHAPTER 4

SANTA INEZ ISLAND

The emerald green island sparkled in the early morning sun. Waterfalls and streams dotted the lush terrain with forests of pineapple, mango, guava, avocado, loquats and cherimoyas. Wild pigs and rabbits scurried under palm trees caressed by a light breeze. A great waterfall cascaded hundreds of feet only to splash harmlessly into three rocky pools far below, where fish jumped and eels slithered to escape the warm sunlight.

Ada Niame, a young woman from Swaziland wearing Bantu hair knots, ran across the wide African village center and called out toward a large thatch and bamboo hut.

"Desta!" she shouted in English. "Desta, please come quickly!"

Desta Kado, a tall and muscular Sierra Leonian, pulled a homemade bamboo knife from his worn pants as he emerged from the doorway. The handsome village leader and elected Head Man scanned the immediate area for trouble before returning the knife to his waistband and focusing on the young woman standing before him.

"Ada? What is it? Arabs? The Asians?"

"It is Chiké. Something is wrong! Something is wrong with him!"

"Fever again?"

"It is his foot. Can you come? Hurry, please!"

As a number of African villagers stepped from their one or two-room bamboo houses with palm-leaf roofs to see what was causing the commotion, Desta followed Ada to her thatched hut where a cooking fire crackled in the center of the dirt floor. Lying on a woven mat with his foot propped up was eleven-year-old Chiké. Ada cradled her son's head in her lap. Desta smiled at the young boy who seemed to light up as he entered.

"Hey, Mr. Chiké? How are you today, sir?" Desta greeted him, taking a seat cross-legged on the floor mat beside the young patient.

"Not too good, I do not know what happened to me. I was out in the jungle helping the day guards and—"

"The village guards?" His mother was aghast. "Chiké, I have told you they are *not* your playmates. A boy of your age must—"

Desta interrupted her, "I think you are a very brave man, Chiké."

"You do?" asked Ada, incredulous, as the boy grinned and nodded in agreement with the village leader.

"All of us must be brave and strong these days. We must be patient as we wait for a ship to take us to asylum in a new country. I believe our ancestors are watching over us, but we must do our part as well." Desta examined the wound on Chiké's foot then spoke slowly to the boy, "You got something sticking in you, little man. You want that I take it out for you?"

"Would you please, Desta?" requested Chiké.

"It will hurt you, Mister."

"I am ready for it." The boy's jaw tightened with determination.

Desta handed his knife to Ada. "Place this on the edge of the fire then go back to my house." Ada jumped to her feet, eager to help. "Bring me the little tin sitting in the corner near the back wall. It is a salve I made to relieve pain." Ada placed the knife carefully on one of the flat rocks circling the fire.

"Are you positive you need it, Desta? I hate to leave the boy, even for a minute."

Frowning, Desta faced Ada. "Yes, woman! I said I need it. Please go!" Desta waited for Ada to hurry out then snatched the knife from the rock and wiped it on his thigh. "Chiké, I did not want your mother here, afraid of all the crying."

"I am not going to cry, Desta!"

The knife dug deeply into the boy's foot. Chiké winced and held his breath as Desta removed a long sliver of bamboo.

"I am afraid of *her* crying, not you!"

The boy laughed then groaned in pain as Ada rushed back in moments later, sweating and out of breath from running to and from Desta's house.

"I could not find the tin you spoke of, Desta! What shall we do?"

"It is all right, Ada. The boy will be fine. We will watch for infection." Desta held the bamboo sliver up and rotated it around and around before tossing it into the fire. "What we need is a good doctor on this island." Desta ripped a piece of cloth from his pant leg and wrapped the boy's foot. "You must stay off this for at least a day or two, Chiké. Do you hear me?"

"That is much too long, Desta. How can I help you manage the village?"

Desta and Ada exchanged grins. "I will have to make do until you are well," said the village leader, standing back up. "But get well soon. I need you with me on the job." Ada walked out of the hut with him. "Keep the boy off his feet for as long as you can, Ada."

"I will, Desta. Thank you."

"I know it will not be easy for you to do that," he said, smiling. "That boy knows *everybody* and *everything* that is going on in our sector." He touched Ada gently on her shoulder. "But I love him like he was my own son."

"I know. He loves you too. We both..." Ada caught herself. "We both *appreciate* your kindness, Desta. Watching over the boy like you do and bringing us food. We thank you for that. Awa would thank you too, if he was still alive. I know you miss him like we do."

"He was my best friend, Ada. Remember, try and keep the boy off his feet." Desta smiled again at the young woman. "Use any means necessary." Ada laughed and watched the handsome Sierra Leonean stride forcefully back across the grassy courtyard.

Desta and Awa Niame's family had arrived aboard the MV *Yap Islander* over a year after the original migrants were shipwrecked on the *Ralik-Ratak*, the rusting old ship still crumpled on the island's eastern reef. Desta and Awa had often hunted together, marveling at the abundance of food on the island and how easy it was to feed village families compared to the problems they encountered in their home countries during times of droughts, floods, and war. Awa had observed that it seemed whatever animal they had decided to hunt that day would somehow appear before them, as if by magic. It was like the island could read their thoughts and provide what they needed exactly when they needed it. Desta attributed it to their watchful ancestors.

Awa Niame's body was found one night after Ada reported him extremely late from hunting wild pig and game birds. Desta had searched the African sector nearly to the great bamboo fence before finding his friend, throat slashed, just off a jungle path. He scooped the dead man up easily in his strong arms and then nearly stumbled over a metal object in the darkness. He searched around his feet a moment before finding a red bangle.

The body of Awa Niame was laid out in his house overnight. The next day, as neighbors sang mournful hymns, Ada managed to set out woven baskets of food in front of the house for all to eat, as was a Swazi wife's traditional duty. Chiké appeared confused as he listened to the adults sing and recite prayers for his dead father. Desta kept the young lad close to him as villagers prepared Awa's body for burial. He was washed several times and draped with a burial shroud made of shaped palm leaves. As tradition dictated, a large hole was cut into the thatched wall of his hut and Awa's body was passed through to mourners on the other side. This was to make it impossible for him to find his way back to the living, as the hole was immediately repaired in his wake. Flowers of lavender and white chrysanthemums were placed around his body. A grave was dug near the house and a drum announced the lowering of his remains while one village elder read from the Bible and another from the Quran. More songs were sung as Ada wailed in anguish. The body was buried with Awa's head pointing east toward the sunrise.

Ada identified the bangle as Asian, and Desta Kado vowed revenge on all the island's Asians and death to the man who killed his best friend. He knew that Jay Rawal, a Pakistani who had also been aboard the *Yap Islander*, often poached rabbits in both the African and Arab sectors. He promised himself to meet Jay again someday.

* * * * *

Jay Rawal had become enamored with the tracking and hunting of rabbits since he arrived on the island aboard the *Yap Islander*. Armed with a bow and arrow, he spent months stalking them throughout the remote Asian sector on the westernmost end of the island, searching for tracks and setting traps near young bamboo plants, where the rabbits liked to feed. At first, he could not come close to actually hitting a rabbit with an arrow and would laugh at his inability to strike his target, even when one sat staring directly at him seemingly daring him to try his luck. Setting traps became Jay's most successful hunting method. He would tie a string made of hibiscus bark around a tree and secure it to a smaller line wrapped around a bamboo stake stuck firmly into the ground. A looped third string became the snare that was triggered by the rabbit bumping into the smaller stick. Jay was successful with his trap the third night he set it in the jungle near the twelve-foot bamboo wall, separating the Asian and Arab sectors.

Although he continued to practice with his bow, Jay's expertise at setting traps grew exponentially with each of his hunting adventures. He learned how to rapidly kill his prey before slipping his fingers through a tiny slit cut in the rabbit's shoulder and pulling away its fur in a single movement. He would gut and clean the carcass in a nearby stream and grill the meat over a wood fire.

Three months later, Jay was hunting one night at the southwestern edge of the Asian sector near the beach, only twenty yards from the great bamboo wall. The fog began rolling in from across the lagoon, but he had just picked up the tracks of a large rabbit and didn't want to lose it. As he neared the sandy beach, the fog grew even more dense, clammy to the skin, and a brisk wind began whipping the branches of the tall trees high above him. Having become fairly proficient with his bow by now, Jay skirted around the end of the tall bamboo fence and entered the Arab sector in pursuit of his evening meal.

Clad in torn camouflaged pants, three pirates walked along a wild pig path not sixty yards from where Jay was tracking his prey. They were armed with bamboo spears and two handguns, and the wet fog slowly enveloped them as they finally emerged on the sandy beach, waves slapping at the shore.

Jay swore to himself. The fog had covered the rabbit tracks leaving him at a loss as to what to do next. Ten yards straight ahead, outlined against a thicket of green bamboo trees, the rabbit appeared as if by magic. Jay's eyes lit up with excitement as he quickly notched an arrow and drew back his bow to fire.

"There you are!" Jay bellowed in his native *Urdu* language. "You are mine!"

Hearing Jay's shout, the pirates, called *Isleños* by everyone on the island, headed in Jay's direction, groping their way through the jungle. Missing his shot and cursing at the intensifying fog, Jay realized he was now trespassing deeper into the Arab sector than he wanted. It was time to return to the safety of the Asian side of the bamboo wall. However, trying to find the path back the way he had come was more difficult than he imagined. Figuring that he would eventually run into the fence and then follow it to the beach, Jay continued to walk northwest.

Holding his bow out in front of him, Jay brushed aside the larger leaves blocking his path. The wind was blowing stronger now, and the fog was virtually impenetrable. In minutes he was soaked to the skin as a light rain began blowing horizontally from the lagoon and across the jungle. One arm out in front of him to avoid being hit in the face by large fronds, Jay stopped, hearing an odd rustling not twenty yards ahead. Listening hard, he was astonished to realize he was not alone. *The Arabs would not be out in such weather so far from their village,* he reasoned. He could only surmise that it was an Isleños patrol looking for a rule breaker: someone trespassing in another sector. Crouching down to hide just off the path, Jay waited as the rain stung at his face.

The Isleños also waited, standing still in the middle of the jungle trail, listening for any additional movement by whomever had called out. The patrol leader motioned for the others to follow, his spear pointed in front of him to clear away low-hanging branches. As the three men passed Jay's hidden position, the Pakistani rushed blindly into the jungle behind them, dropping his bow, and was immediately swallowed up by the thick fog. Crashing through the tangled branches and now almost completely disoriented, Jay scurried northward ducking at the sound of gunshots fired wildly in his direction. He knew the bamboo fence couldn't be far away but worried his pursuers would cut him off before he made it all the way back to the beach. Racing through the jungle undergrowth, he staggered down a muddy embankment and flung himself into a narrow stream, the armed Isleños only seconds behind.

Four Arabs, the heavy fog making them virtually invisible, stood hidden beneath a large banyan tree only ten yards from the stream. Holding spears, their bodies covered in mud and leaves, they watched silently in the rain as Jay struggled to wade across the creek, fish scattering from his splashing. The exhausted Pakistani forded the waist-deep water and crawled out the other side as the three Isleños hurled themselves into the water after him. Jay struggled up the embankment and dragged himself through the mud until he touched the feet of three Asians glaring menacingly over his prone body at his attackers; long bamboo spears raised at the ready. Shocked, the Isleños stopped, midstream, and retreated back the way they had come.

Pulling Jay to his feet, the men turned and disappeared between fruit-ladened mango and papaya trees, in the direction of the Asian sector, fog swirling in their wake. As the Isleños scurried out of the stream and retreated back into the jungle, the four Arabs, still hidden, waited a few moments until they were alone again before turning south towards their own village.

The next morning the Arab patrol reported to Imam Ashraf Agha of the previous night's trespassing event. He asked why they had not interfered or helped the Isleños. The first man said that he recognized Jay Rawal from the *Yap Islander* and knew that he wasn't a bad man. The second man said that Jay appeared to be only hunting, probably a rabbit that had eluded him, and that his Asian rescuers were only trying to return him to their sector unharmed. The third man said the Isleños appeared not to know if the man they were chasing was an Asian or an Arab, so it appeared their efforts were unjust. The fourth man said that killing a man for trying to feed himself or his family was taboo in Islam. The Imam nodded and congratulated the four men for using their heads and not letting their emotions cause the needless shedding of blood.

* * * * *

Approaching the lush scenic island from the northeast, Anna Kruger stepped back inside the bridge of the *Militobi*.

"Helmsman, let's take a ride around the island to see this place a little better. Steer us due west and stay clear of the reef. Follow it around and see if we can find good anchorage."

"Aye, Captain," responded the Helmsman, turning the wheel to starboard.

The *Militobi*, staying seventy yards abeam of the wide reef that encircled the high green island, cruised at *one-third speed*. Kruger, Estrada, and Fernandez took positions together outside at the bridge railing, glued to their binoculars, and searched for signs of life. The hope was for a natural passage through the reef into the calm lagoon that lay between the reef and the shore, which varied in width from a half-mile to several hundred yards. Swaying palm trees and verdant foliage wrapped the island like a warm blanket. Along the island's rocky north coast there appeared to be no sign of human life. Estrada spotted large game birds soaring high above unusually large banyan trees and pointed them out to Fernandez who frowned when he had difficulty spotting them.

The reef angled south, and the ship continued its route along the island's west coast, still without any sign of human life. Two hours later the reef widened eastward, protecting the island's southern coast and forming an enormous azure-blue lagoon. Fernandez spotted loggerhead and green turtles and surmised that this isolated spot was loaded with every variety of fish. As they traversed the southern coast, they saw wide sandy beaches and forests of coconut trees loaded with green nuts. Gabby swore he saw a wisp of smoke, perhaps a cooking fire, but by the time he tried to point out its location, neither Kruger nor Estrada could find it. It was Jorge Estrada, still squinting through his binoculars, who finally located a wide gap in the reef. Anna Kruger re-entered the bridge and ordered the engine room *slow-ahead* through her walkie-talkie. She turned to the Helmsman.

"Can you steer us through this pass without ripping us to shreds?"

The stocky sailor grinned and nodded. "Aye, Captain, will do."

The overcrowded ship eased through the pass and continued east in eight fathoms of water. Anna and Jorge continued to peruse the coast, particularly the beaches, but still could find no signs of life. The lagoon's width now expanded to more than five hundred yards and Kruger ordered the Helmsman to steer toward even deeper water near the southeastern corner of the island.

"Mr. Fernandez, your analysis?"

The Spaniard shrugged. "Captain, we have no information about this island at all. We are in sixty feet of water here so we are in good shape as far as I can see."

"Very well. Let us not drop anchor yet. We will put a boat ashore and see what we find. Mr. Estrada? Prepare the ship for arrival."

"Aye, Captain." Estrada raced down the bridge ladder and hopped down to the main deck.

"All stop," Kruger ordered, nodding her approval when the Chief Engineer correctly repeated her order. Darting between sleeping mats and weathered tarps, Estrada spotted Mohammed Kassab. He grinned and clapped him on the shoulder.

"Prepare for arrival, my friend!"

Kassab grinned back and ducked hurriedly beneath the sea of flapping tarps.

Shouting in Arabic he called out happily, "Hurry! Hurry! This infernal voyage is over. It's time to pack your meager belongings, my brothers!" Within a few moments a roar of grateful voices mushroomed in volume as his words were translated into French, English, and several other languages.

Okeke Ka spotted his friend talking excitedly to a group of Arab passengers. He waited for an appropriate time to ask his question. "Is it truly Santa Inez Island, Mohammed?"

"*Inshallah*, it is," replied Kassab with a smile. "Only God will show us if it is a viable place to stay. Tell your people."

"Praise be to God almighty," Okeke said to himself, hurrying beneath the nearest tarp. He shouted in English for the African and Asian passengers to prepare themselves.

Ashé and Lulu, already at the port railing, looked out on their possible new home. "Not a single building," said Lulu in Wolof, her tone one of disappointment and frustration.

"No, but there may be some good fishing," Ashé responded, his demeanor a bit brighter as he scanned the deep water. "Looks as if no one has fished here for years."

Lulu nodded. "Looks like no one has lived here for years."

* * * * *

Minutes later from a tall banyan tree on the eastern side of the island, a pirate lookout refocused his binoculars and spotted the *Militobi* in the distance easing to a stop in the lagoon.

He called a warning down below, "A ship! A ship!" Within minutes a bell rang in the village and scores of pirates scrambled out of their bamboo and wood-framed houses and thatched huts, searching for their weapons and racing to three Bayline speedboats hidden on the beach.

Commandant Rafael Delgado emerged from the largest wooden house near the village center. The 300-pound pirate leader sported long black hair and a full beard. He was dressed in a worn and much too tight military officer's camouflaged uniform, topped with a red beret and cracked aviator sunglasses taken from the cabin of the *Ralik-Ratak's* captain more than two years earlier.

Rafael Humberto Delgado was the product of the streets of San Sebastian de la Gomera, the capital of La Gomera Island in the Canary Islands. An obese child, young Rafael was the butt of many jokes and teased about his weight throughout his early life. With uncaring and often missing parents coupled with a lack of adult guidance toward a productive and responsible life, young Rafael had dropped out of primary school at the age of ten. At sixteen, he began sitting in on dice games held in deserted back alleys. Because of his size and propensity for violence, Rafael was soon earning extra Euros guarding the backs of gang members who felt much safer when he scowled over their shoulders at their gambling customers, especially those slow to repay their debts. When his gang leader asked him to solve a personnel problem using his prodigious physicality, Rafael felt a valued part of a family, perhaps for the first time in his life.

Rafael's reputation as a local enforcer grew as he reached his late teens but after incessant struggles with the police and the immediate, although predictable, disappearance of his gang friends anytime he was in trouble, he decided to go into business for himself. He started running his own dice games and soon realized there was much more money to be made organizing the games rather than slapping around a few cheaters as the enforcer for others. However, Delgado learned too late that working independently had other risks as well. A disgruntled competitor with local police connections, once a friend, facilitated the introduction of Rafael to the San Sebastian jail for the first time on his nineteenth birthday.

Angered by the betrayal and his first ten-day jail term; the teasing by the police about his size; and, their prediction, to his face, of a long prison term in his not too distant future, Rafael recruited three of his closest friends and moved on to the next level of his criminal career. While continuing to run dice games in back alleys, he located an empty room in an aging park building and operated high stakes poker games. His rapid success in employing his three trusted friends as dealers and charging players for protection along with a hefty entrance fee, persuaded Rafael to leave the streets of San Sebastian forever. Now considered his partners, his three friends branched out on their own as well. Delgado soon was sharing the take from a cadre of pickpockets and purse snatchers targeting tourists on the beautiful Hermiguya Beach in La Gomera.

Keeping in touch with his new partners was at times difficult since Delgado's expanding group of card sharks, pickpockets, and con artists had now reached twelve in number and had spread themselves all over the island. Avoiding the police became a time-consuming effort, so Rafael set up meetings at several isolated mountain locations to manage their growing operations. Often when they were unable to meet in person, Rafael whistled messages to his partners in *Silbo Gomero* from semi-hidden vantage points in the Garonjonay National Park.

Silbo Gomero, the whistling language of the Canaries, was an ancient form of communication enabling villagers to communicate over great distances across La Gomera's high mountains and deep ravines. With a short whistle, the partners, who learned the language as children, could warn each other when local police or the *Guardia Civil* got too close.

Rafael Delgado was emboldened to expand his efforts to other islands in the Canaries as well as La Gomera. As his criminal syndicate burgeoned, so did his reputation as a major island crime kingpin. Rafael's illegal activities spread to Las Palmas de Gran Canaria, the second capital city of the Canaries. Daily European flights brought rich tourists to the exclusive beaches, nightclubs, and casinos and provided Delgado's gang with ample opportunities for adding strong-armed robbery to their criminal repertoire.

Lucha Canaria was the local name for the sport of wrestling in the Canaries. In a large circle, each grappler attempted to throw the other down to the ground or out of the ring. It had the appearance, to the uninformed, of Japanese sumo or Greco-Roman wrestling. Widely popular throughout the island nation, wrestling clubs dressed their members in colorful uniforms and vied in tournaments and championship matches.

Rafael Delgado immediately understood that betting on *Lucha* matches could have big paydays, especially when individual wrestlers or even entire clubs could be manipulated—for a price. In less than half a year Delgado was raking in a minimum of ten thousand Euros a month and that was only from his rigging of wrestling matches on Gran Canaria Island. He returned to La Gomera and was pleased to find that his original gang operation had now ballooned to more than forty members with average hauls of three thousand Euros a week. That success, however, placed Delgado on the radar of the *Gardia Civil* and the *Policia Nacional*.

Local police raided his gambling locations at least every other month both in La Gomera and Gran Canaria. Even with several police lieutenants on his payroll warning him of impending busts, key gang members were jailed and gambling activities often forced to relocate to safe houses throughout the country. Delgado came to the conclusion that the best way to make money on these beautiful sun-drenched islands, and to keep his people out of prison, was to move his operations entirely out to sea.

* * * * *

Uncovering three Bayline speedboats, covered in palm fronds to protect them from the sun, pirates pushed the sleek crafts into the water while others cheered them into battle. Delgado, accompanied by three tall and extremely attractive female bodyguards including Lucia Santos, still serving as his second-in-command, walked calmly across an open area toward the beach. Favoring his right knee, Delgado limped painfully to the water's edge where he was assisted into the first speedboat. Pirates, male and female, jammed the two other speedboats and waited to follow behind their leader. Most were brown-skinned Isleños or Canary Islanders, some were Africans, and a few were Arabs. Many sported tattoos and beards and dressed in ragged shirts and torn pants or shorts, an indication of the two years most of them had spent on the island. Several of the women carried knives and machetes. At the prow of each boat was a male pirate armed with an AK-47 machine gun.

From the *Militobi's* bridge, Anna Kruger watched as migrants struck their tarps, stuffed their pillows with any valuables, and rolled them up in their sleeping mats. Each end was securely tied with rope or twine. As the ship's lifeboat lowered into the water, the accommodation ladder was unlocked and cranked slowly downward. Migrant passengers crowded closer to the ship's port side to watch the lifeboat depart. Estrada found Okeke Ka standing beside Ashé and Lulu, staring at the island's empty beach.

"Captain wants to send one lifeboat ashore first to see if it is better here or along the southern coast. Pick out three men to join us."

Ashé quickly turned to plead his case to join the first lifeboat, but Okeke shook his head and patted the teenager's shoulder. "Not this time, Ashé. Be patient, son."

Commandant Delgado's powerful Suzuki 150 outboard engine propelled his lead boat around the island's southeastern point and, for the first time, glimpsed the *Militobi* just as its lifeboat reached the water. Three African male passengers hurried down the accommodation ladder along with three crew members. Jorge Estrada jumped from the ladder into the lifeboat and revved up the Yamaha 250 outboard as excited passengers watched him from the top deck.

On the bridge, Anna peered through her binoculars and was physically sickened when she saw the three speedboats rounding the point. Focusing on the first boat, she immediately sensed something was wrong only seconds before spotting the pirate standing in the prow cradling a machine gun. Reflexively, she tripped the ship's general alarm. Seven short rings of the bell scattered the migrants and crew, who immediately searched for cover on the suddenly very open and unprotected main deck. Seven short blasts from the ship's horn followed by one long blast, added to the confusion and chaos. In the lifeboat, Estrada yelled at the migrant volunteers and crew members to hurry back up the ladder and screamed for the winch to raise the lifeboat.

In the lead speedboat, Delgado gestured to the pirate standing in the prow who fired his weapon into the air.

Anna shouted into her walkie-talkie, "Full astern! Full astern!" Gabby Fernandez continued to stare at the approaching boats through his binoculars. Kruger was annoyed. "Gabby!

Snap out of it! Get us out of here." Fernandez frantically rifled through the maps on his table as the *Militobi* shuddered and groaned at reverse engines. Short bursts of gunfire erupted from all three pirate boats. Anna was puzzled as to why they were all directed straight into the air. Estrada rushed into the bridge, sweat pouring off him.

Relieved to see her First Officer, all Anna could say was, "Jorge!"

"Captain! Water cannon? Sound cannon?"

The pirate vessels neared the ship at full speed. Anna shook her head. "Too many people on deck. We cannot outrun them. Let us see who they are and what they want."

"But Anna..."

"That's an order! Too dangerous!" Anna found her walkie-talkie and barked into it. "Chief Engineer? All stop!"

"Anna, they may be pirates," pleaded Jorge.

"*Ja*, they will either want money or supplies. Both, I suspect."

CHAPTER 5

"THEY LOOK LIKE PIRATES TO ME!"

Commandant Delgado struggled wearily to climb the steps of the accommodation ladder behind the attractive Lucia Santos and several other pirates. Lucia was Delgado's most beautiful and possibly his most wily gang member. She possessed an air of intrigue about her and a wicked temper. Expert with either knife or pistol, Lucia had risen from working as a dealer in Delgado's Tenerife poker operations to the seducer of the president of the *Federación de Lucha Canaria*. She had rapidly become Delgado's most trusted and reliable lieutenant. Her planned affair with the *Federación* president enabled the gang to fix *Lucha* matches resulting in big paydays and assuring her second-in-command status with the pirate leader.

Delgado sighed in relief as he stepped onto the *Militobi's* main deck and gestured to his Isleños to form a semi-circle in front of him while he caught his breath. He scanned the crowd of migrant passengers who stood speechless, awe-struck by the Commandant's size and the menacing malevolence of his heavily armed pirates.

Enjoying the moment, Delgado grinned and spoke in English, "Good afternoon! How are you today? Welcome to Santa Inez Island!" Uneasy, the crowd murmured until Delgado called out to them again. "Where is your Captain?"

Anna Kruger pushed through the onlookers as more pirates arrived on deck and fanned out along the rusting port and starboard railings.

"I am the Captain, Anna Kruger, at your service."

"Captain! A woman! Nice to meet you. I am Commandant Rafael Delgado. I am in charge of this island. Sorry for the gunfire, but I had to make sure you would stop and allow me to board."

Wary, Captain Kruger put on a diplomatic face. "How can I help you, Commandant?"

Delgado stepped carefully past the semi-circle of pirates and sized up Anna and the passengers watching him. "So many people! How many are there, Captain, five hundred? More?"

"We are over six hundred now."

"Are you smuggling these good people, Captain?"

"We are a rescue ship, sir."

"Ah, a rescue ship. We have many rescued migrants on this island. They are all under my personal protection."

Anna was confounded by his statement. "Your *protection*?"

Delgado motioned to his Isleños who scattered throughout the ship as the huge pirate leader ogled several of the younger female passengers who covered their faces with scarves and turned away.

"Captain, you won't mind if we borrow some diesel fuel, will you? Ships rarely stop here."

Kruger nodded. "Of course, in fact we did not realize anyone lived on this island. It is uncharted, and we were hoping to find temporary shelter."

Delgado laughed. "Very good! Very good! Of course, you are right! It is uncharted because this island is a very remote and dangerous place. There are three villages on the western side of the island, and they are always fighting with each other."

Anna watched uneasily as two pirates climbed the steps to the bridge. "Fighting?"

Delgado scanned the crowd once again. "It is nothing. It is *I* who keep them from killing each other! It is *I* who keeps each of them safe. And, it is *I* who keeps everyone happy. Very happy!"

Still wary, Anna frowned. "And you do this by..."

Delgado waved his arms over his head. The crowd backed away at the gesture, and he laughed at their frightened reactions. He limped forward and, with a big smile, extended his arms wide.

"Ladies and gentlemen! You are all invited to stay here on Santa Inez Island by me, Commandant Rafael Delgado, and my Isleños. You will find there are nice quiet villages on the leeward side of the island, and we will escort you there this afternoon. You will find our island bountiful as well as beautiful. It has been blessed by the Gods. We have fruit, vegetables, meat, and lots of fish and clean water. Just about anything you could ever want. All we ask is that you abide by our rules, do what we ask of you, and do not leave your assigned village areas. If you break the rules... well, do not break the rules. It is that easy. Life is easy on Santa Inez Island. And you are all welcome."

Delgado leered at more of the women and snickered as they covered their faces again. Anxious and uncertain of their fate, the crowd murmured among themselves once again, unsure of whether to be happy to have found food and water or frightened by the look of these, what did he call them? Isleños? Delgado pointed back toward the island.

"In order to facilitate your village accommodations, I am requesting your Captain and, say, thirty of your female passengers to accompany us back to our village to work out the housing, food distribution, and other logistical details of your stay."

Puzzled, Anna stepped toward Delgado. Lucia Santos took a similar step to cut off her path, a warning flashing in her dark brown eyes. Jorge, Okeke Ka, and Mohammed Kassab, now standing at the front of the crowd of passengers, edged forward, but Anna caught Jorge's eye and shook her head.

"Er, Commandant?" she called. "I prefer not to leave my ship."

"Come, come, Captain," scolded Delgado, gesturing for Lucia to back away. "Do not be afraid. Lucia here and a few of my men will guide your ship to the safety of the southern coast and assist your passengers ashore. It is the least we can do to repay your hospitality for the diesel."

"But why all the other women?"

Delgado stepped closer to Kruger and put his arm around her shoulder. Watching closely, Lucia's expression turned to one of disgust and revulsion at the pirate leader. "To tell you the truth, you have more passengers than we have ever seen here before. I have found women easier to deal with than men when it comes to making arrangements for their new homes. As a woman yourself, I am asking *you* to accompany *them*. It will make them feel safer. Do it for them, Captain, not for me. I can assure you everyone will be quite safe. They are under my protection."

In the *Militobi's* musty-smelling ship's hold, two pirates kicked at empty cartons, discarded water bottles, and depleted tins of ship biscuits. They jiggled fifty-five gallon fuel drums until they found the last six full ones and loaded two of them on a wooden pallet for removal. They continued to search for anything of value but found only rolls of barbed wire, boxes of greasy engine parts, scattered life jackets, and large coils of spare mooring lines.

The two pirates returned from the hold, linking up with other gang members who had completed their search of the entire ship. Whispering their findings to Lucia, who waited on Delgado to ask for her report, they fanned out again along both railings to await further orders. The Commandant faced Anna.

"Very well. So, let's get started then, shall we? Please line up all the women on this deck and I will make my selections for the landing party." Anna hesitated for a moment, frustrating Delgado. "Captain, I beg you to do as I say. It will get everyone to safety much faster. There will be a lot of walking and older women will slow everything down."

Standing together among the passengers, Mohammed Kassab and Okeke Ka watched Captain Kruger finally nod, albeit grudgingly, for them to proceed as the pirate leader had directed. Resigned to their task, the men began to disperse the crowd. Estrada joined Anna as migrant women, including Esha and Lulu, began lining up on the main deck. Skeptical, the First Officer kept a watchful gaze on the other pirates, especially those armed with rifles and machine guns.

"Are you sure about going to the island, Captain?"

"Jorge, maybe this is the easiest way to get the passengers some food and into shelter. Seems like this Delgado knows what he is doing. It should not take too long before we get everyone settled."

"But Captain, the guns! They look like pirates to me."

"I am sure they are, but we have no choice. Look, I will go with them to make sure everything is all right. You take the ship leeward and manage the passengers ashore. I will join you there with the rest of the women as soon as I can."

"Let me go in your place, Captain," Jorge pleaded.

Anna Kruger shook her head. "Better that I go with the women. It will keep them calm."

Together they watched Lucia and two other pirates climb the bridge stairs. Jorge edged closer to his Captain, grazing her hand with his own.

"Anna, please be careful." She gazed into the deep pools of his brown eyes and touched his fingertips.

"I will be fine, Jorge. Take care of the ship and keep your eye on that woman."

"I will. I do not trust her."

"I do not trust any of them."

Loaded with two diesel drums and thirty young African, Arab, and Asian women, Delgado's three speedboats headed back toward the pirate village two hours later. A modesty scarf covering her face, Lulu Gaye sat together with Anna and Esha Rao.

"Captain?" Lulu called out, a nervousness in her voice. The Bayline picked up speed, splashing seawater over the prow. Anna took the Senegalese teen's hand and squeezed it.

"Do not worry. We are in this together. We will not be gone long." The women glanced back over their shoulders as the *Militobi* faded in the distance behind them. The three pirate boats sped around the island's southeastern point and Anna wrapped her arm around both women. She had the strangest feeling that she would never set foot on her ship again.

Standing together at the port side railing, Dr. Arun and Ashé watched as Esha and Lulu disappeared from view.

Ashé made a vow. "If anything happens to her, I will kill them. I will kill them all!" Dr. Arun clapped his hand on Ashé's shoulder and could feel the teen's tenseness.

"She will be fine, son. They will all be fine." Ashé kept his eyes trained on Lulu's speedboat until it was completely out of sight.

As the pirate boats drew closer to their village, Anna saw the wreck of the rusting MV *Ralik-Ratak* tilted on its port side, splayed across the reef some four hundred yards offshore. A wide gap in the reef lay just fifty yards away. *That captain had just missed a clean entry*, she thought. Delgado saw Kruger contemplating the wreck.

"Captain, remind me to tell you the story of how we got shipwrecked on this island. That was our ship."

* * * * *

The MV *Militobi* dropped its massive chain and anchor into warm lagoon waters five hundred yards off the island's southern coast. Crew members scrambled to unlock the accommodation ladder and winch down both lifeboats. Jorge Estrada gave orders into his walkie-talkie in Spanish and English as Lucia Santos pointed to a large expanse of sandy beach and identified it as their target landing site. Crewmen prepared all decks for arrival and the exhausted migrant passengers, still clutching their rolled sleeping mats, sat cross-legged in the warm sun to await their turn to be ferried ashore.

The first two lifeboats, carrying African, Arab, and South Asian migrants, were met on the beach by a cadre of armed Isleños. Passengers were ushered through the thick sand and ordered to sit and wait for everyone else to disembark. Hidden in the jungle overlooking the landing beach, Desta, Ada, young Chiké Niame, and a group of Africans watched the new arrivals wade ashore. A hundred yards away, a similar sized group of South Asians also watched the activities from a covered jungle perch. Between the two groups, and covered by heavy foliage, a party of Arab migrants also observed the newest island visitors.

On the beach, pirates began separating the migrants into three distinct groups, each with assigned guards. An overweight pirate, rifle in hand and knife in his belt, motioned for Okeke Ka to guide all the African migrants to an empty section of the beach to wait together. The pirate escorting Mohammed Kassab urged him to identify Arab migrants. They were led to another part of the beach some twenty-five yards from the Africans. Kassab and Okeke exchanged puzzled glances across the distance. Okeke shrugged at his friend, not understanding why they were being separated. A tall wiry pirate, a large machete in hand, directed Dr. Arun and the smaller contingent of South Asians to a third empty section of beach.

After several hours and numerous trips of loading and ferrying passengers ashore, Estrada, Fernandez, and Ashé Gaye, along with Lucia Santos, boarded the last lifeboat. Upon arrival, an armed pirate ran down to meet them, tossed a machine gun to Lucia, then quickly guided a confused Ashé up the beach to join the African passengers. Lucia immediately aimed her weapon at Estrada and Fernandez as they jumped down into the shallow surf.

"No further!" she ordered, leveling the gun at their midsections.

"Whoa!" Estrada exclaimed, staring at the weapon. "What are you doing?"

"New orders for you from the Commandant, sorry!"

Fernandez scoffed, "Orders? We don't take orders from the..."

Lucia pointed her weapon at Fernandez's head. Estrada motioned for everyone to remain calm. Up the beach, Mohammed Kassab spotted Estrada and Fernandez with their hands held high and immediately sensed trouble. He had seen it too many times in Libya where Gaddafi had lined up unarmed civilians who refused to join his Islamic socialists. They had held their hands up too, before they were cruelly slaughtered. Kassab watched as the two *Militobi* officers were pushed back toward their lifeboat. He slid up closer to his pirate guard who quickly pointed his rifle at him. Kassab pointed toward the shore.

"Those people are our friends," he pleaded in English. "Why are they being treated like—"

"They did it for the money!" The guard scoffed. "Don't you know you can only depend on *us* to protect you now from..." He motioned over at the other two groups of passengers. "...*them!*"

A short distance away, the tall tattooed pirate guarding the Asian group yelled at his bewildered captives. He nodded over towards the Arabs.

"You hear them? They say they want to be fed before you. They think they are better than you! You should have known it! They can't be trusted." Dr. Arun tried to object to the outright lie but was almost immediately drowned out by other Asian passengers who stood and yelled back over at the Arabs who, in response, returned with their own barbs. Neither group understood what anyone was saying or why they were saying it. The Africans, not comprehending why the other two groups were yelling at each other, stood and began arguing and shouting themselves. Spurred on by their captors, the beach had become a crazed screaming contest between all three groups of *Militobi* passengers.

Hearing the uproar up the beach, Lucia Santos motioned for the two *Militobi* officers to board their lifeboat. "Your orders are to return to where you came from and bring back a million Euros in cash."

"What? That is impossible!" Fernandez exclaimed.

"You have one month, or your Captain and the other women will die, or worse."

"Worse?" Estrada repeated.

"Unfortunately, the Commandant is a man of, uh, unique... passions. He and the other men have needs that must be met, and they will not wait very long." Lucia scowled as she spoke in a quiet tone almost to herself. "Delgado *never* waits very long."

Estrada pleaded, "Oh God, you cannot do that!"

"You have one month, and if any police or military arrive, they all die. Do not give out our location. We know we are uncharted and wish to remain so. The Captain and the women will be safe until you return with the money."

Fernandez was indignant. "Ransom! I cannot believe that you..."

Lucia aimed the machine-gun at the Navigator. "The Commandant's orders are to let you go to find a million Euros. He does not care where you find it. However, if you fail to return, the Captain and all the nice women will be executed. Clear?"

"Why are you doing this horrible thing?" Estrada asked.

"Commandant's orders! We need cash to get off this island! We *must* get off this god-forsaken island."

"Just take our ship and leave," offered Fernandez. "We will stay. We will stay with the passengers. Just take the ship and go anywhere you want."

Lucia frowned. "Oh, we have a ship. But the Spanish authorities are everywhere. We need cash. Cash gets us anywhere we want to go. You have one month."

Estrada hesitated. "We need to talk to Sea-Sweep, our home office. Maybe they can wire the money to you!"

"Only cash! We do not trust wire transfers, or you. Cash only. Sorry, but it has to be this way. Now, back to your ship. Right now!" Lucia motioned with her machine gun.

The *Militobi* officers took a final glance up the beach at the three passenger groups and then boarded their lifeboat. Estrada peered back at the willowy pirate who continued to point her weapon at them.

"*Señorita,* you are making a very big mistake."

"I hope not," responded Lucia. "I actually hope you make it. We all want to get off of this island."

* * * * *

In the midst of the noise and chaos surrounding him, Okeke Ka watched his friends from the *Militobi* depart and said a quick prayer for them. Lucia returned from the beach and fired her machine gun in the air to quiet all the catcalling and arguing between the groups.

"Listen to me! Listen to me!" All three groups grew silent. "Sit down! Sit!" she ordered in English. "Here's how we will do things." The new arrivals all squatted down in the sand just as Desta Kado and his contingent of Africans appeared from the jungle and trudged slowly toward the migrants. Seconds later, the Arab and Asian observers emerged from their hiding places and also headed in the direction of the new arrivals. The African passengers quickly stood again, confused and somewhat fearful. Okeke pushed his way through his fellow Africans to meet the visitors. Desta stopped first to speak to Lucia.

"Is this to be our ship to the Canaries?"

Lucia frowned and shook her head. "Sorry, Desta, still no word on asylum. We will let you know." She stepped aside and gestured to the pirate guards to do the same. Okeke, upbeat and hopeful, greeted Desta.

"I am Okeke Ka, from Ghana, but we come from many places. We are not sure what is happening to us right now."

"Uncle, I am Desta Kado from Sierra Leone. We will lead you to our village for safety from these people." He gestured over to the Asian and Arab passenger groups who had watched his arrival in silence.

Chiké stepped forward to make an announcement. "We have food and water for you in our village. It is not too far away. You are now in the African sector. That is what we call our part of the island." The African passengers crowded in closer.

"Greetings to all of you," the Head Man said, his voice deep and clear. "My young friend Chiké is right. We are not very far from our village. This is Chiké's mother, Ada Niame. We have been on this island for over a year now and are asylum-seekers like you. Come with us. You will be safe in our village."

Okeke Ka remained wary of the pirate guards. "But these men...and the weapons?"

"The Isleños are here to protect us," Desta explained, sensing possible danger as the Arab and South Asian village representatives arrived and joined their respective groups. The pirate guards backed away again to allow the visitors to mingle freely with the newly arrived migrant passengers. Desta scanned the South Asian contingent looking for Jay Rawal.

* * * * *

"I'm Jay Rawal from Pakistan," the young man said, introducing himself to the South Asian group. He wore a traditional, long brown *kurta* pajama shirt that nearly reached the knees, but his pants had been trimmed into shorts and the shirttail tucked inside the waist to allow for the island's tropical breeze. "You must follow us to safety. Our village is a five-hour walk from here. We will follow along the beach to the westernmost part of the island when it is time." Perplexed, Dr. Arun wended his way through the crowd.

"Excuse me, sir. Why are we being separated from the others?"

Rawal scanned the other two groups then turned back to face Dr. Arun. "*We* have our own village. *They* have their own villages. It is safer for all of us that way."

"Safer? Is there some reason to be afraid of them?"

Jay snorted as he surveyed the entire beach, now swarming with migrant villagers and the new arrivals. "Afraid? You could call it that, I suppose. *They* are murderers and thieves. *We* must stay together to protect ourselves."

"But what about all these other people with the weapons?"

"Isleños is the name we give all of Commandant Delgado's people no matter where they are from. They protect us."

"Why have they sent the ship's crew away? They are our friends."

Jay shrugged. "I do not know about them. Their job is done perhaps, and they return to the safety of their home country." Dr. Arun watched as the African group, still under pirate guard, was escorted due north directly into the jungle. As they departed, he made eye contact with Okeke and Ashé, who waved goodbye. The Arab group, also flanked by several armed pirates, headed west along the beach. Still puzzled by all the guards and weapons and separate groupings, Okeke and Kassab exchanged worried glances as they departed in different directions. The Asian group was ordered to wait for thirty minutes before they were directed to head westward along the shore toward their village, far beyond the adjoining Arab sector.

On the bridge of the *Militobi*, Estrada and Fernandez peered through their binoculars at the landing beach.

"I can still see them. Mr. Kassab is heading west along the beach," Fernandez said.

"*Sí,*" said Jorge, who spoke carefully into his walkie-talkie. "Engineer? Slow ahead. Take us out of here."

On the now empty landing beach, a wistful and solitary Lucia Santos watched the *Militobi* depart and sighed before rejoining her pirate cohorts and leading them eastward toward their own village. *I hope they make it*, she thought. *I have to get away from Delgado!*

* * * * *

During their long walk along the sandy beach toward the western end of the island, Dr. Arun caught up with Jay Rawal as he led the line of Asians through the shoreline that was slowly changing from thick sand to pebbles and rocks.

"What's your story?" asked Dr. Arun in Urdu, "How did you come to be here, if I may ask?"

"Probably the same way you did, sir," replied Jay. "Escaped the Taliban and made my way to Libya. I was a school teacher. And you?"

"I'm a doctor."

"Really?" said Jay, surprised and delighted. "A medical doctor? That is great news! A doctor is sorely needed in our village. We came to this island by chance. We were leaking fuel, at least that is what we were told, and then met by the Isleños, much like you were today. We didn't know anybody was living here. There were already sixty Asians on the island, and we joined them in their village. We must be over a hundred and sixty strong now." Pirate guards continued to escort the group as they walked westward. "We have been attacked by Africans as well as Arabs a number of times," Jay continued. "They steal. They have murdered. They cannot be trusted. None of them can."

"Is your village not safe then?" asked Dr. Arun.

"We are in a very safe spot. We are isolated and protected from the others. It is a mystery how they continue to injure and harm us."

Jay led the group past a twelve-foot high bamboo fence, perpendicular to the beach, whose terminus stopped at the water's edge. The tall fence posts were sharpened into jagged points at the top to prevent climbing.

"Keep moving," Jay called out in English. "We are on Arab land now." Awaiting the Asian group, fifteen Arab villagers armed with primitive bamboo spears and machetes began walking in parallel to them at the edge of the jungle thirty yards away. Jay turned to his followers. "Do not make eye contact with them. They will watch us until we leave their sector. Ours is still further down the beach. Keep walking."

Two hours later, the Asian group passed the endpoint of another twelve-foot high bamboo fence, again perpendicular to the beach.

"From this point on, it is our land," Jay explained to Dr. Arun. He pointed at the fence. "The Isleños had our people build this wall to keep the Arabs and Africans from hunting here but in truth it was constructed to protect us from the other villagers. No one is supposed to trespass, but we know they do." The Asian migrants followed Jay as he turned northwest and entered the jungle. Rabbits and wild pigs skittered away as the group found a worn path that took them through a giant pineapple forest. "We are still more than an hour's walk from our village," said Jay.

"But we are safe now. The path is wide, and it won't take us very long." The pirate escorts headed back toward the original landing area leaving the group to wind its way through the jungle, finally arriving at the Asian village and a crowd of well-wishers.

Welcoming the new arrivals, Mohamed Aboud, a white-haired village elder, was overjoyed to learn Dr. Arun was from Pakistan, his home country. He learned that many of the others from India, Bangladesh, and Sri Lanka had also escaped the grasp of the Taliban, but most had fled poverty, war, and the internecine cruelty that came much too close to their homes and families for them to remain. Aboud decided these tired migrants would be settled temporarily at the council house while volunteers would be sought to host individuals in private homes until new houses could be built for them.

Dr. Arun stepped away from the group as they were led toward their temporary housing to speak with Mohamed Aboud alone. "Peace be upon you," said Dr. Arun, in his native Urdu.

"And with you," replied Mohamed Aboud. "Have you come far?"

"Karachi."

"And I from Islamabad, welcome to our humble village."

"We thank you. We are few in number."

"Still, most welcome. Our village is simple but we will do all that we can to make your stay comfortable. We have been here for more than two years now, some less than that. It is good to meet new people in search of a safe homeland."

Dr. Arun scanned the trimmed bamboo and thatched houses. "This village appears to be well-kept, well-thought out, and most practical."

"Are you familiar with Basti Tabu?"

"The self-supporting Pakistani village north of Sadiqabad?"

"Yes, we are much like that village. Without a true government we have to rely on each other for everything from food gathering to construction to the protection of our women and children. We have formed a village council of elders and post guards outside the village entrance."

Dr. Arun nodded. "Yes, so practical, it reminds me of my grandparents' village, Shimshal, and how they practice *nomus*, working together for the benefit of all. How long do you think we will all stay here?"

"*Inshallah,* it is in God's hands."

"I am missing our homeland already," said Dr. Arun.

"We all do, my son."

* * * * *

The Arab contingent of passengers was led from the landing beach by Hassan Alwan, a young Sudanese fisherman of thirty who had arrived a year earlier on the *Yap Islander*. After several hours they approached the Arab village on a jungle path through sweet-smelling stands of mangos and papayas. The village, a commune of sixty-five thatched and bamboo huts, loomed ahead with two armed guards standing near its entrance.

"But there is so much food here!" Mohammed Kassab said to Alwan in Arabic, astounded as he looked around the lush growth. "It seems to be asking the hungry man to just pick and eat."

Alwan nodded. "Praise Allah. And the fishing is good too. But the Asians and Africans steal from us anyway and have killed three of our people. It is truly a sacrilege." He pointed his thin goatee at Kassab, asking for his acknowledgement of such a reality.

Kassab nodded. "Such difficulty on such a glorious island," he remarked, bowing in return to the many Arab villagers greeting the new arrivals. The men dressed in white, one-piece *dishdasha*s, while *shayla*-veiled women watched the tired migrants drag themselves into the village center, some staggering after the long walk from the landing beach. Imam Ashraf welcomed Kassab and the group of nearly two hundred migrants and ordered the men to be housed in the building currently used as a mosque. Families, single women, girls, and other small children would be housed at private huts and one-room shelters built by Amman Boulas and his group of carpenters.

As they walked past a goat corral along a wide pathway, Mohammed Kassab explained to Imam Ashraf that his group was taken out of Libya at nightfall nearly a month earlier and were met at sea by the Europe-bound *Militobi*. He remarked how well they had been treated aboard ship and that there were migrants in his group from Syria, Iraq, and the Sudan. All were escaping war. Kassab was astonished to hear from the Imam that he had been on the island for over two years. He was astounded that the elderly gentleman seemed, well, *happy* to be living in this hidden jungle village.

"Thanks be to Allah that the Isleños are here to protect us," said Imam Ashraf. "I do not know what we would have done without them. Come walk with me. Let me tell you a story."

Since his arrival on the *Ralik-Ratak*, the elderly Ashraf Agha related how he had taken on a spiritual role in the Arab village and, since he often led villagers in prayer, they now referred to him as *Imam*. Over time he had formed strong opinions concerning the future of his people. A retired teacher from Morocco, he fervently believed the children, and their parents, needed more religious education, both formal and informal. He remembered that the eight Arab children that had arrived with him on the ill-fated *Ralik-Ratak* had secular duties to perform each day. As the village was being built, they would gather fruit and vegetables, carry bamboo poles to the workers erecting the tall fence far out in the jungle, and bring water back from the nearby river in old ship biscuit tins. Those children were busy all day and exhausted each night. Not once had he heard of them getting into mischief. The arrival of the *Yap Islander* a year later however, added at least thirty more children of different ages to the village and with them came the rustlings of boredom and idleness. And today, he pointed out to Mohammed Kassab, even more youngsters had arrived.

"There needs to be more discipline and specific tasks for the youth of this village to do," he said. "They need more religious instruction, otherwise we will soon be living in chaos."

Imam Ashraf also shared his belief there was something curious, almost eerie, about the island itself. While he couldn't articulate exactly what it was, he had no doubt the jungle and tall trees exerted some sort of strange, almost spiritual influence over everyone's hearts and minds. Although not a believer in the supernatural, the Imam reasoned it had to be more than coincidence that brought them all to Santa Inez Island together at this particular time in history.

"Perhaps it is God's will after all," he opined.

"But Imam," began Kassab, responding to the elderly man's story. "When you learned the *Yap Islander* had arrived a year after you landed here, why did you not ask the Isleños to be taken back to Morocco or somewhere else?"

The Imam shook his head. "The arrival of that ship was indeed a complete surprise. By the time our new villagers arrived here they told us the ship had left. But had we known in advance, we still would not have returned from where we came. Remember that we have all made the choice to leave our homelands. There was no place for me to go back *to*, my son. And, now I believe I have found my *true* home, praise Allah. And this home has been good to me. Far better than the one I left behind."

Imam Ashraf escorted Kassab toward the mosque where the new arrivals were unpacking their sleeping mats and finding a place to rest.

"Young man, the original passengers of the *Ralik-Ratak* believed we would attain asylum in the Canaries and that our ship's captain and crew were honest and forthright professionals.

But that was not the case. The crew lost its way, and the result was death, horrible deaths for many innocent people. The evil doers were ultimately punished, of course. It was God's will. Violence is regrettable but we must also believe in a realistic and practical God, no matter what myths the Christians believe about us. '*O Prophet, urge the believers to battle...*'"

"And I understand there are problems with the Africans and Asians?" Kassab added.

"Yes, we have had our troubles with them, at times. And we have worked to protect ourselves with fences on both borders of our sector. We provide food to our Isleños protectors each month to insure their support, as well."

Puzzled, Kassab posed another question as they passed the corral, the goats shying away from them. "It seems to me you do not want to leave this island? Am I correct in that assumption?"

"Is it so difficult to understand? Children needed schooling when we arrived and they still do, now more than ever. Our people need guidance. Libya has been at war for years. Morocco remains in a civil war. War is the cause that brought most of us to this island. Probably you as well."

Kassab nodded as they reached the end of their short walk. "Then you are happy here, Imam?"

"No one feels unhappy with God in their life."

* * * * *

Deep within the pirate village, Anna Kruger sat on a woven mat of pandanus leaves in a one-room thatched house with a planked wooden floor surrounded by thirty female passengers. They spoke to each other in hushed tones of French, Arabic, and English. Sitting in the back of the room with Lulu and Esha, Anna was frustrated at the delay in rejoining her crew. A few women began to sob as the afternoon turned into evening and the light faded inside the locked room. Without warning, the door burst open and two guards stormed inside frightening the women, many who screamed and immediately covered their faces for modesty, clinging to each other for safety.

"Quiet down!" one of the pirates ordered while the other ogled the women lasciviously. "I said, be quiet!" he yelled once more.

The second pirate engaged a bolt on his rifle, and the room instantly became silent.

"That's better," he said. "The Commandant wishes to speak to the Captain." Anna nodded to Lulu and Esha as she stood to follow the guards. *It's about time*, she thought. Fearing the worst, several of the younger women began to weep but Kruger reassured them with a smile. Escorted across a wide pebble-strewn courtyard that bordered the beach, she was led up three short steps and into a large wood-framed house with a thatched roof. Inside, the obese Delgado sat in a large chair rubbing his sore right knee. He removed his beret and fingered the four-foot, mini-bullwhip coiled around his left shoulder.

"Sit down, Captain. We have much to talk about," he began.

"Of course, Commandant. We are all wondering why it is taking so long to—"

"First," Delgado interrupted her. "I need to know how much money you received for these so-called migrants and where you have hidden it!"

Anna was taken aback at his directness. "Money? I do not quite know what—"

"You didn't come all this way for nothing!"

"We are a *rescue* ship. I told you that!"

Delgado guffawed and continued to fondle the whip. "Where's the money, Captain? We searched your ship. You have hidden it somewhere. Perhaps with the migrants themselves?"

Anna was astonished. "You really think we make these people pay us for rescuing them?"

Delgado slammed his fist down on the chair's arm. "Yes! I know you get paid from the smugglers and traffickers! Maybe the families paid you to take them aboard. Maybe European governments are paying you to dump them overboard. I don't care who pays you. I just want the money!"

Anna sat back in her chair, chagrined at how she had allowed herself to be trapped like this. "Commandant, let me explain something to you. Migrants and asylum-seekers are saved from death and starvation by a number of European non-profit organizations. Rescues are made all over the Mediterranean and sometimes even in North Africa. My ship and crew *saved* many people from drowning on this voyage alone! But even with our best efforts, many still died." Anna paused a moment to consider those lost at sea. "You do know we face prison ourselves if we are caught by any of the Coast Guards?"

Delgado grunted. "Sad story, but why this island?"

"Look, we are Sea-Sweep. We are a German non-profit organization with a mission to search for and rescue migrants wherever we find them. Nations like Malta, France, Italy, Spain, and Greece, who once welcomed asylum-seekers with open arms, now will not let our ship enter their ports. We were turned away everywhere. I had an old chart and found this island purely by accident. The passengers decided it was worth the risk to come here and avoid the detention camps. We believed it would be safe, at least temporarily, while we petitioned for their asylum."

Delgado laughed and tapped at a glass cage resting on a table made from a large shipping crate. It contained a coiled black King snake.

"Is it *so* funny?" Anna asked, being as sarcastic as possible. "You told me you wanted our help to get my passengers settled in their villages and—"

Angry, Delgado cut her off by grabbing his whip and holding it inches from her face. "You are a bitch! You and the others will *not* be leaving this camp. And you will *not* be joining your ship. As we speak, it is on its way out to sea to procure your ransom!" Shocked, Kruger could only watch speechless, as Delgado continued. "You *will* do what I say, Captain, or suffer the consequences." Delgado held the whip up again.

Anna surprised herself at how swiftly this crude man touched off her ire and disgust. She erupted, standing up. "I am leaving!"

Taken aback, Delgado hobbled after her to the door. "Get used to it, Captain! You and your passengers belong to me now. Get me that money!" Incensed, Anna turned and came face-to-face with the ponderous pirate, seizing him by his uniform lapels.

"I may be a *bitch,* but you are a delusional *bastard!* And you are nothing more than a thief! A pirate!" Delgado pushed the Captain away as bodyguards entered and rushed to his aid.

"Take her! Take her away!" Anna was quickly ushered out. Seething, Delgado cracked his short whip against the closed door. "*Bitch*! You'll pay for that." He struggled to sit his large frame back in his worn chair, caressed the glass cage and whispered gently to his snake, "Yes, my Diablo, I know she scared you. She *will* pay for that. I promise you. And I always keep my promises!" The snake hissed and slithered to the top of the jar before gliding effortlessly to the bottom of its glass-enclosed world.

Anna Kruger was shoved roughly back inside the one-room thatched house with the other women, tripping over several of them as she hit the floor. Esha and Lulu rushed over to help her up.

"Captain! Are you all right?" Esha asked.

Anna shook her head. "I am fine. I am fine. But we have a problem."

CHAPTER 6

AN ISLAND FORAY

Under the cover of darkness, Jorge Estrada, Gabby Fernandez, and six crewmen scurried from two lifeboats and pulled them up the landing beach to the edge of the jungle where they secreted them under large palm fronds and dead tree branches. Estrada gathered the men together and spoke quietly.

"Listen," he whispered, his voice raspy in the night air. "We will divide up. Gabby, you take three men and find Mr. Kassab. Maybe he knows where they have taken Dr. Arun. You think you can find him?"

"*Sí*, Jorge, they went west down the beach. They must have gone up into the jungle at some point. I do not know where, but we will find them."

"Be careful. Pirates could be anywhere. You *must* convince Mr. Kassab and the others we need their help to rescue the Captain and the passengers."

"*Sí*, Jorge."

Estrada pointed to the remaining crewmen, "You men come with me. We will try and find Mr. Okeke and the Africans. They went straight up into the jungle right here." He pointed north. "Any questions?"

One of the crewmen asked, "Mr. Estrada? What if we meet pirates?"

The men all stared daggers at him without responding. "Oh, got it," the crewman said sheepishly, finally understanding the meaning of their deadly looks.

"Good luck," offered Estrada. "We can stay in contact by walkie-talkie and will meet back on the ship after sunset tomorrow. That gives us tonight and all day tomorrow to find our friends. Watch yourself. You do not want to get caught. Remember the pirates have guns and we do not." He led his team northward into the jungle while Fernandez moved west, following the beach route that he remembered the Arab group had taken.

An hour and a half later, Fernandez spotted the twelve-foot bamboo wall and motioned for his team to stop. He pulled out his walkie-talkie.

"Jorge? Do you copy?"

"I read you," the First Officer responded. "Have you found them already?"

"No, we have reached a huge fence that seems to go on for miles. We will follow it for a while and see where it takes us."

"Good luck, my friend."

"You too, Jorge, out."

In the moonlight, Fernandez used the massive bamboo wall as a guide and reference point. His team made its way silently through a clearing some twenty-five yards from the fence before finding a path west through tracts of guava and papaya trees. Leaving the bamboo wall behind, they sped up their pace, trotting single file along a course lined with elephant ear ferns, orchids, and monkey brush vines. They followed the twisted trail, most likely a rabbit or wild pig track, through vast thickets of wide ferns and shrubs for a half hour. Moments later, before any crew member could even begin to comprehend what was happening to them, a spear whisked past Fernandez's ear and thudded into a breadfruit tree not six feet away.

Fernandez and his team remained motionless as armed Arabs surrounded them. Hands held high, Gabby cleared his throat and spoke in as slow and as clear English as he could.

"Hello! We…are…from…the…*Militobi*. It is the big ship that arrived today. We are trying to find Mr. Kassab, Mr. Mohammed Kassab? He was one of our passengers. Do you know him? Could…you…please…take…us…to…him?"

Miles east of the captured Fernandez team, the African village boasted ninety bamboo and thatched huts that glowed from cooking fires in the warm night. Two African guards, armed with bamboo knives and spears, stood watch. Hidden behind a clump of palm trees, Jorge cautioned his men to remain silent as they edged closer.

Desta, Okeke, and Ashé sat cross-legged on woven mats around a large cooking fire just outside the Head Man's house. Food was served in plaited coconut leaf baskets by Ada and Chiké. The boy hurried to sit beside Desta, drawing a laugh from the African leader who motioned for his guests to eat and drink.

"Thank you for your hospitality. It is appreciated by all of us," said Okeke.

Desta patted Chiké on the shoulder then took a coconut and sliced the top off with two swings of his sharpened bamboo machete. He passed it to Okeke, who immediately closed his eyes in prayer. Desta waited until the Ghanaian opened his eyes.

"My friend Chiké came with us over a year ago after a long voyage at sea," said Desta. "He now helps me run this village." Chiké grinned and Desta patted him on the shoulder once again. "He is the Assistant Head Man." Everyone laughed, and Chiké was embarrassed but Ada was proud and beamed at seeing her son seated on the right hand of the village leader, the man she had grown to love.

"Thank you for the food," Ashé said. "I was very hungry."

Okeke agreed, "Yes, thanks to all of you for allowing us to share in this wonderful and beautiful meal and this charming village. We had no idea it even existed."

Desta held up his coconut in a toast. "It is our way. We are Africans. We must live as one as we join our ancestors in protecting ourselves from all who would harm us." He drank deeply from his coconut.

In the jungle some seventy-five yards from the village entrance, Estrada motioned to his men to stay hidden then took a deep breath and walked straight toward the African guards with his hands held high and his palms wide open.

"Hello! Good evening! Good evening!" The guards sprang to their feet and immediately took defensive positions. "I come in peace!" Estrada shouted. "Hello! Good evening to you!"

One of the guards instantly sprinted back into the village while the other stepped forward to face Estrada, his spear at the ready. "Stop where you are!"

Estrada stopped. *Thank God you speak English,* he thought, relieved.

"We have come to see the passengers from the ship. The *Militobi*? We arrived today. Is Mr. Okeke Ka with you? Have you met him?" Within minutes and clutching a bamboo machete, Desta and several men rushed to join the guard who faced Estrada. Twenty yards behind, Okeke struggled to catch up.

"Who are you?" asked the Head Man, sizing up his potential adversary. He stepped forward, his face determined and his jaw tightly clenched, expecting the worst.

"I am Jorge Estrada, First Officer from the *Militobi,* at your service, sir. We have come to find some of our passengers, our friends. Can you help us?"

Nearly out of breath, Okeke finally caught up to Desta and touched his shoulder. "I know this man! He is from our ship." Desta relaxed his warlike stance as Okeke greeted Estrada with a bear hug. "I was so worried about you, Mr. Estrada. I saw you leave, and I thought I would never see you again."

"We had some trouble on the beach. We need your help."

Okeke shook Estrada's hand. "Of course. Of course."

"I have a few of my men with me," revealed Estrada. "They are out there." He pointed into the darkness.

Okeke turned to his African host. "Please, we must help our friends. There are a few more."

Desta nodded and as they waited for the men to come forward out of the jungle, Okeke made introductions. "This is Desta Kado," Okeke said to Estrada. "He is the Head Man of the village and our host."

"Sir, I am Jorge Estrada, First Officer of the MV *Militobi*, and I am very glad to know you." The three other crewmen slowly moved into the flickering campfire light and then followed Desta and the others back into the village. Motioned to take seats on the woven mats outside Desta's house, the crewmen sat cross-legged next to each other, unsure of the proper protocols for such a situation. Desta asked Ada to prepare food baskets for each of them.

"Mr. Desta, we thank you," began Estrada. "I know we are not supposed to be here, and we know it could be very dangerous for you."

"I am not afraid," the African leader said, confident that there was no other place on the island as safe as his own home.

"Good, then let me request your help. More precisely, we *need* your help. These pirates have taken our Captain and many women from our ship as captives." Desta continued to slice off the tops of the coconuts with no facial expression or reaction to Estrada's words. Chiké took each coconut from Desta and delivered it to the visitors.

"Pirates?" Desta finally responded. "You mean the Isleños?"

"Sir, they are *pirates*! They have kidnapped our Captain and many of our female passengers and are holding them as prisoners." Desta smirked as he drank from his coconut.

Okeke nodded. "Desta, it is true that women were taken from the ship soon after we arrived. We were told they needed them to make the living arrangements."

"There is more," added Estrada. "On the beach we were told they would kill the Captain and all the women, if we did not pay a ransom of one million Euros."

Astonished, Okeke tried to put a more hopeful spin on this stunning piece of news. "Perhaps they did not mean it quite like that, Mr. Estrada. Perhaps you misunderstood them. Perhaps it was a language problem that—"

"They pointed their guns right at us! Did you not see that we were forced off the beach and back to the ship? There was no language problem I can assure you."

"Their guns protect us from the Arabs and Asians," explained Desta, as if lecturing a child. The crewmen exchanged worried looks. Estrada tried again.

"The Arabs and Asians on our ship are not your enemy, sir."

"No, they are not!" agreed Okeke. "God knows we are all one. God cares for all of us."

Desta slammed his empty coconut to the mat, splitting it in two. "Where was *He* this last year? Where was *He* when the Asians killed Chiké's father, Awa, my best friend? Why doesn't *He* stop the Arabs and the Asians from stealing and killing us? It is only our ancestors and the Isleños who protect us. No one else!" Desta stood, his anger quickly subsiding. "You are all welcome here. But tomorrow is our village's turn to take food to the Isleños. If you are not afraid to go with us, you will see there is no reason to worry. I will ask them about the women and your Captain."

"Can I go too, Desta?" Ashé asked. "I will ask about my sister."

"No children are allowed, but I will ask for you," Desta replied. He pointed to Ada sitting in the doorway to his hut. "Ada will show you where to sleep tonight. We will leave at sunrise." He checked a final time to see that Chiké had enough in his basket to eat. He stopped momentarily to gently touch Ada's hand and then entered his hut. Ashé was infuriated.

* * * * *

African men and women lined up across the village center early the next morning toting coconut-leaf baskets of fish, pork, breadfruit, pineapple, and mango. Desta greeted the new migrant passengers from the *Militobi* who joined the line for the first time, trying to fit into village life as quickly as possible. Food baskets balanced on their heads, villagers followed the Head Man through the main entrance and out into the steamy jungle. Estrada and his men watched as the long line disappeared into the lush foliage then followed behind them, walking slowly and taking in the sights and sounds of the warm green canopy cradling the island like a protective mother cradles her newborn child.

Carrying a huge stalk of bananas over one brawny shoulder, Desta glanced back at the file of villagers winding their way along the path behind him. Seventy Africans, food baskets still teetering on their heads, walked east in the direction of the massive bamboo wall that divided them from half the island. Hours later, Desta motioned for everyone to rest. Estrada and his men walked up to join him at the head of the line, gazing at the imposing twelve-foot high bamboo divider up ahead. A gate had been pushed opened from the eastern side. Curious, Estrada contemplated the purpose of the wall but before he could say anything, Desta turned to speak.

"This is the border of our land. The other side is Isleños land. There is a waterfall not far away. If the jungle was quiet, you could hear it from here. It is where we leave our baskets. The Isleños take the food they want back to their village on the far side of the island."

Fascinated at the willingness of the people to complete this onerous task without question, Estrada asked, "And you do this each week? They open the gate for you?"

"Every three weeks; the Asians will do it next week, then the Arabs, then we do it once more."

Estrada studied the wall. "This is incredible! How long has it been here?"

"It was here when I arrived. They say the first villagers, the shipwrecked ones, built it for protection more than two years ago."

"The poles are all sharpened at the top."

Desta picked up his heavy banana stalk and slung it easily over his shoulder. The other villagers stood and prepared to follow him.

"No one is to cross over to another sector. Find a place to hide before we reach the waterfall. It can be very bad if their rules are broken."

"And are there many rules?" Estrada asked.

"Not many but they are punishable by death."

Okeke Ka joined the men at the front of the line. He stared at the wall, his glance following it northward until it disappeared into the tall trees.

"My God! We are all birds in a bamboo cage."

Estrada asked Desta, "How many pirates, er, Isleños are there?"

"Not enough to protect us!" Desta said, as the line moved toward the opened gate. The deafening sound of the great waterfall raged in the distance as the African villagers finally reached their destination. Water cascaded two hundred feet into three widening pools that teemed with eels and fish, each one shallower than the next. In the clearing, twenty armed pirates awaited the Africans who placed their food baskets carefully in piles near the widest pool then turned away without saying a word. Pirates immediately began sifting through the baskets, selecting the food items they wanted to bring back to their own village, discarding the rest.

Lucia Santos, machine gun in hand, acknowledged Desta with a nod as she watched the Africans pile their baskets. Hidden from view behind a stand of seventy-foot bamboo trees, Estrada's team watched as the pirates, each fingering a rifle, pistol, or machete, watched the line of Africans complete a long loop to the nearest pool to drop their baskets before returning again to the opened fence gate. As Okeke Ka set his food basket down on the pile, he took a step toward Lucia.

"Excuse me, madam." Startled, Lucia stared back at the Ghanaian. "I was wondering when we can expect our women folk to return? The ones from the ship?"

Lucia scowled at him. "Soon, very soon."

"Thank you. Thank you," replied Okeke. "Oh, and will Captain Kruger be with them?"

Wary, Lucia eyed Okeke then scanned the line of Africans, searching for their leader.

"Desta?" she called out. "Desta? Get your man out of here!"

The Sierra Leonian rushed to Okeke's side. "He is one of the new ones, Lucia! He just arrived and wanted to come with us. Many of them are worried about their women. And one asks about his sister."

Lucia nodded. "I understand, but the women will be released when the Commandant says so. Not before! Don't ask anything more about it."

Confused by her answer, Desta frowned. "Released? You mean they *are* prisoners?"

Uneasy with the direction the conversation was taking, Lucia pulled the bolt back on her machine gun. "No more questions. You both had better be on your way now. Back to your village."

Sensing trouble, other pirates stepped closer causing the line of villagers to stop and remain motionless, fearing violence. Unafraid and growing angrier, Okeke took another step toward Lucia.

"*Prisoners?* They have done nothing but offered to help the Commandant!"

Lucia leveled her machine-gun at his midsection. "Like I said. It's up to him. I don't want to hear anything more from you."

Desta gently took Okeke by the arm and steered him back toward the line of villagers, whispering to his new friend, "Something *is* wrong, Uncle. I can feel it. She is not telling us the whole story. The Spanish sailor may be right after all."

* * * * *

Santa Inez Island

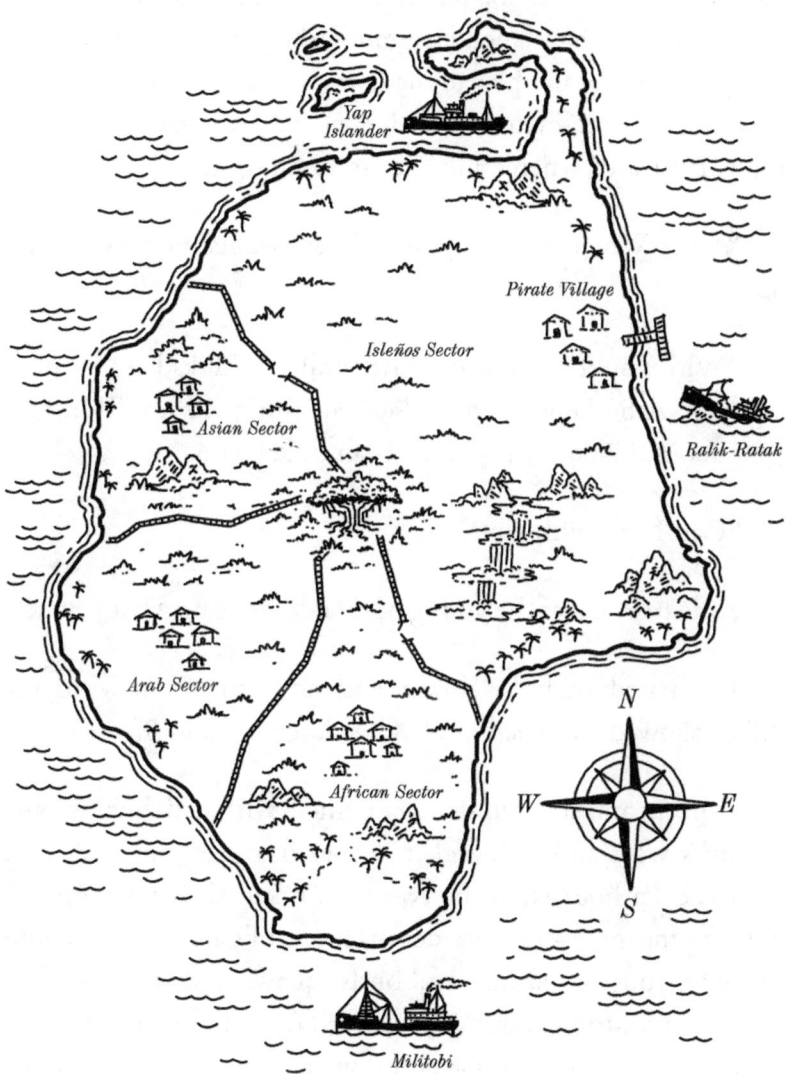

Yap
Islander

Pirate Village

Isleños Sector

Ralik-Ratak

Asian Sector

Arab Sector

African Sector

N

W   E

S

Militobi

At the northern edge of the African village, Ashé was determined to find a place where he could be alone to think about his sister and plan how he might rescue her. *It was a brother's duty to do so*, he told himself. So far, he believed he had failed miserably in that duty. He had failed his grandfather, and he had failed to live up to the promise he had made to protect his sister. Jumping easily over a knee-high garden fence, the teenager entered the jungle, frustrated when Chiké ran to catch up with him.

"Ashè? Where are you going? Desta wants me to stay with you."

"Why would he want that? After all, he thinks I am a child." Annoyed, Ashé kept moving. He had things to do. Things to think about. Chiké shrugged and ran to keep up.

"Can I stay with you?"

Ashé frowned at the young boy. "I do not care what you do!"

Fascinated with his brash and adventurous new friend, Chiké followed close behind. "Where are you going?"

Ashé promptly found a trail lined with red bugloss and St. John's wort and followed it deeper into the jungle. A mile north and an hour later, the two boys hiked their way through fields of pineapple and a ponderous forest of date palms. Rabbits scurried through the brush and birds squawked their displeasure as the boys continued, ducking beneath rubber tree branches and passing through acres of passion flowers and orchids. In the far distance, two long twelve-foot high, bamboo fences dovetailed precisely at a massive, hundred-foot banyan tree whose branches and broad leaves seemed to block out the entire sky.

Tired and his foot still sore, Chiké had fallen behind his new friend and called out to him, "We are going much too far, Ashé! It is not allowed."

Ashé was amazed at the size of the fences and the great banyan tree. "Just look at these walls and this tree!"

"We are not allowed!" Chiké warned.

Ashé stared up at the sharpened points atop the bamboo fences. "What are these fences for? It looks like they do not want you to climb them."

"They are the boundaries of our sector. On the left is the Arab sector. On the right is the Isleños sector. We cannot go to other sectors."

"Why not?"

"It is a rule! And we cannot climb the great tree either. It is forbidden! It is an Isleños rule."

Ashé stood at the base of the enormous banyan and peered up at its broad intertwined branches, most were thicker than a man's thigh.

"So you are telling me that you are afraid to climb this tree?"

"I am *not* afraid! If the Isleños catch us, we could be shot."

"Shot? They will shoot you for climbing a tree? Maybe just a quick look over the fences then." Ashé began to climb. Chiké was dumbfounded at his new friend's recklessness.

"Stop! It is not allowed!"

"Just a quick look. It will be fine."

Ashé climbed until he could see over both bamboo walls.

"Hey! There are two *more* walls on the other side of the tree! Come on up!" Curious, Chiké hesitated then climbed until he reached Ashé's branch. He peered through the thick foliage to see that the main bamboo wall that bordered the Isleños sector extended northward beyond the huge tree. However another fence extended west as far as the eye could see. All three fences intersected at the banyan tree to form three rough triangles to the west of the main fence. The two boys scanned the horizon and could see miles of tree-topped forests in all directions.

"Just look at that!" Chiké said, in amazement. "That is Arab land to the west and the Asian sector to the north, straight ahead. I have never seen that before."

"Asian sector?" Ashé repeated. "My friend Dr. Arun is Asian. He is from Pakistan, I think. Follow me!" He made his way through the branches and around the imposing tree trunk before Chiké could say a word.

"Ashé, no! We are not allowed to even climb this tree. Desta will be angry with us."

"I know, I know," replied the Senegalese teen, trying to calm his little friend. "I will take all responsibility. You will not be in any trouble. We will be safe with Dr. Arun. Come and follow me." Ashé lowered himself down to the Asian sector and watched as Chiké slowly wended his way around, over, and under the wide branches. He guided the youth to the ground and brushed dead twigs and leaves off his back and shoulders.

"See, you made it! It was easy."

Over the next two hours, Ashé enjoyed their stroll through the lush jungle while Chiké, more anxious than at any time in his short life, continuously scanned the trees and bushes for danger. The boys stopped only once to watch a female rabbit followed by four kits cross the path in front of them. Ashé pulled a short-bladed knife from his belt and held it up to Chiké, as if reassuring him they would be safe against the soft furry bunnies. Both youngsters laughed out loud. Suddenly, a crackling noise close by stopped the boys in their tracks. Ashé held up his hand to be completely still.

"What is it?" Chiké whispered, instantly regretting his decision to climb the great banyan tree. They found a hiding place behind a stand of wide-leafed bushes and waited. "Is it the Asians? They will kill us!" Ashé shook his head. "Isleños? *They* will kill us!" Ashé rapidly covered Chiké's mouth with his hand.

Twenty yards from their hiding place, three pirates crept stealthily past them then crouched down to reconnoiter. One of the younger pirates, a Malian, gripped his rifle.

"Quiet! The village is just up ahead," he said in English.

"You have the necklace?" A thin Canary Islander asked the third pirate, whose jagged white scar along his right cheek looked painted on by a drunken tattoo artist. He sported a dark beard and stood nearly six feet.

"I said I *have* it," retorted the scarred pirate, annoyed since he had been asked the same question at least three times that morning. "I'll leave it near the bodies." Ashé attempted to move closer for a better view but Chiké held him back, wrapping his arms around his new friend. They continued to listen closely to the three intruders.

The young pirate was angry and nervous and scowled at his two partners. "Let's go! Let's go! I want to finish and be done with it. I told you we should have waited until dark."

The scarred pirate scoffed, "Anybody can make the shot at night. No one can see you. You need to earn the Commandant's respect, man," he chided in English. "What's that proverb of yours from Mali? 'You can't wage a war without the sound of gunpowder'? Or, something like that."

The young pirate smirked. "I never knew what that meant." The pirates continued carefully up the path, focused intently on their deadly mission. Sixty yards ahead at the entrance to the Asian village, two guards, both armed with sharpened bamboo spears, talked quietly while drinking from green coconuts. Wedging himself between two mango trees for balance and arm support, the young pirate aimed his rifle as Ashé and Chiké drew closer.

"Hurry it up," whispered the gaunt pirate with a hiss in his voice. "They're right there in front of you. Take the shot!"

"I will. I will!" The young pirate checked his aim once again. "I see them." Unexpectedly, the wind picked up and blew a harsh gale through the tall canopy of trees high above. Ashé and Chiké glanced up simultaneously to see large branches rocking back and forth like long thin arms pointing down repeatedly to where the pirates were hiding not ten yards away. The boys braced themselves against the wind that seemed bent on preventing their forward progress. With a final push, the boys turned off the path then screamed in unison, horrified as the sniper fired, the loud crack reverberating through the forest. One of the guards was killed instantly, spinning awkwardly before hitting the jungle floor while the second found cover behind a thicket of bamboo.

The pirates bolted to their feet. The scarred pirate yelled, "C'mon!" Frantic, they turned back to the jungle path and nearly ran over Ashé and Chiké. The scarred pirate drew his handgun and shot Chiké through the heart, killing him. Ashé was bowled over and smacked his head on the ground as the African necklace was purposely dropped beside him. Losing consciousness, Ashé's mind raced back to a conversation he had with his grandfather in Bitenti, seemingly ages ago.

* * * * *

The Gaye family sat in their reed and millet stalk house, one of four buildings on their fenced-in compound overlooking rice and millet fields in the vast Saloum River estuary.

"Are you a *griot*?" Ashé asked his grandfather one evening, referring to a traditional Senegalese storyteller.

"Do you think I am?" Pap replied with a question of his own. Ashé grinned and nodded.

"Well, then I am," he answered.

Ashé's mother, Khady, laughed at the old man. "Father, you are the worst *griot* in all of Senegal," she said, and they all laughed again. Pap began a traditional song that named relatives dating back a hundred and fifty years. His sing-song voice, rooted in Senegal's story-telling culture, delighted Ashé who could listen for hours, mesmerized by his grandfather's voice.

"Grandfather, why do you sing the names of our relatives so often?" Ashé asked. "They are long dead."

"So we do not forget them, Ashé! When we sing their names they stay in our memory forever. Will you remember me even if I have been reincarnated as one of your fish?"

"Of course! Come back as a big bass, Grandfather, please. I will catch and release you!"

Pap chortled. "I sing the names of my grandfather and his grandfather and his grandfather, so I will remember them all. Some were fishermen like you are, and I was. Some were farmers like your father."

"I will be a fisherman," said Ashé, proudly.

"Yes, you will Ashé. You will someday be a great and prosperous fisherman. The owner of a fleet of canoes."

* * * * *

Groggy, Ashé could barely discern the outline of adult male legs standing around him in the Santa Inez Island jungle. He tried to call out but only managed a feint whisper before losing complete consciousness.

"Dr. Arun. Dr. Arun. Find Dr...." And then his mind wandered back to his trip through the Sahara.

The four propellers of the Niger Air Douglas DC-6B constantly vibrated and the numbing hum kept Ashé awake the entire three-hour flight from Diori Hamani International Airport in Niamey to Agadez in the suffocating heat of central Niger. The large plane landed with several bumps at the secluded Mano Dayak International Airport at the edge of the sand-swept town of over one hundred thousand inhabitants. Ashé and Lulu had made their way to the restrooms in the stifling tan and green terminal and changed clothing. Lulu emerged ten minutes later dressed in dark pants and a grey hoodie pulled up over her head. Ashé almost didn't recognize her. She looked like a tall teenaged boy.

The oven-like heat was so intense and overwhelming it nearly took the siblings' breath away. Rising at midday to 113 degrees, the debilitating Agadez temperature was worsened by strong gusts that whipped sand and dust around the tiny airport in swirling brown siroccos. They followed other passengers toward what appeared to be a bus stop where they sat and waited. Several dusty taxis pulled up and many of the passengers seemed to know the drivers and greeted them affectionately. A passenger in one of the late arriving taxis scanned the remaining travelers until he eyed the two teenagers sitting together and approached them, speaking in Wolof.

"You are from Senegal? I am a friend of your Uncle Dallah."

Ashé and Lulu breathed long sighs of relief. "We are his family," Ashé said. "We were told to wait for Aliou Sow."

The man grinned. "Good! I am Aliou Sow, and I work with the Toubou people who run the trucks to Libya. You are lucky. If we hurry, we can get you on tomorrow's caravan through the desert." Sow ushered the Senegalese teens into the back seat as the taxi sped off along the airport road and headed for town. Sow turned to the teenagers from the front passenger seat.

"I was told you would have money to pay for your journey, yes?"

Lulu and Ashé exchanged concerned glances. "We have enough," Lulu responded.

"How do you know Uncle Dallah?" Ashé asked.

"I am Senegalese too. I have known Dallah for many years. We went to school together. I was ahead of him by two years. I have lived in Agadez for five years now. I help many migrants, especially those from Senegal to cross the desert."

"Lulu is going to school in France," Ashé blurted out, for no apparent reason. "She will become a teacher."

"Yes, your uncle mentioned that," replied Sow, glancing at the hooded teenager who looked like a boy. The old taxi sped through the dusty Nigerien streets, weaving between Chinese made scooters, Suzuki motorcycles, and donkey carts. Mud-brick, one-story houses lined both sides of the busy roadway.

"You know about Agadez? The history of it?" Sow asked.

"No, not really," replied Ashé.

"It was a very famous place. It is a World Heritage site now, the Grand Mosque, that is. Built in the sixteenth century. Many tourists used to come here to see it, but no more. Now it is only migrants. Either going to Libya or coming back from Libya. Agadez was also famous as a great oasis for camel caravans."

Ashé sat up in his seat and spoke directly, "How will *we* get to Libya, Mr. Sow?"

Sow looked back at both teens and grinned at their determination. "As I said, you are very lucky. Tomorrow is what they call the *Monday Caravan* to Libya. It is a line of trucks that follow each other all the way to Tripoli. It is the safest way to go, but you will be crammed in the back like goats. My friends are from the Toubou tribe, and they will handle everything for you, for a price. I always bring my customers to them."

They pulled up outside a mud-red fence with a blue painted iron gate. It was propped wide open with young men and women walking in and out of the bleak compound. The siblings got out and brushed sand from their clothing.

"This is called a ghetto," Sow announced, and led his two passengers to the gate. "It is the Toubou ghetto. Thousands and thousands of people come through here each year." Lulu and Sow entered but somehow Ashé couldn't follow them. His legs felt heavy and wouldn't move.

Lulu called out, "Ashé? Ashé?" But his legs were frozen in place and he began to slowly sink into the sand, nearly up to his knees. And then Lulu's voice morphed into the distant but familiar soft tones of Dr. Arun.

"Ashé? Ashé?"

The Senegalese teen moaned and moved his head, exerting every effort to draw closer to the doctor's voice.

"Ashé? Ashé?" Dr. Arun called again, a bit more loudly this time to his young patient who sported a large and very ugly welt on the side of his head. "Ashé? Can you hear me?"

The teenager mumbled as he finally regained consciousness. "Dr. Arun?"

"Yes, I'm here. I'm here." The doctor wiped Ashé's brow with a handkerchief and conducted a pupillary examination to check for traumatic brain injury. "You have a bump on your head, but you'll be fine in no time."

"Chiké! How is Chiké?" Ashé tried to sit up, but the doctor held him down, his face darkening. He shook his head and Ashé closed his eyes.

"Oh, no! It is all my fault. It is *all* my fault."

"Now, now," the doctor soothed. "It was not your fault."

"Yes, I brought him here! He told me not to come. He said it was against the rules. But I was angry and wanted to show him I was not scared, but I was scared, Dr. Arun!"

"Now, now, you just rest."

Jay Rawal approached Ashé. Irate, he dangled the African necklace over the youth's face.

"Does *this* belong to you?"

Ashé cocked his head to look at it. "No, it belongs to those Isleños."

Shaken by the teen's statement, Jay repeated what he had just heard, "Isleños? What Isleños?"

"The ones who shot Chiké and that other man!"

Jay and Dr. Arun exchanged puzzled glances. "Isleños shot them?"

"There were three of them. A tall man with a beard and scar and two others. We followed them through the jungle. We did not know they were going to shoot that man and then they pushed us down and shot Chiké. They ran away and I could not move and I—"

"It wasn't *Africans* that attacked?" Jay asked, incredulous.

Concerned by Jay's awe-struck reaction, Dr. Arun handed the teenager a coconut shell full of water. Ashé took a sip and nodded his thanks before sitting up.

"Are you sure, Ashé?" Dr. Arun asked.

"Desta and the villagers are taking food to the Isleños today." Jay realized he was right.

"Yes, it's their day."

"I wanted to explore the island and Chiké followed me. He told me not to come here. Not to climb the tree." He searched the face of a puzzled Dr. Arun for understanding.

"Yes," Jay explained. "There is a giant banyan tree where all the border fences meet. No one is allowed to climb it or to cross over to other sectors. The Isleños believe for some reason the tree symbolizes their strength and absolute control over the island. I know it's a bit odd."

Dr. Arun turned back to Ashé. "But you are saying it was the Isleños who left the necklace?"

"I saw them drop it as they ran away."

Pausing for a moment to consider the situation, Dr. Arun finally realized what happened. "They wanted to *blame* the Africans for the murder of the guard!"

Jay grew very serious. "I know this boy, Chiké. He is like a son to Desta, the Head Man in the African village. We must get him back to his people or things will get much worse for all of us. Isleños rules do not matter now."

* * * * *

A litter containing Chiké's body, covered in green banana leaves and large palm fronds, was carried by four strong Asian men. In the late afternoon sun they approached the massive bamboo wall that bisected the island, protecting the Isleños sector from the other three. Two sinewy villagers looped vine ropes over the tops of the sharpened fence posts and pulled themselves up and over. Moments later the large gate was pushed open and the funereal procession, led by Jay, Dr. Arun, Ashé, and six others, passed slowly through.

"We are now on Isleños land and must turn south toward the African gate," explained Jay. "We are not allowed to be here except to bring food to the Isleños."

"Not allowed?" Dr. Arun repeated, pointing to the covered bier. "After what they did to Ashé and this young boy?"

"There are rules. Rules to keep us safe," said Jay.

"Perhaps it is time to revise the rules," suggested Dr. Arun.

Hours later in the African village, Desta, Jorge Estrada, and the three other *Militobi* crewmen jumped to their feet in alarm as an African guard raced into the village shouting a warning of intruders. Walking solemnly into the village, Jay Rawal led the procession into the central courtyard as a pathway was made by the African villagers who watched silently as the litter was carefully placed down near a large fire pit encircled with large stones.

Tears in his eyes, Ashé met Desta who stared menacingly at Jay.

"Desta," he sobbed pointing to the litter. "It is Chiké. He is dead. He was killed by the Isleños. He was very brave. He saved me. I am so very sorry." Ashé burst into tears and fell to the ground in despair, his arms encircling the legs of the Head Man. Weaving through the large crowd of onlookers, Ada Niame, Chiké's mother, learned the news and threw herself across her son's lifeless body, screaming in agony. Estrada and Dr. Arun shook hands, their expressions somber, as Ada's mournful wails echoed throughout the village.

"Mr. Estrada, good to see you," said Dr. Arun, almost in a whisper. "This is a sad situation. The villagers are extremely angry. One of their guards was killed and they are concerned the Africans will blame them for the death of the young boy." Estrada steered the doctor away to speak to him privately.

"I have something to tell you and it is bad news," Estrada began in a low voice. "These pirates, Isleños they call them, have threatened to kill the Captain, Esha, and the rest of the women they took off the ship, unless we bring them ransom money. A million Euros!"

Staggered by the news, Dr. Arun could barely speak. "Esha? They want ransom?"

"They gave us one month or they will execute them all. But we are not leaving. We will not leave them alone. We will try and rescue them, but we need help. There are not enough of us and we are basically unarmed. Do you think some of your villagers will help us?"

"My villagers?" Dr. Arun shrugged. "I hardly know any of them."

"We have to try and get more help."

"You must talk to this man, Jay, right away. He seems to be one of the leaders in the village. He will know what to do."

Desta's rage grew in intensity the longer he stared at Chiké's palm-covered litter. Jay approached and tried to placate him.

"Desta, I am sorry this happened. We are all sorry. The two boys were coming to find the doctor and saw the Isleños kill one of our guards. As they escaped, they shot Chiké." Jay held the African necklace up for the village leader to examine. A fury raging inside him, Desta snatched the shell necklace from Jay's hand and gazed at it.

"What is this?"

"The Isleños dropped it as they ran away," Jay explained.

Estrada and Dr. Arun joined the two enemies. Jay pointed at the necklace.

"It is African. They wanted *us* to blame *you* for the guard. I suppose they wanted *you* to blame *us* for Chiké, in retaliation."

Dr. Arun introduced Estrada to Jay Rawal. "This is Mr. Estrada, from the ship that brought us here, yesterday."

They shook hands but Jay turned back to face Desta.

"I know we are not friends, and you believe I have done terrible things to your people. It is not true, but I know you believe it to be. At first I thought it was this boy, Ashé, or someone from your village who did these killings, but I know now that it was the Isleños. For that I am sorry."

Still sobbing with anguish, her body convulsing, Ada was consoled by a number of African women. Okeke Ka stood by the grieving woman and offered a silent prayer.

"I am sorry about Chiké," Estrada said, offering his condolences to the African Head Man. "He seemed like a fine boy."

Desta fought back tears. "He was a son to me."

"Know that he suffered no pain," said Dr. Arun. "The bullet pierced his heart."

Desta turned to the Pakistani doctor who continued in a calm, almost soothing tone. "I am Arun Rao," he said. "I examined the boy." Estrada explained that the doctor and his wife were also on the *Militobi* with Okeke and Ashé. Desta walked to Chiké's litter. He brushed away a tear and stared morosely at the boy's uncovered face before turning away, his heart broken.

Estrada pleaded his case with Jay as they watched Desta return, his head bowed.

"Do you know that our Captain and many female passengers were taken from our ship when we arrived? These pirates, the Isleños, have threatened to kill them unless we pay a ransom. My crew and I are going to attempt a rescue, but I need help from your village." Desta rejoined the conversation and overheard Estrada.

"I will help," the Head Man said, his voice cold and detached. "The Isleños will *pay* for Chiké. They have always said they were protecting us, but I know now they were lying. They said the Asians and the Arabs were my enemies, but that was a lie too, was it not?" He turned to Jay Rawal who nodded.

"They have lied to all of us," Jay said, agreeing with his former nemesis. "*They* are the real enemy!"

Estrada saw the resolve in the face of the African leader. "My friend, tomorrow morning we will be on the beach where we first arrived. Please join us. We will meet at sunrise, and I will take you out to our ship. I want to show you something that might help."

"I will be there with some men," said Desta.

"I will join you as well," added Dr. Arun.

"Good," responded Estrada, taking out his walkie-talkie to contact Gabby Fernandez. "Now we must return to our ship before it gets too late. We do not want to get caught in the jungle by these pirates."

"I will ask some men to lead you," said Desta.

"Thanks," Estrada said, turning again to Jay Rawal. "And you? Anything you can do to help us fight the pirates will be appreciated."

Jay finally accepted the use of the term. "*Pirates?* Yes, they are pirates, aren't they? I never looked at them that way before."

"There is no doubt in my mind," said Estrada.

"But my people will be hard to convince," explained Jay. "We have many elders who are set in their ways and are happy the way things are right now. They won't believe the Isleños are really pirates."

Estrada scoffed, "You have to convince them that the *pirates* are their real enemy. Not the Arabs and the Africans"

"*Inshallah,* they will believe," Jay said, and shook hands with Estrada, Dr. Arun, and even a surprised Desta Kado. "I will do my best to convince them."

As Dr. Arun prepared to depart with Jay and the other members of the Asian entourage, Desta approached him. "You are really a doctor? A medical doctor?"

"Yes, we will be happy to help in any way we can."

"We?"

"My wife, Esha, is a nurse. But she is a prisoner of the pirates right now."

* * * * *

That afternoon Desta made his way through the throng of women comforting Ada and took her aside. Tears streaming down her face, they embraced.

"Desta, what are we to do? Our boy is lost."

"He will not be forgotten, Ada. We will always think of Chiké with respect and honor. He was a good boy."

"He was. He was the best son a mother could have."

"He will be avenged, Ada. Believe me when I tell you that. He will be avenged." They embraced once more. "Do not worry about anything, Ada. I am here for you as I have always been."

"I know," Ada said.

CHAPTER 7

PLANNING A RESCUE

In a calm sea bathed in light by a waning yellow moon, the MV *Militobi* floated out of sight of land, a mile directly south of Santa Inez Island's wide coral reef. On deck, Estrada, Fernandez, and the rest of the crew ate from bags of mangoes, guavas, and stalks of bananas brought by both search parties.

"What about the Arabs?" Estrada asked, munching on a guava.

"Jorge," began Gabby Fernandez. "They caught us before we even got close to their village. We did not hear a thing. Luckily, Mr. Kassab understood our situation and promised he would help. He is scared, I think, but said he would gather as many people as he could. But he does not really know that many people in the village except for our passengers. They will help us though. They know many of the women taken by the pirates. Some are even family members."

"Mr. Estrada," the stocky Helmsman added. "Rescuing the Captain may prove to be very, very difficult. What will we do about weapons?"

Estrada frowned. "What weapons *do* we have?"

"Aboard ship we have only water and sound cannons, and we still have our sniper's rifle. They didn't find it but we have only a few boxes of ammunition."

"What about on the island?" Estrada asked Fernandez.

"The Arabs have homemade spears and bows and arrows. I saw a few bamboo knives. Primitive stuff at best. No guns though. Are you sure we should go through with this plan, Jorge?"

Annoyed, Estrada confronted his friend. "Gabby, do you really want to leave the Captain with those pirates? I cannot do that! I will *not* do that!" He faced the other crewmen. "Anybody else think we should *not* try and rescue the Captain?"

Fernandez tried to calm his friend. "Relax, Jorge, I did not mean that. I meant the shooting of the young boy may scare away others from helping us. Maybe we should try and sneak into the pirate's village alone, maybe late at night. We could get lucky."

Estrada shook his head, now understanding his friend's meaning. "Sorry, I know you all want to save the Captain and the others as well. There are just too many guns and weapons against us. It would be suicide to try it alone."

"On the other hand," said the Helmsman. "It sounds like the boy's death has riled up some people, like the African leader you spoke about. Maybe the time *is* right for them to fight. The trust may have been broken with the pirates."

"The Africans will fight, I am sure of it. They are angry," said Estrada, yawning as he stood up. "Let's get some rest. Early tomorrow morning we will move the ship closer and use the lifeboats to bring some of them here. We will see just how riled up they are and whether or not they will join us to fight for their freedom."

Gabby grinned. "Just like in *The Professionals,* Jorge, except this time Claudia Cardinale *wants* to be rescued."

Estrada stared blankly at his friend. "I have no idea what you mean by that and *why* are you always talking about old movies?"

Fernandez grinned and turned to the other crew members. "That's what the American ambassador use to ask me all the time when I was a teenager in Salamanca. He was the one who called me *Gabby.*"

The Helmsman laughed. "The Salamanca District in Madrid? Were you with that snobby embassy crowd growing up, Navigator?"

Gabby nodded and grinned again. "My father was a lawyer and, I must say, a very heavy contributor to the People's Party."

Estrada laughed. "Gabby even attended the IE Business School, right?"

The Helmsman was impressed. "One of the best schools in the world yet you ended up on this old rescue ship instead of becoming a successful businessman or a diplomat?"

"My parents did want me to go into business in Madrid, but I enjoyed staying in San Sebastián."

"Biscay Bay! Beautiful area!" The Helmsman exclaimed.

"We had a villa. Summer vacations on the sailboat. What can I say? I loved the ocean."

Estrada smirked. "And that took you to the Barcelona School of Nautical Studies where we met."

"But I had special navigation training at *Escola Port Barcelona* while you studied, what, ship's defenses? How brutal!"

"And I served as an intern every summer," Estrada said, proud of his accomplishment.

Fernandez frowned and shook his head in disgust. "Internships! Course requirements! I called it forced labor aboard dirty, filthy stinking tubs that induced nausea and were captained by Europeans with haughty attitudes. No thank you, Senōr!"

The crew roared with laughter.

* * * * *

Anna Kruger sat cross-legged on the mat floor of the one-room house that served as the makeshift prison cell for the captive passengers. Lucia Santos and two pirate guards entered and scanned the crowded room. Most of the women turned away to avoid eye contact. Anna, Esha, and Lulu, however, stared back defiantly, as if daring them to fight.

Lucia pointed directly at them. "You three! Come with me." The guards stepped between the captives to force them up, but the fearless women sprang to their feet under their own power.

Lucia, a scowl on her face, pointed at random to three additional women who screeched and struggled as the guards grabbed and shoved them roughly toward the door. As most captives turned away in fear, Anna was proud to see some of the younger women huddled together, staring back obstinately at their captors. She made eye contact with them, and they returned her grim half-smile.

Outside, Lucia separated Anna, Esha, and Lulu from the other three captives and led them along the main path that ran in nearly a straight line through the center of the pirate village. Anna stared at the tall statuesque pirate.

"Where are you taking us? Why are you doing this?"

Lucia stopped and nervously glanced around to insure she was not overheard. "It's not my doing. It is the Commandant."

"Where are you taking those other women?"

"Orders. They have other jobs to do," said Lucia. "They will be returned when they finish."

"You should be helping us, not treating us like animals."

"Look, Delgado is no friend of mine," said Lucia. "He is a pig and has done nothing but lie and cheat to get what he wants. He is disgusting, and I would stick a knife in his back myself, but the other Isleños would kill me without thinking about it." Lucia saw Delgado approaching and quickly handed Anna a small knife. She immediately hid it inside her blouse. "Protect yourself. Your night guard easily falls asleep and you may be able to..."

She stopped as Delgado motioned for Anna, Esha, and Lulu to follow him back toward the galley. Waiting until they disappeared completely from view and out of earshot, the remaining three captives were pushed and shoved toward the nearest wooden shack where three pirates awaited them. The women shrieked as their clothing was ripped from their shoulders and they were forced inside. Lucia turned away sickened and ashamed at being a part of this ordered assault. *Pigs*, she thought. *Just like the Commandant.*

Led by Delgado to a huge wood and tin cookhouse that served as the galley, Anna, Esha, and Lulu hesitated momentarily at its flimsy tin door, wary of what lay in store for them.

Delgado scoffed, "I hope you are hard workers, ladies. If not, there are other duties I can assign to you!"

Inside the enormous smoke-filled cookhouse, stalks of yellow and unripened green bananas hung from the rafters. Woven baskets filled with pineapples, mangoes, avocados, and breadfruit lined two walls on overflowing tables. Assorted crockery and orange plastic fishing balls half-filled with water were piled and jammed together on long tables and stacked upon bulky wooden crates. Along the near wall, two pirate women, their faces in perpetual frowns, chopped fish, wild pork, and rabbit on two abutting tables whose legs were lashed together with thin rope. They purposely did not look up at Delgado, both unhappy with their forced assignments in the cookhouse. The Commandant pointed at the women.

"These Isleños work for me, as you do," he announced to the captives, claiming personal authority over even the most basic of village activities.

Alonso Rivero, the fat and balding head cook, nervously eyed the pirate leader and the three female captives as they stood before him. Then, as if receiving a stage cue to begin his performance, he broke into a wide grin and spread his arms out in a friendly greeting that surprised all three women.

"Welcome, my friends! Welcome! I am so glad to meet you!" Delgado scowled at the man who nervously avoided making eye contact. "So, you come to work for Alonso? Good! You are very welcome. You can cook?"

The three women stared insolently at him and did not answer. Anna gestured at the pirate women. "What about them?"

"These do not cook!" Alonso said. "They hate Alonso! They will only help Alonso prepare the meals to feed all the peoples in this village. It is much too much work and I do it every day." He glanced at Delgado for a sympathetic reaction, but the pirate only glowered at him. Nervous, Rivero mopped his brow with a dirty rag. "Maybe you clean the galley then, yes? Alonso will show you. Alonso will show you everything! Do not worry! Alonso take care."

In his sordid past, Alonso Rivero was always a good cook but a very bad pickpocket. After a number of run-ins with the law as a young man, he decided he could make more money in the kitchen than out on the street repeatedly bumping into unsuspecting tourists. Rivero was well known on Las Palmas de Gran Canaria as a somewhat crazy, albeit brilliant, cook who had learned traditional recipes from his grandmother, great aunt, and mother. He was hired by the Amigo-Amigas Restaurant in Gran Canaria as a roast chef where, over a period of only three months, he was promoted to sauté chef concocting spicy *Mojo Picón*, a sauce made from garlic, olive oil, red peppers, cumin, salt, and vinegar. Using his grandmother's secret recipe, Alonso's sauce was added to a number of meat and fish entrées like *papas arrugados, miel de palma,* and *ropa vieja,* which garnered him a renowned reputation and a loyal following with local diners and visiting tourists.

A prima donna behind the stove and a tyrant around the four-star restaurant, Rivero had wasted no time in commanding and thoroughly insulting station chefs, junior chefs, porters, waitresses, and even dishwashers. He was adept at detailing perceived errors and correcting everyone's job performance, except his own. Most frustrating for the staff, he would continually remind them that he was carrying most of the workload on his rounded shoulders *only* because of their poor work habits. Besides, he would say to them in a condescending manner, the success of the Amigo-Amigas depended solely on his prowess as a chef. His well-earned reputation as a bully resulted in an almost immediate dislike by other kitchen staff, particularly the sous chef and head chef, who quickly demanded the owner fire him or they would walk.

The restaurant owner, under almost constant pressure from all his other employees, painfully realized that this flamboyant newcomer had to go. Rivero was fired, much to the consternation of new patrons who were disappointed to learn that the restaurant's unique sauces that accompanied their expensive beef and fish platters, would no longer be available. Alonso made a departing speech chastising the owner and declaring that his grandmother's secret recipes would be leaving with him and would soon be making a competitor's restaurant very famous.

Rivero moved on to the *Restaurante Hosea* in the beach town of Arinaga, some twenty miles from downtown Las Palmas. Located a stone's throw from the water, this well-known restaurant specialized in spicy seafood. The owner, Timoteo Hosea, was overjoyed, at first, to have a chef with Rivero's ability and gastronomic reputation. His *sancocho canario*, a blend of whole fish, sweet potatoes, and *papas arrugados* topped with his special *Mojo Picón* sauce, resulted in more plentiful and satisfied customers, including many crew members and officers from local shipping companies. Rivero's culinary skills, however, were heavily outweighed by his exasperating and demeaning behavior to the other staff. Chef Juan Hosea, as other head chefs had before him, fired Rivero within three months of his employment.

Contemplating a return to a life of crime and, inevitably a police lockup, Rivero was delighted to be offered a job as a ship's cook on a freighter bound for the Mediterranean. While he was promised total control of the kitchen and staff, Rivero also demanded that his title be changed to *Head Chef.* This new title appealed directly to his burgeoning ego and his need for power over shipmates assigned more menial kitchen support duties.

Over the next year, Alonso Rivero worked across the Mediterranean on several ships until one night, while having a smoke on the Esplanade de la Marina in Tangier, Morocco, he met Hassan Al Bourké, the Libyan captain of the MV *Yap Islander.* The port itself, some thirty miles east of Tangier, was the largest in the Mediterranean and the eighteenth largest in the world. Ships of all sizes and under many flags filled the deep water port that served as a central location for sailors from the Middle East, Europe, and Africa. This seafaring crowd intermingled with employees from over 750 companies with representative offices at the huge port complex. Blocks away from the main dock, several dingy bars catered specifically to French, Spanish, or Arabic speaking clientele.

Captain Al Bourké had been searching for a ship's cook for some time and Rivero's name had come up, recommended by one of his own crew as a great chef but with a checkered criminal record. This background did not bother Al Bourké in the slightest. In fact, it enticed him to learn what ship Rivero was on and to arrange a meeting when next they were both in Tangier. Over several bottles of cheap wine at the Port Luna Bar on the grimy Rue des Postes, Rivero was persuaded that complete authority and control over his own kitchen aboard the *Yap Islander* was, in fact, his dream come true. What he didn't realize was that the ship was about to rendezvous with a load of smuggled migrants several nights later off the coast of Misrātah, Libya.

The kitchen on the two-hundred-foot *Yap Islander* was not exactly what Alonso Rivero was expecting. In the first place, there were only three other staff to support his culinary efforts: a junior chef, if you could call him that, and two dishwashers who were also charged with serving food to the crew as well as cleaning up after them. The filthy mess hall was composed of two picnic tables with long benches on either side. Rivero was able to prepare *papas arrugados* and *miel de palma* the first two nights at sea but was told to make larger quantities of rice and to open numerous tins of ship biscuits for the African, Arab, and Asian passengers they would soon be picking up at sea.

As migrant passengers boarded the ship from three overcrowded dinghies the next night, Rivero sensed a change in the demeanor of Captain Al Bourké and the rest of the crew. Guns were now on display everywhere. Crew members pushed the women and children below and forced the men to make crude shelters out of tarps on the top deck. Any arguments or disagreements over how they were treated were met swiftly with the back of the hand and a reminder that the crew was well-armed. Rivero's junior chef informed him the ship was headed to the Canary Islands to drop off all the passengers and then return to Libya for more. Rivero now realized he was the Head Chef on a ship full of smugglers and captive migrants. He also realized that, if caught, the police would consider him to be a smuggler too. It was a critical moment in Alonso Rivero's life. Like for most men, there comes a sobering moment when one realizes life is short and spending it behind bars is not the ideal use of that precious resource.

In the pirate galley, Alonso Rivero stole another peek at Commandant Delgado who, completely disinterested, brushed specs of dirt from his uniform and then exited with two pirate guards the way he had entered.

Rivero stepped closer to Anna and whispered, "I am so glad you are here to help Alonso. I am so unappreciated. I am really not with them." He gestured with his nose in the direction of the departed Delgado. "These Isleños are mean to Alonso. Especially him!" Rivero's voice remained just a whisper as he glanced furtively back at the two pirate kitchen workers. "And them!" He took a step closer to the three captives. "Alonso cooks for everybody! Alonso takes care of everybody! But who takes care of Alonso? Nobody!"

Anna, Esha, and Lulu frowned derisively at the cook then turned their backs on him, almost grinning to themselves at his over-the-top manner. Rivero watched as the women began slowly roaming through the galley.

"Okay, scraps go to the pigs in the back, those four-legged garbage buckets. They are so dirty! Ugh! Each morning you will always check with Alonso, and he will tell you what to do. And ladies, please do not be late!"

The women lifted tops off teapots, examined the backs of plates, noted all the silverware, and ran their fingers across food-stained tables. Anna palmed another small knife and hid it beneath her blouse with the other one. Lulu picked a mango from a basket, smelled it, and tossed it back on the pile before staring curiously back at the cook. Rivero watched her with a keen eye. *She is a smart one*, he thought. *Be very careful around her or one day she will be giving you orders instead of the other way around.*

Rivero continued to watch the women explore the galley and spoke to himself in a whisper, "Very good! Very good! They will be fine. Alonso is fine. Everybody is fine."

* * * * *

Two of the three migrant women assaulted by the pirates earlier that day were returned to the captive women's house that night. They were by no means fine. Clothes torn, hair disheveled, and faces and arms bruised, they were shoved through the doorway, falling atop several sleeping women. Weeping, their fellow prisoners gathered around them, sensing the horrors that had befallen the two Africans. Awakened by the crying, Anna and Esha pushed through the crowd to learn what had happened. Anna recognized the women from earlier that morning. Esha examined each of victims and used wetted strips of material from their torn clothing to clean and bandage them. The women were comforted until they were finally able to fall asleep. Esha turned solemnly to Anna, who did not need to be told that the pirates had taken a fateful next step in cruelty. The women had been sexually assaulted. *Things are turning ugly,* Anna thought. *Something has to be done and soon.*

Anna and the other captives tried to sleep that night in the dimly lit room. The only light a kerosene lantern hung high from a rafter. Her forehead perspiring, Anna grimaced and tossed, caught up in an all too vivid memory from long ago. She was a college student again and back aboard the *Gitane* with her grandfather, Dirk. He had looked at her in the strangest way. It was a look she had never seen before and it had given her the shivers.

"What is it? Why do you look at me so oddly?" Anna had asked him in German.

"Sit for a moment, Anna. I would like to talk to you." Grandfather Dirk poured them each a glass of schnapps and stared at his beautiful granddaughter as she relaxed in the sailboat's teakwood cabin. He sighed deeply and took a sip. "Anna, I saw the doctor last week and he says my heart is not so good."

Shocked, Anna leaned forward and stared directly at her grandfather. "How bad is it?"

"It is failing me, I'm afraid."

"Oh, Grandfather, that is terrible news!" She got to her feet and hugged the elderly man. "What can I do? I can stay here with you, if you want me to. I can take care of you."

"No, *meine kleine,* there is nothing for you to do," he said, calling her by his pet name, my little one. "It is what it is." He motioned for Anna to sit back down. "I know you will be leaving again for school very soon. There is something I want to tell you. It is a story that I have not told anyone before except your wonderful grandmother."

"I miss Grandmother Brigitte," Anna said.

Dirk nodded in agreement. "*Ja,* as I do, but I will only tell you this story once and then I never want you to bring it up again. Agreed?"

Anna's curiosity skyrocketed. "Agreed," she said, sipping her drink. "At least until I know exactly what it is you are talking about."

"Agreed?" Dirk asked again, his stern tone indicating there was no room for debate on the matter.

Puzzled, Anna stared back at him. "Yes, then of course, if you insist. I agree."

"Very well. Have you heard of the *Sicherheitsdienst*? It was also called the *SD*?" Anna shook her head that she had not. "It was the intelligence service of the Gestapo and the Nazi party.

I was part of its clerical support unit." Anna's eyes blinked in surprise. Her grandfather rarely spoke about the war. Her own father had never spoken about it in front of her, not once. "I was only seventeen or eighteen years old at that time. I was carrying file folders and typing reports for the officers, nothing important really. But I had studied English in school so I could both speak and read it fairly well. The *SD*, in the beginning, was an information-gathering agency. They had me monitoring all the British and American papers and radio broadcasts for stories about the Reich. Other parts of the agency were tasked with detecting and neutralizing actual or potential enemies, but I had no part of that."

Dirk paused to take a sip of schnapps. Anna could only stare, astonished. Possibly for the first time in his life, her grandfather was exorcising personal demons right before her eyes.

"By 1938, at just the beginning of the war, all I did every day was read the papers, listen to the radio, type reports, and carry heavy briefcases to meetings. I would wait outside with other young men just like me and then carry everything back to the office, nothing more. My immediate supervisor was a tall evil man named Krausnich, and one day he ordered me to accompany him on a trip to Austria because the army had invaded and new orders required us to cooperate more with military leadership. I was happy to go, actually. Happy to get out of Berlin for a while."

Both Anna and her grandfather took sips of their drinks at the same time. "We arrived in Saltzburg and were immediately taken behind the lines where we followed our troops through the outskirts of town, maybe a few hours behind them. I did not know what Krausnich and his fellow officers were about to do. He just told me to follow him in case he needed anything, and I did. We were a group of six *SD* officers, two other clerical support staff, and me." Dirk finished his drink in a single gulp and then poured a more generous one. Anna frowned, concerned that the schnapps was not likely what her grandfather's doctor had prescribed for his heart condition.

"I heard the Reich had been rounding up Jews, Latvians, Bohemians, Gypsies and other minorities. I did not believe it was true, of course. But in Saltzburg, as we walked along the empty streets, the officers began shooting at anything they saw. They just drew out their pistols and shot at storefront windows and at parked cars and at streetlights. They laughed about it.

"They just kept shooting and laughing. This went on for some time and then Krausnich saw an old man, an Austrian, running between buildings and shot him down!"

Stopping for a moment to consider the gravity of what he had just said, Dirk Kruger sighed before continuing, "When he killed that man, the others began looking for other people to shoot. It became a game for them. They shot men, women, and even children. It became a competition. They laughed as they watched those people die in the street like animals." Dirk grew silent for a moment and Anna waited, unsure of what he would say next. After an agonizing moment of silence, she felt compelled to say something.

"But you did not know they were going to do that, Grandfather. It was not your fault. They were monsters."

Dirk Kruger looked back at Anna and gently nodded. "Yes, they were monsters. But I was there too and did nothing and said nothing. I was a monster too."

"No! What could you do?" Anna exclaimed, leaning forward. "What could you say to them that would make any difference? They would have shot you."

"Perhaps, perhaps they should have."

"No! Do not *ever* say that!" Anna moved across the cabin and sat next to her grandfather whose eyes had filled with tears. She put her arm around his broad shoulders. "Never say that or even think that." Dirk took his schnapps and drained it before wiping his eyes.

"That was the only time I ever saw people get shot. Nothing was ever said about it, even after we returned to Berlin. I went back to reading the papers, listening to the radio, and typing up reports again." Dirk seemed to have caught his breath. "Let's go out on deck, *meine kleine*. It is too hot in here."

It was a fine summer's night and Anna positioned her deck chair to take advantage of an evening breeze, amazed at what her grandfather had just related to her. "Did my father know all this?"

"No, not really, he knew I was in the war and that I eventually escaped Berlin to Hamburg and then to Bremerhaven where I worked on the ships for a while before meeting your grandmother in Frieburg."

Anna stared at Dirk's lined face, permanently sunburned from years at sea. He still appeared trim and vigorous to her notwithstanding his bad heart. "Why did you tell me this story?"

"*Meine kliene*, you are very special to me. I am seventy-eight years old and before I die I want you to know of the sorrow and guilt I have carried for so many years. When I think of the Jews and the Gypsies and all those other people that died, I think, no, I wish I could have done something to help them...just one thing...anything. But I did nothing. I thought only of myself and of escaping the nightmare of the Third Reich. My wish for you is that you never carry such a dark weight that will eat at your soul. In your lifetime you will face many opportunities for helping people but you will not always be able to do so. You cannot help everyone. However, there will come a time when you must try, and I know you *will* try! You won't be like me and run away."

"How will I know who to help, Grandfather?"

Dirk smiled at her and finished his drink. "You will know, *meine kliene*, you will know it in your heart. It will gnaw at you until you can't stand it anymore. And then you will do your best. You will do what you never thought you could do."

* * * * *

Bathed in sweat, Anna realized Lulu and Esha were now sitting beside her, whispering in hushed tones to avoid waking the others. "Are you all right, Captain?" Lulu asked.

"You seemed to be almost delirious," added Esha.

188

Anna sat up. "I am fine. I am fine. Thank you."

"How do you feel?" Esha asked, concerned about the mental strain on her friend.

"How do I feel?" Anna repeated, a determined look returning to her face. "I feel like something is gnawing at me and I have had just about enough of it! How about you two? Are you ready to get out of here?" The two women nodded, and Anna surveyed the sleeping bodies scattered throughout the room. She signaled for Lulu and Esha to remain quiet then tiptoed carefully to listen at the door. Just outside, a sleepy pirate, Bartolo Molina, sat near the doorway. Bored, he stared blankly into a flaming campfire, his rifle balanced across his knees. Anna noiselessly led Lulu and Esha to the rear of the house. On her knees, she revealed the two short-bladed knives now wrapped in a handkerchief at her waist.

Esha was astonished as Anna gave her a knife. "Where did you get—"

"Shh! From that tall pirate woman and the galley." Anna made a cut into the thatched wall, stopping to listen for any type of reaction from Molina outside. Hearing nothing, she began cutting. Esha joined her as Anna whispered to Lulu, "Wake the others but be very quiet about it. I think the guard is asleep."

Making their security rounds for the night, two pirate guards found Molina, eyes closed, beside the fire. "Idiot! Wake up!"

One of the pirates kicked the sleeping sentry who was startled and bolted to his feet, grasping for his rifle.

"Stay awake, you miserable sea dog," the second pirate guard barked. "Don't let us catch you asleep again!"

Anna guided Lulu, the last captive, through the rectangular hole in the back wall, then led all the women behind several bamboo shacks until they stopped, frozen in place, by the sounds of laughing and shrieking nearby. Motioning for the others to wait in silence, Anna cautiously stepped closer to the next house and peered inside its open back window. Three pirates, two men and a woman, half-dressed, poked at a young naked Arab woman who attempted repeatedly to protect herself from their roaming hands. She dodged and ducked repeatedly as mouthfuls of liquor were spit at her. One of the male pirates forced her down on his lap as she slapped at him, to the sheer delight of the others. The female pirate stood and yanked the woman's hair back before pouring rum down her throat from a large bottle, nearly gagging her. Anna motioned for Lulu and the others to keep moving. *There is nothing I can do for that woman*, she thought, *at least not now.*

The next morning, Alonso Rivero marched up to Bartolo Molina, who remained sitting on a log at his campfire post outside the locked house holding the captive women.

"Okay, bring them out! I need to speak to them."

"Who?" Molina asked.

"You know who, or there will be no food for you today." Rivero pointed dramatically at the door that Molina had been guarding. "Wake them up! They are very late!"

"Who are you talking about?"

Exasperated, Rivero pushed past Molina and called out, "Captain! Miss Lulu! Miss Esha! Get out here you naughty ladies. You are late and you know it. Alonso cannot make the breakfast all by himself now can he?" Molina peered over Rivero's shoulder but was pushed away by the chubby cook who was growing more and more impatient. Rivero called out again in a sing-song voice, "Oh, Captain? Where are you? This is Alonso calling. I'm waiting for you."

Delgado and three pirate guards approached from the main path. "What is happening here?" Completely intimidated by the tone of Delgado's voice, Molina shrugged and stepped back from the door. Rivero tried to explain.

"The Captain and the two other women...Miss Lulu and Miss Esha; they did not come to the galley this morning." Rivero pointed his thumb back at Molina. "*He* does not know where they are." Delgado glared at Molina who swiftly unlocked the door and stepped aside again as the Commandant barged up the steps. Stunned by its emptiness, Delgado immediately saw the precisely cut rectangular hole in the back wall. Peering through it, he rushed back outside, pushing between Rivero and Molina to bark at his guards.

"They escaped! Get some men and go after them. They can't get very far in the jungle. And where is Lucia? I haven't seen her all morning." The guards sprinted down the main path to find more help. Delgado turned back to Rivero and Molina, glowering at them in anger and a growing rage. "Did they not come out during the night to relieve themselves? Did none of them knock at the door?" Molina shook his head, angering Delgado even more. "None of them?" Molina shook his head again then shrugged. It was the last straw. Delgado took a pistol from his holster, shot Molina dead and faced Rivero. "Is my breakfast ready?"

Wide-eyed and afraid for his life, the head cook nodded repeatedly and ran toward the galley, talking to himself, "Breakfast! Breakfast! Alonso must make breakfast!" He rushed through the galley's entrance and squawked at his kitchen workers, "We must make the breakfast for the Commandant! Drop everything! Drop everything this minute!" The two pirate women scowled at him and continued at their own pace. Rivero fell into a chair and put his forehead on his crossed arms. "Oh, my goodness! Oh, my goodness! Alonso, you were almost dead!"

* * * * *

A half mile offshore, the early morning sunlight cast a golden glow on the distant horizon as the *Militobi's* two lifeboats, loaded with African and Arab migrants and each towing a long African canoe, tied up at the lowered accommodation ladder. On the main deck, crew members opened the cargo bay doors and watched the ship's heavy winch drop a hook down into the unlit cargo hold.

Desta Kado, Mohammed Kassab, and Gabby Fernandez jumped on the winch's rusty chain and rode it down, the rancid smell of the musty, near-empty bays assailing their nostrils. Coils of ropes, half-filled fuel drums, a few scattered boxes of biscuits, torn bags of rice, discarded water bottles, and large empty storage containers were piled along both the port and starboard sides. Fernandez, a scented handkerchief held tightly under his nose, led the men through the skids of engine parts, diesel drums, and spare machinery replacements to the bow where two-foot-high rolls of tightly wound barbed wire lay stacked and wrapped in forty-pound spools. He opened a carton of gloves and began distributing them to other migrant volunteers who hurried down the hatch and stairs to join them.

"Put these on!" Gabby shouted. "Biggest problem we have with this nasty stuff is taking it out and putting it away. We need to move all these spools over to the winch."

Desta was puzzled. "Why do we want this wire?"

Fernandez smirked. "It is our secret weapon. Trust me." A path was cleared allowing the wire spools to be dragged directly to an empty wooden pallet situated beneath the winch's cable and hook. Desta carried two heavy rolls by himself and slammed them down on top of each other. Kassab and the others took one roll at a time and often needed help to wrestle and reconfigure the unwieldy spools onto the pallet to maintain balance. An hour later, fully loaded and securely placed to avoid the shifting of weight, Fernandez linked the hook to the guide ropes from each pallet corner.

"Take it away! Slow does it!" Fernandez shouted to the crewmen above on the main deck. The winch creaked and groaned under the strain. The pallet was carefully guided by many hands until it rested gently on deck. Relieved at their successful effort, Estrada signaled for everyone to rest. Sweating profusely, the workers flopped down on the deck and were cooled by the brisk morning breeze. Estrada approached Dr. Arun and sat beside him on deck.

"Any word from Jay Rawal and the other South Asians?"

Dr. Arun shook his head. "Like I told you. I don't really know them. Jay seems to be a good man. I'm sure he will do his best to persuade the elders to help us, but I left the village before dawn to meet you on the beach. No one was awake except the guards."

"We will just have to hope and pray," said Estrada. "We cannot rescue the Captain, or your wife, without more help."

"Let us hope and pray then," said Dr. Arun. "What more can we do?"

Estrada ordered the *Militobi* to move even closer to the reef, allowing for a shorter ride to the landing beach. The two African dugout canoes bobbed in the swells just below the thirty-step accommodation ladder along the ship's port side. Crewmen and several of the African and Arab volunteers leaped into the lifeboats to await the lowering of the wooden pallet filled with the heavy spools of barbed wire.

Estrada peered over the port side and acknowledged Fernandez's signal that all was ready.

"Very well." He gestured to the crew member manning the hoist controls and the old winch creaked and groaned again as it precariously lifted the straining pallet. Migrants and crewmen guided it carefully over the side. The heavy wooden litter was lowered to within four feet of the closest lifeboat—the full extension of the winch's cables. Each of the barbed wire rolls was lifted or rolled off the stack until all were secured safely into both boats. The dugout canoes were lashed alongside each lifeboat to reduce teetering from the increased weight of the wire rolls and the rising and falling of sea swells.

Ashore, waiting patiently in the soft golden sand, nearly a hundred Africans and Arabs of all ages and genders hurried to meet the arriving lifeboats and canoes. Okeke, Ashé, and Ada greeted Desta as he jumped into the surf and helped push the first lifeboat up on the beach. The migrant volunteers quickly understood their task and began unloading the wire rolls. A large blue tarp was laid out in the sand near the edge of the jungle, and the barbed wire was stacked side by side in rows.

"Desta, there are no Isleños for miles," reported Ada, awed at the perspiring village leader carrying two rolls up the beach by himself, shirt off and muscles straining. "We have sent scouts all the way to the bamboo wall, as you asked."

"Good, Ada; we must not be seen by the pirates today. They will see us soon enough!"

Within an hour both lifeboats were unloaded, and the African and Arab migrants sat together in the sand to rest. Estrada surveyed the numerous rolls of wire on the tarp.

"*Amigos* and *amigas*," he began. "Thank you. Thank you for your help. I know you are very tired, but there is only one more job to do. The wire that you have brought here will be used to fight against the pirates, the Isleños. The next step is to link the wire together into two very long lines, like a rope."

"I will do that," Desta responded, determined to finish the job. "The rest can go." The African villagers, nearly as one, sprang to their feet and began uncoiling the wire rolls. Estrada marveled at Desta's leadership and the way his followers jumped at any of his orders without question. *I will do that* meant *we will do that* to his followers. Estrada thanked Mohammed Kassab and the Arab volunteers again as they prepared to return to their village.

"My friends, we will use this wire to fight the pirates and bring back our Captain and your women! Now we need you to make as many weapons as you can: spears, bows, knives, slingshots. Find anything else you can use to fight the pirates. When the time comes, you will be contacted."

The Africans milled around Desta who led the arduous task that remained ahead of them. The barbed wire was uncoiled from each roll, stretched and straightened, then linked together by twisting and locking the ends to each other. Hours later, two razor-sharp lengths of wire, each thousands of feet long, were coiled like giant lassos. Sand and palm leaves covered the folded tarp, providing a natural covering to keep away prying pirate eyes from the new weapon.

Dr. Arun shook hands with Jorge before leaving on his long walk back to the Asian village. "We will need more than bamboo spears and barbed wire to fight against guns," he opined.

"We also need God's protection," added Okeke Ka, who joined the men, wiping sweat from his brow.

"Yes, and I will pray for it," said Estrada. "But we also need guns. We cannot match the fire power of the pirates with only barbed wire ropes." Desta overheard the men and joined them. He had an idea that had been circling inside his head.

"I know how to get some guns. At least one or two, if we are lucky. We need to set a trap tonight. A pirate trap!"

* * * * *

Emerging from the steamy jungle late that afternoon and arriving at the most magnificent waterfall any of them had ever seen, Anna Kruger and the mud-splattered captive women, still holding hands, ran for the closest of the three clear pools. Physically spent and thirsty, they scooped drinking water with their hands and washed the mud from their faces, arms, and legs. In the distance, the twelve-foot bamboo wall loomed ahead. Three long and very thick bamboo poles served as horizontal locks that secured the large gate, separating them from the African sector.

"Let's rest here for a bit," suggested Anna. "I'm beat!"

"I am too," agreed Esha, dropping to her knees, exhausted and tired.

"We cannot stay here too long," warned Lulu, glancing up at the sun's location in the cloudless sky.

"I wonder what this fence is for?" Anna asked, scanning the long bamboo structure that disappeared into the jungle in both directions. She marveled at the beauty of the waterfall. "This island is absolutely magnificent," said Anna, pointing up toward the top of the waterfall and across the green mountain range.

"It really *is* beautiful," said Esha. "But I'm too tired to enjoy it."

"How are you doing, Lulu?" Anna asked.

"Very well, Captain. I am wondering how long it will take us to get through this wall."

Esha stared at the fence that bisected the entire island. "It seems to go on forever." Anna was puzzled by its very existence.

"It must be there for a reason, but I have no idea what it is."

"Either to keep something in or to keep something out," offered Lulu. "I do not know which."

"I'm guessing to keep people out," said Esha. "Anna, what do you think is on the other side of that wall?"

"I am hoping it is Jorge and my crew. I know he is trying to find us. I do not believe he has left to find ransom money. He sensed something was wrong from the very beginning."

Esha nodded. "Yes, Mr. Estrada is a good man. I watched him on the ship with the passengers."

"He *is* a good man but early on I misjudged him," Anna admitted. "Now I miss him. More than I ever thought I would."

Lulu edged in closer to the two women. "How did you misjudge him, Captain?"

"I thought he was overprotective, considering we are a rescue ship from a humanitarian non-profit organization. It seems now that he was right to be overprotective."

Lulu tittered. "Well, *I* misjudged our cook!"

Both Anna and Esha blinked in surprise. "What did you say?" Anna asked, flummoxed by Lulu's comment.

The teenager grinned. "Alonso, the cook; at first I believed he was just like the rest of them. But now I do not think so. He was the only one who treated us decently, but I have to admit he is one crazy man." The other two women roared with laughter.

"You are right," agreed Esha. "He may be the *only* decent man in that entire village, and he is as petrified of Delgado as the rest of us."

"Come on, ladies," said Anna getting to her feet. "Somehow we have to get through this fence."

"It will take all of us to move those poles," responded Esha.

Calling the other women together, they lifted the heavy gate poles one-by-one, dumping each to the ground at their feet. They rested momentarily after dropping the third pole when Anna spotted the pirate patrol emerging from the jungle and fanning out some forty yards behind them.

"Quick!" Anna shouted to the others. "Push!" The women shouldered the massive gate, opening it just enough for one person to squeeze through.

"Lulu, go! Go!" Esha implored the teenager standing next to her. Lulu stared wildly at Esha and then Anna, hesitating half-way through the opening.

"Lulu, you must go now! Save yourself," Anna shouted, shoving the teen through the gap. The women pulled the gate closed again just as a pistol was pointed at Anna's temple, forcing her to her knees.

"Commandant Delgado ordered us to bring all of you back," said the male pirate patrol leader holding the pistol. He glanced briefly through the fence, but Lulu had completely disappeared. The pirates had no inclination to chase her into the African sector.

"Please, just let us go!" Esha pleaded. "We mean nothing to you. We have families."

"It will be all right, Esha," Anna said, eyeing the five pirates. "We will be fine." The captives were herded into a makeshift line and led back toward the waterfall. As they neared the closest pool, Anna shoved two of the pirates into the others, knocking them to the ground like tenpins. Anna pushed Esha toward the jungle.

"Run! Run everyone!" As the women scattered in all directions, Kruger hurled herself atop the patrol members, giving Esha even more time to escape but the pirate leader regained his footing almost immediately and aimed his rifle at the Pakistani nurse. He called out once for her to stop before firing. Hit in the back, Esha rolled forward into the underbrush, lying completely still.

"No!" Anna cried. The pirate aimed his rifle at Anna who stopped and raised her hands. Realizing his possible error in shooting the woman, he gestured for her to go to Esha. Anna raced to her friend, cradling her in her arms. "Oh, Esha! We will get you some help. Just do not move." Esha smiled weakly and shook her head.

"Lulu?"

"She got away," whispered Anna with a slight grin.

"Tell Arun that I..." Esha's brown eyes flashed brightly for a moment before dimming and fading away forever. An enraged yet determined look grew in Kruger's eyes.

"I will tell him, Esha. I will tell him how we got through this because of you." Steeling herself, Anna raised her hands and stood to face the pirates. "All right. All right. No more shooting."

Crouched at the base of the bamboo wall on the African sector side of the fence, Lulu had returned to peer between the sharpened poles and watched as Esha was killed and the Captain and the rest of the women recaptured. She burst into tears as the patrol led her friends away. Her jaw tightly clenched, she turned and sprinted into the jungle.

CHAPTER 8

SETTING A PIRATE TRAP

Late that same afternoon in his spacious house, Delgado drank rum and tapped at the glass cage containing his pet snake, Diablo. Lucia Santos entered and scowled at the sight of the reptile.

"You were looking for me, Commandant?" Delgado leered at her and motioned with his forefinger for her to spin around. Used to her leader's debauchery and ogling, she sighed and did as she was told, as she had done seemingly hundreds of humiliating times before. *It is a price I am willing to pay, for now*, she thought.

"Nice," the pirate leader said watching her. "Very nice, indeed!" Then, remembering how she had been missing all day, his face lost color and he grew very angry. "Lucia, where were you this morning? I had to send some other guards after the women when I couldn't find you."

Lucia feigned innocence. "I *heard* they escaped last night. How could that happen?"

Delgado scoffed, "That idiot Molina was standing guard. He did not even hear them."

"Why do you think they left *last* night, Commandant?"

"Who knows? That Captain is such a mean bitch of a—"

"But I know why!" Lucia snorted, incensed. "It was because *you ordered me to give* three of them to my men yesterday!"

"*My* men, Lucia, *my* men! But the others were not touched! I was sending a message that there will be consequences if they defy me." Sickened, Lucia shook her head in disgust at her obese leader.

"Do not worry, my dear," Delgado grinned and gestured for her to sit beside him. "They will be recaptured very soon. There is nowhere they can go where we cannot find them." Delgado tapped at the glass jar again and the King snake hissed. Lucia frowned at the black reptile and Delgado laughed at her reaction. "Tell me about the other new arrivals to our island paradise."

"The Africans brought food yesterday, and I saw some new faces. They were asking about the captive women; when they would be released. Desta and one of the new ones were asking. They were upset. I handled it before they caused any trouble."

"Desta is not a problem. He is as docile as a *Pastor Garafiano* sheep dog. What about the ship's crew? You gave them their orders?"

Lucia scowled at the snake again and picked a ripe mango from a woven basket and began to peel it. "I watched their ship leave. They know they have one month to return with the money. Oh, there is one other thing. Three of *our* men nearly got caught out at the Asian village. They killed someone. I heard it was a young boy."

Delgado shifted uncomfortably in his chair. "Idiots! I thought I made it clear to everyone that I do not want anymore killings! There are too many migrants here now. I do not want someone coming after me bent on revenge because we killed his son or his daughter! Steal from them as you like, but don't kill them."

"Yes, Commandant; I will give *our* men the message."

Delgado sat upright with an idea. "Lucia, I have a new job for you. Take those same three idiots out again with you tonight but go to the African village this time. I know Captain Kruger has hidden money with some of the new arrivals."

"We just had people there a few days ago watching them. We have had people watching all the villages."

"Never mind that! Search around the African village tonight. Leave an Arab or Asian trinket in the bushes for them to find. I know there is money out there somewhere. We need to find it."

"Yes, Commandant!"

"And, do *not* let them kill anyone!"

"Yes, Commandant!"

Lucia turned to exit but Delgado stopped her. "Before you go, Lucia."

"Yes, Commandant?"

Delgado leered at her and gestured with his finger for her to turn around again. Sickened, Lucia did as she was ordered. "Slowly Lucia, let me take a good look at you. Take your time."

I could kill him now, she thought. *No one would know it was me.*

"Lucia, you get better looking every day. Now, find those three idiots and head out immediately," directed Delgado. "It's a long way to the African village."

"Yes, Commandant," Lucia said and exited, thoroughly ashamed and disgusted with herself. *I know he will eventually ruin all those captive women*, she thought.

Delgado grinned as his coiled snake hissed at him. The pirate's face close to the glass, he stared directly into the snake's dead eyes.

"This will be a warning to those Africans about asking too many questions." He reached into a covered bucket and pulled a live field mouse out by the tail. He carefully opened the top of the glass jar and dropped it in, then watched fascinated as the black snake immediately constricted itself around the rodent and began to squeeze. "Diablo, you poor thing, are you still hungry?"

* * * * *

That evening, down on one knee, Desta searched for signs in the jungle less than a half-mile from the African village. A light fog was rolling in from the south, although visibility was still good enough for tracking. He found broken branches and matted ferns in a clearing just off the sector's main path. Rubbing his hands together, he lowered his head until it nearly touched the ground, listening quietly as if waiting for the jungle to tell him a story. Jorge Estrada, Ashé, Okeke, three *Militobi* crewmen, and several African villagers, watched in utter silence until he motioned for them to draw closer.

"This is the right place. I found this spot a few days ago, and I could tell that at least three people sat here. Whether they were pirates or Arabs or Asians I do not know, but no one from our village would sit so close to the path. We will set our trap here. I have sent scouts ahead to the bamboo wall. They will signal if trespassers come our way tonight."

Frustrated with Desta's reluctance to accept what, for Estrada, was obvious, the First Officer challenged the Head Man. "Desta, I do not understand why you still believe Arabs or Asians would go over or through all the walls and gates on this island just to sit here in the jungle near the main pathway to your village and, do what? Spy on you? I suggest we need to focus on the pirates. The Arab villagers so far have been nothing but helpful." The village leader remained silent as Estrada continued. "And remember the necklace the pirates left after shooting Chiké? Remember that they were trying to blame you and your people for killing the Asian guard? The pirates are your real enemy. Not the Arabs and not the Asians!"

"I remember the necklace, Spanish," Desta shot back, his anger growing . "And, you do not have to remind me that pirates killed Chiké. The pirates will pay with their blood. Chiké was only a child. They killed a child."

Concerned about the underlying anger in the tone of their voices, Okeke tried to calm things down. "Yes, Chiké was only a child and we all miss him. I know you miss him most of all,

Desta. '*The Spirit himself bears witness with our spirit that we are children of God.*'"

Lucia Santos led her pirate raiding party through the opened bamboo gate and headed quickly into the African sector. Gripping an AK-47, she studied the surrounding area now dark and rapidly filling with a swirling fog. Listening for signs of movement she felt safe enough to proceed and motioned for the men to hurry. Less than a hundred yards from the gate and well-hidden behind a thicket of avocado and guava trees, an African scout heard the pirates before he saw them. Grumbling about the lateness of the hour and how this trip was nothing more than the Commandant's punishment for doing something that had been considered a right of passage for the past two years, the team struggled to keep up with Lucia. Remaining completely still, the scout waited as the pirates passed within fifteen feet of him. When clear, he signaled to another scout hundreds of yards away with a sharp bird call. Within minutes Desta had been alerted to the intruders.

"People are coming!" he announced.

Astounded, Estrada strained to peer through the darkness and thickening fog at the trees surrounding the small clearing where they waited to spring their trap. "I heard nothing at all!"

"We still have some time," said Desta, sitting cross-legged. "I will tell you when."

Sitting close by, Ashé stared at the ground, lost in his own tormented thoughts. *How could I have let my sister go with these pirates*, he asked himself. He had tried to hold her back, but she pulled away from him and got in line with all the other women. He couldn't stop her. *Perhaps she was still angry with me for what I said on the ship*, he thought. She was always a strong-willed young woman. He remembered their perilous trip though the Sahara and how their new friend Mashoul believed Lulu was Ashé's brother because she had dressed like a man for safety. Lulu thought it was hilarious and was determined to keep the act up until they reached Libya.

In Qatrun, still seven hundred miles from Tripoli, Lulu had wandered off to the marketplace and Ashé had been worried that she had gotten lost. He spotted her browsing a rack of colorful headscarfs. A young Nigerian vendor approached her and spoke in English. Ashé had overheard their conversation.

"Sir, may I help you? A gift for your wife?" The young woman suggested a bright red scarf with an embroidered gold African shield. Lulu sniggered at the success of her ruse and had adjusted her sunglasses, replying back in English in a low voice.

"It looks very nice. Can I touch it?" The young woman handed it to her to feel its soft texture and marvel at its traditional design. "You are not from Qatrun?" Lulu asked.

"No, sir, we are from Nigeria. Many people from Africa make their way to Qatrun. We have Somalis, Ugandans, Sudan people. We are from many places."

"Why here?"

"Qatrun is the ancient path to the Mediterranean. People come from the West, the East, and even the South. We are going to Tripoli."

"And then?"

"And then we shall go to Europe, sir."

"Why did you leave home?"

"There is no work there. Only begging or prostitution and we are not like that. That is not for us. My family is better than that."

"I will take this headscarf," Lulu said, searching her clothing for her stash of Libyan dinars.

The young woman folded the item and presented it to Lulu. "I am sure your wife will be happy to receive such a gift. Thank you, sir."

Lulu paid for the headscarf and gave the young Nigerian a large tip. "Good luck to you, miss. I am happy to have met you. You are to be congratulated for the sacrifices you are making for your family." Lulu had worn the red headscarf under her hood for the rest of the journey.

Jorge Estrada watched Ashé, who appeared to be lost in his own world of thoughts. He was impressed with the teen's courage and bravery to be out in the dark on such a potentially dangerous mission.

"Are you ready, young man?"

Ashé glanced up, a firm look on his face. "I am. I have vowed to save my sister."

"She was one of the women they took?"

"Yes, and it is my duty to bring her back."

Estrada nodded. "We will bring her back. We will bring them all back."

Another bird call signaled it was indeed time to bait and set the trap. Desta motioned for Ashé to take his place, and the teenager hurried to the center of the clearing and played dead. The rest of the group fanned out, hiding in the surrounding jungle, nearly invisible in the heavy fog. Minutes later, Lucia spotted Ashé's prone body and motioned for the scarred pirate to check on him.

Silently, Desta approached the thin pirate and clapped his hand over his mouth before stabbing him to death. Ashé sprang to his feet as Estrada flung himself at the second pirate, tumbling them both to the ground. He thrust his knife deep into the Malian's heart. Okeke Ka grabbed at Lucia's machine gun and in their struggle it discharged, strafing gunfire across the clearing, wounding the scarred pirate above the knee. Shoving Okeke to the ground, Lucia leveled her machine gun at him then stopped abruptly, dropping it and raising her hands.

"Take their guns," Desta ordered, shocked and confused at Lucia's action. Keeping his eyes glued on the tall woman, he carefully picked up the machine gun at her feet.

"I don't want to fight anymore," she said.

The bodies were searched. Sidearms, rifles, and knives were taken by the *Militobi* crewmen. Estrada clapped Ashé on the shoulder. "You did well, young man." Relieved and still somewhat stunned at their accomplishment, Ashé watched as Lucia and the scarred pirate were secured with vines and he found himself reminded of Chiké and that tragic afternoon in the Asian sector. Suddenly Ashé recognized the wounded pirate's scar and beard and grew animated and anxious. Estrada saw the boy's petrified expression.

"Ashé, what is it?"

"He killed Chiké! He was the one," Ashé whispered. Estrada placed his arm around the boy's shoulder and took him aside as the two captured pirates were pushed forward along the path toward the African village.

"Are you sure?" Estrada whispered. "Absolutely sure?"

Ashé nodded as they edged between the dead pirates. He peered closely at the other dead bodies. "And *they* were there too! That one shot the guard."

Estrada turned Ashé around and gripped his shoulders. "Please trust me on this, my friend. Do not tell Desta. We need to find out more about the pirates. If you tell him, Desta will kill the pirate and maybe the woman too. Promise?" Ashé nodded. Estrada patted the teen's back as they followed the prisoners through the jungle. "Good man."

* * * * *

The next morning, the horrific screams of the scarred pirate reverberated throughout the large African village. Spread-eagled on the ground, Chiké's murderer watched in horror as Desta dropped fire ants on his open gunshot wound. Desta, Estrada, and Ashé, their eyes narrow and focused, reflecting the seriousness of the situation, watched solemnly as the pirate screeched in fear and pain. Okeke Ka turned away, nauseated by the entire proceedings. He felt faint.

"Must we do this? It is not right. We should be ashamed of ourselves," he remarked, shaking his head in disbelief at their actions.

Lying next to the scarred pirate, Lucia Santos was also spread-eagled. Her wrists and ankles were knotted with vines. Fire ants swirled over her bare stomach, but she didn't flinch, not even once.

"How many of you pirates are there?" Estrada asked them both.

The scarred pirate glanced over at Lucia. "Tell them nothing!"

"There must be another way!" Okeke exclaimed.

Scores of village onlookers watched the unsavory scene unfolding from twenty yards away. Estrada took a deep breath and walked the pious Ghanaian toward them.

"I am sorry, my friend. We do not have much time and the ants will not kill them. You do not have to stay for this."

Okeke shook his head. "No, I must stay. I must see it all. It is my penance."

Estrada returned to his questioning. "How many?"

The sweat poured from the scarred pirate's brow, his eyes reflecting fear as Desta dropped more ants on his wound. "Make him stop!"

Estrada knelt close to his head. "You can make him stop. How many?"

"Sixty! About sixty!" Lucia cried out. "I don't know for sure."

The scarred pirate shouted, "Liar! You miserable bitch…"

"Only sixty?" Estrada asked, moving closer to Lucia.

"Maybe more," she replied.

"Weapons?" Estrada asked her.

"Don't!" The scarred pirate shouted, struggling with his bindings. In response, Desta sprinkled even more of the frenzied ants across his wound. The pirate yelped even louder as Lucia began to talk.

"We have six or seven working AK-47s and many rifles and handguns," she said.

"She's lying! We have many more than that. Many more!" The scarred pirate swiveled his head toward Lucia. "Delgado will kill you for this! I will kill you myself!"

Lucia snorted. "Delgado is an animal! I'm sick of his lies and his pawing and his groping and his—"

Okeke confronted Lucia, stepping closer to her. "Why did he take all the women?" Desta and Estrada exchanged knowing glances.

"The Commandant is demented. He's a—"

"Liar!" The scarred pirate bellowed. "He needs them to cook, gather firewood, haul water, and—"

"He's lying!" Lucia yelled.

Astounded, Okeke stepped closer to the scarred pirate. "Slaves? You mean you are using the women as slaves? How could you do such a thing?"

"They're only migrants! Nobody wants them. Nobody cares. They've been abandoned." The pirate strained to blow puffs of air repeatedly at the ants weaving their way up his hairy chest.

Okeke shook his head. "Never! God never abandons anyone, not even you!"

"How did you come to this island?" Estrada asked Lucia. "We thought it was uninhabited."

In a calm voice, even with the unscientifically named *crazy ants* swirling over her stomach and crawling into her belly button, Lucia explained, "Shipwrecked in a dense fog just over two years ago. Our ship is still on the reef, the *Ralik-Ratak*. About a year later a smuggler dumped another shipload of migrants here on another ship, the *Yap Islander*."

"That was my ship!" Desta interjected. "I was with Ada and Chiké and Awa and Balla Mendy. Captain Hassan Al Bourké was in charge." Estrada gestured for the African village leader to sweep the ants off Lucia's stomach to encourage even more cooperation.

"Al Bourké was an animal just like Delgado," related Lucia. "He was paid to bring back more supplies and weapons, and he did. Enough guns and ammunition for everyone. But he brought lots of rum too and there was trouble. Al Bourké and Delgado were drunk and a fight broke out over the money that Delgado owed him. Delgado was never going to pay him anyway, but Al Bourké was stabbed to death, and we took his ship."

The scarred pirate shouted, "More lies! She's Delgado's whore. She killed Al Bourké herself."

Estrada was puzzled. "So you *do* have a ship! Then it really *is* for the money? All of this just for...money?"

"Spanish Coast Guard is everywhere. The money is for bribes and to pay off the police." Lucia squirmed at her bindings. "Look, I'm telling you the truth. Let me go and I will help you. I'll even fight for you, but you have to take me with you. They'll kill me if they know I'm telling you this."

"*Bitch!*" The scarred pirate thundered, shuddering as the ants began to swarm around his neck.

"You want us to trust you?" Estrada asked Lucia. "After what you have done to our Captain, our passengers, and the people of this island?"

"Everyone is safe as long as they believe we are protecting them from each other."

Estrada, Okeke, and Desta exchanged looks.

"Let's get them up," said Estrada. Desta cut their lashings and pulled the captives to their feet.

"Let me finish them," requested Desta matter-of-factly, but Estrada shook his head. Fear flashed in the eyes of the scarred pirate as Desta grabbed him by the bicep, but Lucia did not register even a hint of dread.

"These two might still be useful to us," Estrada said. "And, we are not murderers like them." Believing the captives should be put to death, Desta led them away, hoping they would attempt an escape so he could personally break their necks.

Ashé grabbed Estrada's arm. "I must tell Desta about him now!"

"Please wait," pleaded Estrada. "There may be more they can tell us. It will not be too much longer, I promise."

Pushed ahead toward the empty hut that would serve as their temporary jail cell, the scarred pirate whispered to Lucia under his breath, "You are dead, you lying traitor!" Close behind, Ashé overheard the threat and turned back to Estrada.

"He is right. They are both liars and they both deserve to die."

Estrada tousled the teen's hair. "No one deserves to die, young man."

Inside the hut, Desta secured the scarred pirate to the back wall with vines. As she waited for the village leader to take her inside, Lucia turned to Estrada.

"I know you don't believe me, but I have been telling you the truth."

Estrada stared at the beautiful pirate then motioned for her to sit on the ground.

"So, how did you get involved with Delgado?" Lucia shrugged, a rueful expression on her face, almost bemused at the thought of her origins with the pirate.

"It was the biggest mistake of my life. I was a dealer in his poker games in Tenerife and then I ran the games while he would go to other islands to check on his people there." She shook her head as if to rid herself of the memory. "Then he had me blackmail the president of the *Federación de Lucha Canaria* to rig the wrestling matches. He made lots of money. His operations grew larger and larger, and he trusted me to keep everything running smoothly."

"So what happened between you two?"

"He said he would share it all with me: the money, the men, everything! But that was all a lie. He just used me. And I went along with it for a long time. Too long. Then he promised me a way out."

"How was that?"

"On La Gomera they had begun to rob tourist sailboats and then hide out in an old Spanish colonial house near a sheep and goat farm not far from the Garajonay National Park. The police never found them. So Delgado realized there was lots of money to be made at sea. He set up raids on the Boluda Line freighters that made stops at Santa Cruz every other day. That's when Delgado bought the Bayline speedboats and moved everything to San Sebastian. We had a few weapons, but guns were officially banned and difficult to buy, even on the black market. So, he started to smuggle some over from Tenerife but was always looking to find more. Delgado even went out after a freighter himself, something he had never done before, but called it off at the last minute when a police patrol boat appeared on radar. It was that police boat that changed his entire approach."

Desta exited the hut and Estrada gestured for him to sit and listen as Lucia continued.

"We had been paying a police informant and he told us that ships filled with African immigrants were arriving at an unusually high rate. This was about three years ago. Smugglers were charging the asylum-seekers thousands of Euros to bring them the 675 miles from Morocco and dropping them off on various islands throughout the Canaries. The police had even tried to stop one of them and had a Molotov cocktail thrown at their boat."

Estrada nodded. "That was in the papers, I remember."

"Delgado thought that the smugglers themselves could be the best targets, and he knew his three speedboats were fast enough to catch any ocean going freighter. What was missing was the information on the location of the ships outside the twelve-mile international border. The Canary police wouldn't go beyond that point. That's when Javi Mujo came into the picture."

"Javi Mujo? Who is he?" Estrada asked.

"He was the radio operator at the Tenerife Rescue Coordinating Center. It is part of the Department of Public Works. They get the first call from the authorities at the Barcelona Maritime Rescue Service when a smuggler's ship is spotted on its way to the Canaries."

"So he was your informant?"

"That was the plan. Mujo's organization had responsibility for coordinating the government's search and rescue efforts."

"So the idea was for Delgado to get the ship's location from Mujo before anyone else."

Lucia nodded. "We had to get Javi Mujo working for us."

"Again, more blackmail?"

Lucia nodded. "Mujo enjoyed playing roulette and drinking at the Playa Beach Casino in Tenerife. Delgado had men keep watch on him for two weeks until one night at the casino, without his wife of course, he lost a hundred Euros in a couple of minutes. Delgado's spotter called me and I…"

She paused and Estrada filled in the blanks, "Just happened to meet Mr. Mujo at the casino bar."

Lucia nodded again. "Something like that. Later that night some photos were taken—"

"And Delgado had his new informant. I got it."

Lucia nodded. "So I convinced Mujo I could get the pictures back and save him from getting fired at work and a divorce at home. Delgado had me wait a week before contacting him to say he would need to provide shipping information or he would never get the photos back."

"And he went along with it."

"Of course. He was afraid of his wife like most men. He told us right away the Spanish Maritime Rescue Services had found nearly ninety African asylum-seekers two hundred miles south of Tenerife and that more than 1,500 immigrants had legally arrived in the Canaries from Africa the last year alone."

"That is a lot of traffic."

"He even told us that many of the migrant women and children had been placed in luxury hotels for up to two weeks because there was no other place to put them."

"But that was before the ban on asylum-seekers. How long did Mujo provide you with information?"

"For nearly a year and up until the time we went after the *Ralik-Ratak*. I told him the pictures of our...time together would be returned to him soon, as long as his reports were accurate. We had no problem with him at all."

"What about the shipwreck?"

"Mujo said the ship was carrying at least three hundred fifty immigrants and was well off course a hundred miles northeast of Tenerife. Delgado thought this could be his biggest haul yet and pulled out all the stops. He brought in everyone from all over the islands and crammed us into the speedboats and a big *Luhrs Tournament 350* fishing boat he had stolen. We loaded it with the rest of his gang and as much fuel as we could carry."

"What was the problem then?"

"He lied to me about the whole thing! He said the money and weapons we made on this job would set me up on my own, and I could leave with some of the men who were loyal to me."

"What happened?"

"What happened was, he was never going to let me go. We got caught in the fog. I was checking the radar while we were waiting, and the ship nearly ran us over. Three thousand tons! There was no crew aboard. They had all been killed. Only the migrants were left, and they were in bad shape. They had been beaten and shot up. All of a sudden, Delgado announced he was taking over the ship! That's when he started calling himself, Commandant. I couldn't stop him. We ended up crashing over the reef here in the fog."

"But you said another ship came later."

"The *Yap Islander* stopped just over a year ago, purely by accident."

Desta nodded. "Yes, we were headed for the Canary Islands seeking asylum and they said our fuel was leaking."

"Delgado made Al Bourké a deal," Lucia explained. "He would leave his passengers with us on the island and return with more men and supplies. And he did that, for a price."

"What happened then?"

"A knife in the back happened."

"The other pirate said *you* killed him," Desta said in an accusing tone.

"Does it matter who killed him?" Lucia responded. "The result was that we had a ship and I thought Delgado would be giving it to me and my men to get off the island, as he promised."

"But that didn't happen, did it?" asked Estrada.

Lucia shook her head. "He told me some lie about not having enough money to let me go off by myself with the ship, and I was to wait until we could all go together. More lies."

"So, that's why the ransom then; it's to get you all off the island."

"Everybody but the migrants, of course."

* * * * *

Anna Kruger and the captive women, still under armed escort, arrived back in the pirate village in late afternoon. Worn out from their long trek through the jungle, the women were led back to their one-room house where they entered and sprawled on the matted floor, falling immediately asleep. A female pirate guard, armed with a rifle, entered and locked the door behind her.

* * * * *

Sitting cross-legged around a cooking fire that evening, Estrada, Okeke Ka, and Desta Kado drank from coconuts and discussed what they had learned from their *questioning* of the pirates. Ashé sat alone near the doorway of Desta's house, lost in thoughts of his sister and how he had failed her and his friend, Chiké. Ada joined him and wrapped her arm around the morose teenager's shoulders.

"And, how are you doing, Ashé? What are you thinking?"

"I am thinking about Chiké and my sister." The youth stared into the face of the mother of his lost friend. "Ada, when do you think we will try to rescue Lulu and the others?"

"Soon enough, the men are talking about it now."

"That is good, but when is *soon enough*?"

"You miss Lulu, don't you?"

"Yes, I do, very much. I am supposed to take care of her. I promised my family. We are Serer people. Our parents and grandparents must be obeyed, and they are getting very old. They must think we are all dead by now." He glanced up at the bamboo rafters and pointed to the roof. "Our house is very much like this one, you know. But it is made of reeds that we harvested and carried back from the river. And, we grow rice and millet and have a few goats as well. It is a nice farm, Ada. I miss it."

She was glad the teen was speaking out more since Chiké's tragedy and watched the sparkle in his eyes grow as he spoke about his family and his home in Senegal. "It was our grandfather who convinced Mother and Father that it was best that we leave and make our way to France for our education."

"It was your grandfather? Not your parents?"

"No, Grandfather was convinced that fishing along the Saloum River, growing rice, and tending our goats was not a sensible future for us. Mother agreed but it took Father a long while before he allowed us to go. I am sure that he regrets his decision even more, now." Ashé remembered the family argument that seemed to go on for days.

"Why must they leave here to go to school?" Ashé's father, Mousa, had shouted at his grandfather in Serer. "What is wrong with Dakar? There are five universities there. We have a good life on this farm. The children were born here. Even if we have to move to the coast someday if the soil turns salty, we will need our children to help with the goats and fishing."

Pap Gaye nodded his head showing his daughter's headstrong partner that he understood his point of view, even if he didn't agree with it. "Yes, we have had a good life here. Yes, there are a few good schools in Dakar. Yes, we may need help tending goats if we ever have a new farm. But does your religion not say that a father gives his child nothing better than a good education?"

Moussa was surprised at the reference to the Quran since everyone knew Pap was not a religious man. In fact, he was quite the opposite in many frustrating ways.

"Yes, it does," he replied.

"And does the Quran not say that seeking knowledge is obligatory for every good Muslim?" All eyes were now trained on Pap, who had jarred them with his knowledge of Islam. He snorted at their reactions. "Just because I do not celebrate or practice your religion does not mean that I have not learned some good lessons from it. I believe the education of our grandchildren is of utmost importance and should be to all of you as well. If our son Dallah, who has worked in Paris for three years, can be of help in obtaining an education for our grandchildren, we should explore it. Do you not agree, Moussa?"

Flustered, Moussa had to concede the point. "You are right, of course. I share your sudden belief in what the Quran says about our children receiving the best education we can provide them."

"It is settled then," said Pap, dismissing Moussa with a wave of his hand. "We will write Dallah at once for his assistance and advice on the matter."

Ada interrupted Ashé's thoughts. "And Lulu was happy to go to France to study?"

Ashé nodded with a smile. "Oh yes, she wanted very badly to become a teacher. She hated the smell of the West African dwarf breed goats that we raised. It was only a herd of thirty or so but that was all we could afford. During the dry season we would even have to sell some of them for meat and skin. The larger *Sahelian* goat was a much better breed to have but dearer than we could afford. And, Lulu hated carrying the buckets of water and the beans and *groundnut haulm* for the goats. It would always spill over her clean, traditional *boubou* outfit." Ashé giggled at the thought and laughed out loud. "She told me once that no teacher should ever be seen in public in such a messy state."

"I know you miss her, Ashé."

"But when she was taken from the ship, she was angry with me."

"That cannot be true."

"Yes, I told her that I would not be staying with her in Paris and that I wanted to return home to become a fisherman. I never wanted to be a businessman. That was my grandfather's idea."

"I am sure she was not mad at you."

"My sister is very serious about teaching. She thought our family might force her to return with me."

"I am sure that was not the case. And, a teacher is needed in this village too."

Ashé grew solemn once more. "I hope it is not too late. I am supposed to take *care* of her, Ada. But she was the one who has taken care of me."

"Oh?"

"Did you know Lulu saved my life in Libya? We were in Sebha and a man tried to rob us while we awaited the truck caravan to Tripoli, but she put a knife to his throat. Actually, I was quite scared but Lulu was not. She was not scared in the least. It was the second time she saved my life on that trip."

Ada gently rubbed the back of Ashé's neck. "I know you will be with her again very soon, Ashé." She stood and dusted off her skirt, then touched the teen's shoulder. "You remind me of Chiké so much. It will not be too long, child."

Ashé watched Ada return to join the men at the campfire and then he thought to himself. *No, I know it will not be much longer.* Later that evening, he waited for the moon to disappear behind a dark cloud then made his way quietly through the village and entered the jungle, heading due east.

Desta, Okeke, and Estrada sat eating carp and mangoes just outside Desta's house and discussed battle plans.

"So," began Estrada, setting a drinking coconut down on the mat. "We will need to get as close as possible to wherever they are keeping the Captain and the women. We must surprise them or we will fail. Has anyone here ever been to the pirate village?"

Desta nodded. "Those who first arrived on the *Ralik-Ratak*, the one that was shipwrecked, and those of us on the *Yap Islander*, but that was over a year ago now. The village is right on the beach."

"Perhaps you could make a drawing of it and..."

All eyes suddenly turned to Ada, who rushed to Desta's side and whispered in his ear. He immediately sprang to his feet. "Ashé is gone!"

"Gone?" Estrada repeated.

"He has left the village," said Ada. "I think he has gone after his sister."

"Oh, Lord," cried Okeke. "The pirates will shoot him like they did poor Chiké!"

"I will go after him," declared Desta.

"Desta, no!" Ada said, worried. "The Isleños will shoot you too! It is much too dangerous."

Desta ran inside his house, emerging seconds later with a long bamboo spear. "Wait here," he ordered the others.

"I can come with you," Estrada offered, but Desta shook his head.

"I can travel faster alone, Spanish. You must reach the Arab village tonight and tell them we will need more help from them than some of your ship's passengers." He turned to Ada, his face serious and concerned with the possible loss of Ashé. "Ada, ask one of the village guards to accompany these men to the Arab fence and help them cross over." Ada nodded and Estrada shook hands with the African leader.

"Tomorrow morning then, as agreed?" asked Estrada.

"Tomorrow is the day," said Desta, hurrying out the doorway.

* * * * *

Deep within the African sector, Ashé carefully tightroped between long rows of sharp pineapple leaves then hurried through a forest of mango trees. He took his short blade and slashed at the vines to clear his way as he searched for a faster route through the jungle foliage. Checking the position of the moon and stars as he ran, he noticed the shadowy tree limbs seemingly pointing the way to an unusually wide rabbit trail, and he took it at a full trot.

An hour away, Lulu emerged from a clump of thick banana trees and checked the position of the bright moon before pausing, listening for sounds of danger in the unfamiliar jungle. *Where are all the people*, she wondered, searching for a clearer path to take her through the dense brush. *Odd how the branches of these tall trees are all pointing west.*

Okeke sat alone with Ada inside Desta's house finishing their meal of fish and mango. Ada was nervous about Ashé out all alone in the jungle but even more worried about her true love, Desta Kado. *If the pirates kill him I will be completely and hopelessly lost*, she realized.

"You have been most kind and gracious, Ada," said Okeke.

"Oh, uh, more food, Uncle?"

"No, thank you. You seem worried though."

"What if he is caught, Uncle?"

"Ashé or Desta?" Okeke chortled at her flummoxed reaction.

"Both of them, of course."

"They will be in God's hands. We are all in God's hands. The Asians, the Arabs, and, even the Isleños...the pirates."

"But they are all outsiders, Uncle!"

"Outsiders?"

"Not Africans; not like us."

Okeke considered her statement. "You can say such things even when you saw these *outsiders* help us unloading all the wire, yesterday? Even when you realize that many of them will die alongside of us trying to save the Captain and the women, tomorrow?"

"But they are not one of us. You know that, Uncle."

Okeke reflected again on her words and repeated them to himself. "Not one of...*us*? Yes, but who are *we*, Ada? Who are we *really*? Even back home, were *we* better than our fellow man? Were we smarter? Were we kinder? Does God look upon *us* any differently than *He* does our neighbor or our enemy? It would seem to me that on this island, no one is really different. In fact, more than ever, we are the same. We eat the same food. We drink the same water. And soon we will fight the same enemy."

* * * * *

Lulu had remained hidden in the jungle only a few hundred yards from the bamboo fence the night of her escape. The next day, worried that she might be spotted by an Isleños patrol, she found a good hiding place in a stand of bamboo and waited for dark. Sweating profusely, she had now been running for what seemed like hours. Nearing exhaustion, she slowed to a walk, her dwindling energy nearly depleted. She knew she couldn't go on much longer without rest. *Odd how quiet the jungle had become tonight*, she thought. The wind was barely noticeable but those massive fern leaves up ahead seemed to be beckoning her to take shelter beneath their inviting green canopies. She nestled under the nearest one to rest, willing herself not to fall asleep.

Less than a mile away, after picking up Ashé's trail, Desta rushed through a forest of cherimoya trees and splashed through a narrow stream. He raced past a thicket of tall bamboo before noticing how quiet the jungle had become. He stopped, straining to listen for movement. A distant bird squawked and flew off. A soft breeze wafted through the banana and mango trees, gently rustling their broad leaves. *Odd*, he thought, something seemed to be guiding him along a new pathway; a shortcut through the forest. Was it the ancestors?

Ashé remained motionless behind a large banyan tree, peering through the darkness. *Odd*, he thought, nearly overcome with a warm and almost pleasurable feeling about this particular place in the jungle. No fog; the moon brighter than ever before, and even the tall trees were completely still. The virtual tranquility of the quiet forest generated a strange but pleasant feeling of calm and contentedness within him. Without realizing it, he felt the inner rage that had been brewing inside him since he and his sister had left Senegal, disappearing. He sighed at the serenity of his surroundings as he continued along a westerly path. Passing through an orchard of thirty-foot avocado trees, he had stopped for a moment to listen to the murmuring of branches high above the almost idyllic landscape when a large hand clapped over his mouth and pulled him to the ground.

"Quiet! Listen!" Desta ordered. Relieved at the sight of the Head Man, Ashé remained silent. They could both just barely make out the distinct sound of footsteps in the distance. Desta gestured for the teen to stay hidden then disappeared into the jungle. Anxious, Ashé pulled out his knife and waited, but after a few moments found himself edging back into the pathway and moving forward one careful step at a time.

Eighty yards ahead, Lulu moved cautiously from beneath the large fern. *There is something out there*, she sensed, *but what?* She crept forward for several minutes staying as quiet as she could before grunting loudly when she was tackled from behind and flipped over, the point of a spear inches from her throat.

"Who are you?" Desta bellowed, glaring down at the girl. Hearing the voices, Ashé ran up the path toward them.

"Wait, Desta! It is my sister! It is Lulu!" Desta pulled the girl to her feet, and she embraced Ashé.

"My brother!" Lulu cried, relieved at finally seeing him again.

"Sister!" Ashé shouted, before Lulu pushed him an arms-length away.

"Why didn't you rescue me?"

Desta grinned at Ashé's startled look then motioned for the pair to follow him back to the African village.

Hours later, Okeke and Ada lay half-asleep on mats in two corners of Desta's hut as the Head Man burst through the doorway. "Ada! Food for this girl! She is safe!" Okeke and Ada awakened with a start.

"Praise God!" Ada grinned at the village leader, relieved and thankful for his safety. She turned to Ashé and smiled. "You found your sister after all!"

"This is Lulu!" Ashé announced, his face beaming.

"You escaped, Miss Lulu!" Okeke exclaimed, hugging the girl. "Thank God!"

"Mr. Okeke! Yes, we did with the Captain and Miss Esha and the others."

The Ghanian glanced over the teen's shoulder. "Where are they? Where's the Captain?"

"They found us again," Lulu explained, a sadness coming over her face. "The Isleños, they...killed Miss Esha. I saw it."

"Oh no!" Okeke cried.

"How did you escape?" Ada asked, motioning for everyone to sit.

"The Captain saved us. She fought them, the Isleños. She was very brave."

"Is she still alive?" Okeke asked, a solemn tone to his voice. Desta sat beside Lulu as Ada brought a food basket. Proud of his sister's sheer bravery in escaping, Ashé watched as she bolted down fish and mango slices, washing it all down with a green coconut.

"I don't know," replied Lulu, between bites. "I think Commandant Delgado wants to keep her alive."

"And the other women? They are alive?" Desta asked.

Lulu nodded as she drank once more. "For now, but they are in danger. They have assaulted at least four women, maybe more."

Ada put her arm around Lulu's shoulder. "Let this poor girl rest."

"I am fine!" Lulu exclaimed a bit too loudly. "We have to save them! We have to save the Captain!"

"We will, child. We will!" Desta declared, taking a deep gulp from a coconut. "Ashé? Tomorrow you and your sister will guard our two prisoners. Tomorrow we fight. Tomorrow we fight these pirates. We will fight them for Chiké!"

Desta threw his empty coconut through the open door and turned to Lulu. "You will need a weapon, young miss."

Lulu wiped her mouth with the back of her hand. "Do you have a bow?"

CHAPTER 9

THE BATTLE BEGINS

Sixty-five thatched huts encircled a rectangular common area in the Arab village where large cooking fires were ablaze, bathing the curious villagers in deep shadows as they gawked at Estrada and his three crewmen. Mohammed Kassab and several others who had worked with them to unload the barbed wire greeted the *Militobi* crewmen and led them to their Imam.

"Peace be upon you and welcome! I am called Imam Ashraf. I am one of the elders in our poor and humble village."

"This is Mr. Estrada and members of the ship's crew," Kassab said, introducing the men. They need our help to rescue their Captain and many female passengers including some destined to come to our most welcoming village." Imam Ashraf motioned the visitors toward a central campfire where water was provided in coconut shell cups.

"Complete peace has eluded us since our own arrival on this rich and charitable island," the elderly Imam said. "The Africans and the Asians continue to trouble us and now I understand you wish us to fight the very people who protect us from our enemies."

"Thank you for seeing us at this late hour. We *do* seek your help, sir," explained Estrada. "But we believe the Africans and Arabs are *not* your enemies. You have been tricked by these pirates, er, Isleños, as you call them."

"Perhaps you are right, *Inshallah.* Come and tell us what you seek."

The Arab Council of Elders, sat in a large circle around the fire. Younger men, including Hassan Alwan, Amman Boulas, and a few women, including Akila Samar, sat outside the circle.

The Imam faced the Council and spoke Arabic in a voice loud enough for all to hear, "You all know me. I am Agha from Morocco and have lived on this island for more than two years now. We have agreed to Mr. Kassab's request to listen to this man from Spain who has assisted our new Arab brothers and sisters reach us. Now he seeks our help."

Estrada scanned the many Arab faces as the Imam spoke. He could sense their skepticism as the elder extended his arm indicating it was his turn to speak.

"*Gracias,* we appreciate the help that many of your people have already given us. We are now asking for even more help. These pirates, I do not know where they are from, perhaps Africa, perhaps Asia, perhaps as close as the Canaries. They have taken our Captain and many of your women as prisoners. They did not take them to help plan the settlement of new migrants on the island, as they told us, but have kidnapped them for ransom, for money. And they also took African and Asian women, as well. We wish to rescue them all and believe that, together with your help, we can bring them back to safety."

The Imam translated and the elders talked loudly among themselves, reacting to his words.

"Council members ask why do you not save your Captain and let us worry about our own women? Why do you think they are in danger?" All eyes turned to Estrada.

"The pirates told me that my Captain and all the women will be put to death in one month unless I return with a million Euros for their release!" The crowd waited momentarily for the Imam's translation and then exploded with confusion and anger in their voices, many disbelieving the Spaniard's claim. The Imam attempted to calm them but was soon embroiled himself in arguments with several of the other elders. Frustrated, Estrada raised his hands and the crowd quieted. "I have also captured two of the pirates who admitted that your women, and my Captain, are being held as prisoners, hostages in their village on the eastern coast of the island. These pirates, and I call them pirates because that is exactly what they are, have stolen and killed from you for years. They have blamed the Africans or the Asians for *their* crimes. Just two days ago they killed a young African boy who witnessed them murder an Asian man. The Africans have pledged to help us."

An astonished Imam Ashraf translated Estrada's words into Arabic. Council members recoiled in shock then continued to argue with each other.

"The Captain of my ship," continued Estrada in a loud voice to recapture the audience's attention. "She also happens to be a woman, and is very special and close to my heart, although I am not sure that she knows it." Estrada paused for a moment, surprising himself at his brief welling of emotions. "She has rescued hundreds and hundreds of migrants, including many who sit here right now. It is her life's work. And it has become mine." Estrada's crewmen nodded in agreement.

Council members listened intently as the Spaniard's words were translated simultaneously by Alwan, Boulas, and Samar sitting around the circle behind them. Estrada continued, "The crew of the *Militobi*, our ship, cares for the safety of all our passengers, no matter where they come from. *We* feel responsible because it was *our* suggestion to come to this island after being turned away from every European port, the last being France."

"We know of your arduous journey," said the Imam in English, with an understanding smile. "We have all made similar voyages, but the Isleños are helping us to reach asylum."

"They will *not* help you!" Estrada quickly responded. "They are lying to you! They are being hunted themselves by the Spanish authorities. They are criminals. They are pirates!" The crowd erupted again as Estrada's words were translated. He continued, his voice booming, "It is the *pirates* at fault here! They are your real enemies! Help us! Please help us!" The elders continued to shout and argue with each other in Arabic. Some appeared confused by the shocking revelations while others were consumed with rage. Estrada made a final plea. "Please! Please! We cannot defeat these pirates without your help!"

The debate grew in volume and intensity. Hassan Alwan, frustrated with the bickering of the Council, stood to speak directly to Estrada in English.

"We have always believed the Isleños protected us. From our first days on this island two years ago when they banished the

Africans to another part of the island to protect us, we believed Commandant Delgado was our friend. It is inconceivable that he would deceive us. To what purpose? Why would he do this? Perhaps it is just a few of the Isleños at fault."

Estrada exchanged worried glances with his crewmen and cleared his throat. "Sir, I thank you for speaking up. I understand this situation is very difficult for you to believe. It is difficult for all of us. You have villagers here who were on our ship, like Mr. Kassab here. They all saw the pirates take away our Captain and many of your women. Have they been returned? No, and they will not be returned. We have heard it directly from the lips of two pirates who admitted they keep you under control with a big lie about the illegal behavior of other migrants on this island. They want you to hate the other villages. As long as you keep hating, they control you. We are asking you to *break* their control. Tomorrow is the day to do that. Tomorrow is the day you take control of your own lives!"

Imam Ashraf translated for the rest of the Council as the First Officer sat down on a woven mat. Mohammed Kassab patted Estrada on the knee and whispered, "Very good, very good. I am sure they will argue all night but we will be ready tomorrow."

Rising to his feet, Estrada gestured for his crewmen to leave. "Thank you, my friends. Those who are willing to fight, meet us at sunrise where we first landed." He thanked the Imam, who momentarily stopped mid-argument to shake his hand before rejoining the debate. Estrada shook hands once again with Mohammed Kassab and was surprised when Hassan Alwan stepped forward to do the same.

"I will show you a path back to the beach, follow me."

* * * * *

The next morning in the center of the pirate village, the recaptured women cried and wailed in horror as Anna Kruger, tied to a post, had the shirt ripped from her back by a bare-chested and muscular pirate. The three women assaulted earlier sat together trying to hold back tears, comforted by several African and Arab captives. Delgado, his short whip unfurled, lashed out and a red welt appeared across Anna's bare back. The captive women wailed in sympathy, as Kruger grunted in pain, tears welling in her eyes.

"Silence!" shouted Delgado at the sobbing women. "You were told this would happen! If you try and escape, we will find you and you will be severely *punished*!"

The lash cracked again as Delgado focused his anger on the leader of the escape: Anna Kruger.

"We don't *want* to hurt you," shouted Delgado, spittle flying from his mouth, "But we must have *respect*! Respect for the rule of law. And *I* make the law!" He hobbled closer to examine Kruger's bleeding back and yanked her hair back, leaning in close so only she could hear his words. "Sorry, Captain," he whispered wickedly. "But I have to make an example of you for the others. I'm sure you understand." He shoved Kruger's head forward as she slumped to her knees nearly unconscious. A final lash and Delgado yelled at the onlookers, "Cut her down! Take her back inside!"

The women half-dragged, half-carried Anna back to their house and lay her face down on the matted floor. A young Chadian woman daubed at her wounds. A Moroccan girl peeked over her shoulder and asked in English, "Will she be all right?"

The Chadian nodded as Anna opened her eyes. "Oh, Captain, how do you feel?"

"Fine. I'm fine," said Anna, grimacing in pain. Thirty minutes later, two male guards entered the room and pushed several women aside before pulling Kruger to her feet, disregarding the multitude of pleas to leave her alone. Gripping each arm, they dragged her across the room and through the door. They hurried her across the pebbled main path, her toes barely touching the ground, and carried her up the stairs into Delgado's house. The Commandant, his bad leg propped up on a barrel that had been cut in half, tapped at the tall glass jar containing his black snake. Wincing, Kruger was thrown into a chair. She tried to focus on her immediate surroundings but ended up staring straight into the black eyes of the reptile.

"Wait outside," Delgado ordered his guards. He eyed Kruger and enjoyed her obvious discomfort. "Captain, I hope you can understand my position." His voice sardonic and vicious. "We must maintain discipline, no?" Anna snorted but remained silent. "I must tell you that you are quite a unique visitor to our village. In fact, you are quite impressive. We have had very few guests escape our...hospitality."

Anna adjusted herself in her seat. "Hospitality? Is that what you call raping and killing these helpless migrant women, you pathetic bastard?"

Delgado guffawed. "Now, now Captain; let me tell you a story about your *helpless* migrants. Two years ago, we were made aware from an informant that a freighter had been located off course north of Tenerife, possibly carrying several hundred migrants. My entire crew of Isleños quickly headed out to meet it at full speed."

Anna shifted in her chair again, her back stinging as she tried to find just the right position to ease the pain. Droplets of blood seeped through the back of her shirt, forming a line of tiny circles down her spine.

"The fog was so thick you couldn't see your hand in front of your face, and the ship nearly rammed us." Delgado took a long swig of rum straight out of a bottle.

Anna frowned. "A bit early isn't it?"

Delgado grinned back at her and took another long gulp. "When we boarded her, there must have been at least three hundred migrants sitting around staring into space like zombies. No one said a word. Their eyes had a far away look to them. Glassy, you could call them. As if they knew we were there but couldn't see us. It was like they were awaiting God's final judgement. A young Arab and his girlfriend stepped forward and asked if we were the police."

Anna snorted. "The police? Of course you told them you were."

"That we did, Captain. That we did. Their clothes were torn and blood was everywhere. I asked them about the Captain. He's dead, they said. I asked where the crew was and they said they were dead too." Delgado stopped for another sip of rum and shook his head. "They said the crew was *evil,* and they had killed them all! But there wasn't one dead body anywhere. Not a one to be seen. You know what they said?" Anna said nothing. "They said they threw them all overboard because they didn't want the authorities to find out and ruin their chances for asylum. Can you believe that?"

Anna adjusted herself in her seat once more. Delgado waited a moment then made direct eye contact with her. "These are your precious migrants, Captain. The ones you are protecting. They killed the Captain, the First Mate, and every single crew member and threw them all overboard!"

Anna wondered if this story was just another pirate lie. "Things happen at sea. I am sure you realize that."

Delgado chortled. "And we knew the Spanish authorities would be coming after us, but the ship's passive sonar system showed we had about an hour to get away. So we headed northwest in the fog."

"Northwest? The Spanish would suspect you would head south toward the Canaries," Anna said.

"Right. We disengaged all tracking devices and lights; left our boats tied up alongside the ship to be towed and in fifteen minutes or thereabouts, we were headed into open ocean. We told the passengers they were being temporarily taken to a shelter because asylum-seekers were no longer allowed in the Canary Islands."

"You were going to rob and kill them."

"Hadn't really decided, to be perfectly honest. Maybe take them as hostages if we ran into the Spanish." Delgado took another long swig of rum before continuing. "So, everything was going our way, at least that's what we figured. But we smashed into the reef in the fog. That's when I hurt this bum knee of mine and that's when we all became prisoners of this island."

"You did say that was your ship on the reef."

"The *Ralik-Ratak* in all her splendor, what's left of a four-hundred-foot, three-thousand-ton vessel. We stripped her of everything valuable: food, fuel drums, rope. Even the ship's bell. There was a lot more we could salvage, but we had to wait on the tides. We took doors, hatch covers, hand railings, diesel oil, and several kerosene-burning lanterns. Everything went into building this village."

"But what to do with all the passengers? That was your biggest problem."

Delgado laughed. "Right again, Captain. There were too many to kill, well over three hundred when we counted them all up, and that included the children. We set up camps along the beach and the migrants were happy to help. They went about making shelters and gathering food. It was everywhere. Somebody must have farmed this place years ago and then left it to grow wild. The Arabs formed into a number of groups of friends and relatives. They explored the northeastern part of the island. The Africans divided into groups too. The French speakers worked together to find palm fronds and driftwood.

They built even more shacks and huts. The West Africans who spoke Yoruba, Igbo, and other dialects, tended to stay together farther down the beach and explored the southeastern part of the island. They all would fish and hunt for wild pig, and rabbit and birds. There were only about twenty-five or thirty Pakistanis, Indians, and Afghanis."

"Sounds like everyone was getting along pretty well. You must have hated that."

"Oh, Captain," Delgado chuckled, "I knew it would only be a matter of time before they started to question my authority. And I only had about thirty or forty men and women with me. But, for my money, they were becoming too friendly with the migrants. They would eat with them, hunt with them, fish with them. Something had to be done before it got out of hand."

Anna nearly laughed at the pirate. "*That* was your problem? People were becoming too friendly with each other?"

Delgado scowled at her. "Yes, there were too many migrants and not enough Isleños."

"So?"

"So, on the beach one night I had Lucia steal a bracelet from an Arab woman after the camp was asleep and plant it under the sleeping mat of one of the Africans. When the Arab woman realized it was gone we had a massive search for it."

"Let me guess, the Arabs were angry with the Africans?"

"It was a shocking discovery, Captain, and it resulted in all the Africans banished to the other end of the island."

"You, of course, served as judge, jury, and executioner?"

"Of course, and we had weapons to avoid any...problems with my judgment. Later we accused the Asians of spying on the Arab women."

"Same result?"

He nodded. "Each group made their way to the other end of the island and away from this village. The trick was to have each group think we were protecting them from the other. The Arabs believed we were protecting them from the Asian voyeurs and perverts by allowing them to set up their own village. And the Asians believed we were protecting them from both the thieving Africans and the hysterical Arabs who, for some reason believed the Asians were trying to steal their women! They found a place way out on the western corner of the island, as far as you could go."

"So the Arabs and the Asians thought you were protecting them. What about the Africans? You had banished them. They could not have been happy with you."

Delgado took yet another swig of rum. "Yes, that was my best idea yet. I had Lucia and some other female Isleños visit the Africans after they had set up their own village. Lucia has a way about her that attracts men like bees to honey. She said I did not actually blame them for stealing that bracelet because I knew they didn't do it. She said that I knew the Arabs and Asian migrants were plotting against them and that it was the Arabs who planted that bracelet and wanted them banished."

"And the Asians?"

"That the Asians knew all about everything and were in favor of their banishment." Delgado laughed at his own deviousness. "Lucia testified to them I knew the only way to avoid bloodshed and to save their lives was to banish them. It was my way of protecting them. The Africans believed every word of it. I even had them build long fences so they could feel safe from each other and gave them rules not to trespass into other sectors. We told the other villages about the Africans building fences and they all wanted to build their own. They all thanked me for telling them the truth. I tell you, Captain, they love me. They all love me."

"I have news for you, Commandant. They do *not* all love you."

Delgado's eyes narrowed. "For the last time, Captain. Where is the money you got for the migrants? I know it is somewhere on this island."

Anna painfully laughed then winced at the effort. She moved in her chair once more to relieve the pain. "Again, there is no money! What do you need money for anyway? What can you possibly buy here? You have taken everything from these people."

Delgado's eyes flashed in anger then settled back into a fiery glare. "Money is not for here, Captain. Money is for *leaving* here. Again, where have you hidden it?"

"Again, we are a humanitarian rescue ship carrying migrants from Africa, the Middle East, and even South Asia."

"As you have said before."

"And again I am telling you, we are rescuing migrants. Men, women, and children, farmers, laborers, truck drivers, students, doctors..."

Delgado abruptly sat up in his chair. "Doctors? Where are the doctors?"

"Really?"

Dead serious, Delgado stared ominously at Anna. "You don't know where they are?"

"I don't know where anybody is because you pulled me off my ship to work as a galley slave!"

"I should have had you killed."

Incensed, Anna scoffed at her captor, "Why didn't you?"

Delgado eased back in his chair. He tapped at his snake once again. "You intrigued me, Captain. It's nice to have someone like you to talk things over. Someone who is intelligent and can appreciate the world I have created here."

"You have a unique way of showing it, Commandant, I will give you that."

Delgado called for his guards. "Captain, you will tell me from what country are the doctors you brought with you. I need to know this in precise detail, if you please."

"I never ask anyone their nationalities while I try and keep them from drowning."

"If you don't tell me, I will send my Isleños to each village until they find them and bring them here. For every day it takes, I will kill one of the captive women."

Shocked, Anna sat up, her back now throbbing. "You wouldn't! Even someone as ruthless as you would not dare to—"

"It is all up to you, Captain. It is all up to you. I will send the first patrol out immediately."

* * * * *

Desta Kado tested the strength of his bowstring. Okeke, Lulu, and Ashé watched him pull the finely woven hibiscus twine to his chin before letting it go. He nodded at its pinging sound and handed the bow to Lulu with a bundle of arrows tied together with vine, comforted in knowing the weapon was ready for battle. Outside, a cadre of African fighters practiced throwing spears, swinging bamboo machetes, and slashing at imaginary opponents with their knives. Desta held his captured machine gun high in the air.

"For Chike!"

His followers shouted the name back to him. Satisfied, Desta and his warriors raced through the village entrance and into the jungle as elderly onlookers and children cheered and waved in support.

In the Arab village, Mohammed Kassab completed his prayers then took up a makeshift bamboo spear and tested it in his hand for balance. He greeted Hassan Alwan, Amman Boulas, Akila Samar and a contingent of armed Arab warriors, both men and women, standing just outside his bamboo house.

"Let us go with God. *Inshallah*, we will be victorious! *Allah akbar!*" The Arab warriors repeated Kassab's words as elderly onlookers, lined up on both sides of the main path, cheered and waved in support. Women performed an ululation, or tongue-trilling, as the fighters passed them and headed into the jungle.

In the remote Asian village that same morning, Jay Rawal continued to plead his case on the seemingly deaf ears of his village elders. Women sat behind the circle of old men and whispered loudly to them whenever they wished to add their opinions to the conversation.

"But they are our friends!" Jay argued. "Unlike the smugglers who abandoned us here!"

Dressed in a dark turban and a worn tunic, a thin Sikh elder waved his hand to be heard and rose to his feet in response to Jay's arguments. "But we do not know their intentions, young Jay. They partner with our enemies, the Africans and the Arabs. Helping them will be quite dangerous." Jay shook his head in amazement at the unwillingness to listen to what seemed to him so obviously a beneficial act.

"No, they want what *we* want and that is *peace*! Their Captain is a prisoner along with *our* own women! And with the doctor's wife! He left before sunrise to join the ship's crew. The battle is today! Esteemed elders, our women are not coming back until we free them ourselves." Two old men began to argue and nearly came to blows until they were separated by several younger men and women.

The thin elder stood and called for order with a wave of his hands. "We understand the Isleños have rules that must be obeyed. Young Jay himself has broken these rules a number of times when he hunts outside of our sector. He has nearly paid for it with his life while chasing after mere rabbits!" Jay lowered his head, admitting the statement to be true as the old man continued. "His actions have often placed us in great danger, but we have always come to his rescue, even facing down the Isleños at times. Brothers, we are not afraid of danger, but we *are* afraid of ruining the life we have made here on this wondrous island." Many elders nodded and applauded in agreement. "And we understand completely how the doctor is concerned about his wife. A man must fight for his family. Perhaps it is just a misunderstanding with the Isleños."

Frustrated, Jay shook his head again, angered that his message was not getting through. "Yes, I agree Dr. Arun is *right* to fight for his wife. I tell you, these sailors are our friends! They have rescued many of our own people. Rescued them from cutthroat Libyan traffickers who overflow their flimsy boats with those of us desperate to escape the dangers of our own countries!"

The Sikh elder stepped forward to respond. "Be it known, I have no quarrel with the Spanish sailors, and I understand their wish to save their Captain! It is the joining with the Africans and the Arabs that I do not understand. I do not trust them. None of us can trust them! None of us *should* trust them." The crowd murmured in Urdu, Hindi, and other South Asian dialects, although English was the lingua franca within the village. As the final translation of the thin elder's comments was completed, the crowd exploded with shouts and handwaving as each village elder attempted to add their views to the growing controversy.

Jay held up his hands to be heard once more. "The Africans and Arabs are *not* our enemies! It is the *pirates* who have made us hate our neighbors. It was the *pirates* who killed Ahmed, our brave guard, and the African boy, only yards from our village! It is the *pirates* who make us live behind bamboo walls and fetch their food like the slaves we have become! I say it is the *pirates* who must be defeated. We must join our neighbors or they will all be dead by this evening. The time to act is now!"

The discontented crowd continued to rage as many of the women argued with each other and then with the men who tried to step between them.

Jay yelled loudly again to be heard, "Remember that most of our Arab neighbors are also Muslims! And they are *not* Taliban! They do *not* force us to pray their way nor stop us from doing as we please. It is this old way of thinking about strangers that must change. The Quran says, '...*and do good to parents, kinsfolk, orphans, the poor, the neighbor who is near of kin, the neighbor who is a stranger, the companion by your side, the wayfarer.*'"

Village elders and onlookers shouted even louder at each other as they now argued over the interpretation of the Quran's passage.

The thin elder called out again, "We left the terrors of our home countries because of those who would tell us how to live and how to worship God. No other country wanted us. Many of us were set adrift, and God delivered us to this magnificent island where there is sustenance for all. Yes, we all know there is a serpent in our garden. These Isleños rule over us. *Their* way has become *our* way. Regretfully, this is the way of our new world."

"But it does not *have* to be that way!" Jay countered. "Whether it is the Taliban or Isleños, there will always be those who try and prevent us from finding the peace we seek." Still frustrated, Jay shook his head and appealed to several of the other elders who, for the most part, had remained silent. "You know many of us believed the Isleños when they told us the Canary Islands would soon lift their ban on immigrants. But that was just a lie. Gentlemen, since the first settlers, including many of you, built this village, we have tried to avoid trouble and justified our isolation as the price we must pay for our protection! But now that price is too high!"

The thin Sikh elder nodded his head, seemingly in agreement. "Yes, young Jay is right. We have chosen to *avoid* violence and have made many sacrifices, but we are not *afraid* of violence. We have long awaited a chance for asylum, but now I know I will die here one day, and I am at peace with that. But we cannot allow our Asian brethren to join this fight against the ones who have always protected us because some believe a few of the new arrivals are in danger." After saying his piece, he sat back down and many in the crowd nodded their approval at his words.

Jay made a final plea. "I say to you one last time, join me today to help the Spanish sailors rescue our women. Realize that peace is only for those who seek it and are willing to fight for it." Jay sat down, out of breath and out of argument. Mohamed Aboud finally stood, helped to his feet by two of the younger men. He had been one of the elders who had remained silent, listening to both sides of the argument. The crowd quieted as the old gentleman spoke in English.

"Now we have heard two very different points of view. One quotes the Quran that we must help our neighbors. The other says we must not fight against those who protect us. The differences are clear, and it is now time to decide our fate. I ask all of you to consider both sides of this conundrum and let your hearts tell you what to do."

* * * * *

Jorge, Gabby, and two crewmen boarded one of the *Militobi's* lifeboats and headed for their original landing beach in the African sector. Just down the shore, Mohammed Kassab and Hassan Alwan led a cadre of thirty armed Arab warriors toward the rendezvous point. Bows, arrows, spears, slingshots, knives, and bamboo machetes were the weapons of choice. Through the jungle north of the landing beach, Desta, Ada, and a large contingent of forty-five African fighters emerged from the jungle. As the Arab and African groups mixed there was pushing and shoving between them. Scuffles broke out and a woman screamed. Desta and Mohammed fought their way through the crowd to separate the combatants.

"Brothers! Sisters! Please!" Okeke cried.

"Calm down!" Desta ordered.

"Quiet!" Mohammed shouted in both English and Arabic.

Speaking as if he were preaching to his own flock, Okeke raised his arms to calm the growing din, "Please! Please! My friends! We all know the *pirates* are the real enemy, not each other! It was the *pirates* that took away our sisters and have caused all of us great pain. I know you do not all know me, but I speak the truth. Now is the time to put away our differences and work as one."

Estrada and Fernandez jumped from their lifeboat and hurried up the beach to join the anxious crowd of warriors. A cooling breeze swept over the group, adding to the efforts to pacify long pent-up anger and distrust. Mohammed Kassab patted Okeke's shoulder indicating solidarity with his plea for peace and understanding. He faced the combined migrant army himself.

"Many of you have friends and relatives who have been killed or mistreated on this island. These pirates have forced you to live in bamboo pens like animals. You have been treated like slaves and have followed their demands like sacrificial lambs in order to keep their protection. We now gather together to battle for our freedom. *Inshallah*, we will be rewarded."

Estrada and Fernandez uncovered the large tarp to reveal the two elongated ropes of barbed wire. The migrants formed rapidly into two teams, each carrying one long length. Hands wrapped with vines and banana leaves for protection from the barbs, stretched and pulled the long coils to straighten out kinks and knots. Desta, Mohammed Kassab, and Dr. Arun joined Estrada and Fernandez at the tarp.

Drawing a rough sketch of the pirate village in the sand with a stick, Estrada gave his final instructions. "Like we said before, Mr. Kassab, your team will string wire around the western side of the village. Take it as far north as you can and then east toward the beach. Desta's team will cover the southern end. Take it as close to the beach as possible without being seen. The wire will cut off their escape and hopefully trap them. Wait for the shooting to start. That will be the signal to attack. Drive them into the wire, if you can. Let those with guns lead the way."

"Then kill every one of them!" Desta said grimly.

"Remember, we do not kill those who surrender. We will take them prisoners," Estrada reminded both men.

"We will remember," Mohammed Kassab acknowledged, rubbing his goatee.

Although he did not agree with sparing any of the animals who killed Chiké, Desta nodded that he understood the instructions. "We have sent scouts out early this morning to prepare the way."

"Good luck to you both!" Fernandez said, shaking their hands. Desta and Mohammed signaled for both groups to enter the jungle. Lucia Santos and the scarred pirate, wrists bound, marched with Desta's team under the watchful eyes of Ashé and Lulu. At the lifeboat, Dr. Arun joined Estrada, Fernandez, and the other *Militobi* crewmen.

"I'm coming with you. I won't take no for an answer."

"You are most welcome," responded Estrada. "We are undermanned and I can guarantee there will be casualties."

"It is what Esha would have wanted me to do." The doctor's eyes were filled with tears.

Estrada was puzzled. "What? What's wrong?"

"The pirates killed her. They shot her trying to escape. Lulu saw it happen," he explained.

Estrada embraced his friend. "Dr. Arun, I am so sorry. So very sorry!"

"Desta just told me. She will be missed. It is inconceivable she is really gone."

Finally realizing the inherent danger in the news, Estrada grabbed the doctor's shoulder. "And the Captain? Any word on her? Was she..."

Dr. Arun shrugged. "No news about the others. I just don't know."

Estrada grew solemn, his face grim and serious. "Gabby, let's go get our Captain!"

"*Sí*, Jorge, we're as ready as we will ever be!"

CHAPTER 10

THE BATTLE OF SANTA INEZ ISLAND

Deep in the African sector, birds squawked high overhead as the long line of Africans and Arabs marched together through a mango forest still wet with morning dew. A sweet scent wafted from the ripe yellow and orange fruit. Men, women, and teenagers struggled to avoid snagging the wire in the tangled brush. An African scout, waiting long since before sunrise, spotted a five-person pirate patrol pushing open the heavy bamboo gate. He immediately alerted the next nearest scout hundreds of yards away with the call of the Timneh African grey parrot. The trilling signal was passed across the jungle until it reached Desta Kado. An hour later he motioned for the large migrant army to stop and rest. He pointed directly at Lulu and several African fighters, all carrying bows, and gestured for them to follow him deeper into the jungle. Fearing the worst, Ada set down her coil of wire and sighed as she watched the African leader depart with the archers.

The armed patrol, on their way to the African village in search of a doctor for Commandant Delgado's knee, trekked through groves of guava and papaya trees until they arrived at a clearing and stopped to rest. Fatigued from their laborious jungle journey, the team flopped on the ground, breathing heavily and wondering why they were chosen for this disagreeable duty.

Drinking deeply from a water canteen, the patrol leader glanced upward, his eyes registering in incomprehensible horror

261

as the sky above filled with a lethal shower of sharpened bamboo arrows. Before he could utter a word of warning, he and the rest of his men were killed instantly, their bodies riddled with the lightweight shafts. Desta and his team of archers made their way down to the clearing to search the bodies for weapons. Shocked, Lulu gaped openly at the dead, their bodies twisted in their final frozen poses. Several pistols, knives, and two rifles were found. Desta wrapped his arm around Lulu.

"You did well, sister."

The MV *Militobi's* anchor clanged into its locked prow position as the worn ship got slowly underway. On the bridge, Jorge Estrada gave a *slow ahead* order into his walkie-talkie. The crew hurried to make ready as the ship rattled and moaned and gradually entered the lagoon just inside the southern reef. Estrada and Fernandez peered through their binoculars.

"Hold her steady," Estrada ordered. "We have to time this just right for Desta and Mohammed."

"Aye," replied the Helmsman.

"When I give the order, we will be getting as close to that pirate beach as we can without going aground."

"Aye, right down their throats, sir."

"Gabby?"

"*Sí?*" Fernandez replied.

"Prepare all weapons."

Grinning at the order, Fernandez nodded to the Helmsman who grinned back. "You mean *battle stations*, Jorge?" Estrada nodded then shook his head at the two men.

Fernandez patted the Helmsman on the back as he pulled the sniper rifle from a bridge closet then hurried out the door. "Aye, aye, *Captain*," he replied.

Fernandez flew down the stairwell to the top deck to join the crew members who were checking the two other rifles and limited ammunition on hand. The Helmsman steered the ship northward and whispered to himself, "Here we go!"

* * * * *

The bamboo gate dividing the African and Isleños sectors, still ajar, was pushed wide open as the combined African and Arab migrant army marched through, stopping to rest at the great waterfall. Many warriors drank from the nearest pool while others carefully set their lengths of barbed wire aside and attended to annoying cuts and abrasions on their hands, a result of the wire slipping through their vine and leaf wrappings. Immediately recognizing the waterfall, fence, and opened gate, Lulu edged away from the others and ducked into the underbrush. It took her only a few moments to find Esha's lifeless body. Her eyes brimming with tears, she said a quick prayer and covered her friend with banana leaves before returning to her place in line. *I will be back for you soon, dear Esha*, she vowed.

263

Minutes later the word was passed to get back underway and the long line of migrants, less chatty now as the seriousness of their journey began to sink in, continued their arduous trek eastward through green forests of banana and breadfruit. Along the way, Ada's wire became snagged in branches and Desta stopped to help her. They exchanged smiles and she touched his arm.

"You must be careful, Ada. This wire can cut through your skin."

"But the wire is important, Desta? That is what you said."

"Yes, it will trap our enemies."

"I miss Chiké," Ada said softly. "I know he is watching over us."

"He is here with us in spirit, Ada. I miss him too." He checked her hand to ensure that she was holding the wire safely then joined Mohammed Kassab at the head of the line of warriors. As he glanced back again at Ada, who met his gaze with a half-smile, he whispered to himself, "Oh ancestors, protect this woman from harm."

* * * * *

Anna Kruger lay on the floor of the captive quarters trying to find a comfortable way to rest with her bleeding back still feeling like it was in flames. Finally giving up on sleep, she sat cross-legged and took several deep breaths to ease the pain. Still guarding the door from the inside, a female pirate watched as several of the captive women moved closer to the Captain. The Arab woman violated by the pirates on the night they made their escape, touched Anna's shoulder and spoke in low tones so as not to be overheard.

"Captain? Are you all right? Why do you do this for us?"

Anna smiled wistfully at the young woman. "I regret I was not able to help *you.*"

"There was nothing you could do. We are all in danger here."

"You have faced more than anyone should ever face."

"I am not brave, like you."

Anna shook her head. "Brave? No, *you* are the brave one." She stole a look over at the guard. "People have died. People have gotten hurt. People like you. People I should have saved."

Tears welled in the woman's eyes. "You cannot save everyone, Captain."

Anna patted her on the knee. "The people I rescued were only trying to stay alive. Just like you. All we can do is to try and help the ones we *can* help. That was what my grandfather was telling me a long time ago."

"I am frightened."

"I am frightened too, and I am angry. *We* brought you to this island. *We* convinced you it was going to be safe. *We* asked you to trust us. It is *our* fault you are here. It is *my* fault." Anna made eye contact with the guard who looked away uneasily. "And my anger is growing by the minute."

* * * * *

After slogging through the jungle for hours, Desta and Mohammed halted the long line of fighters and gestured for all to rest and stay quiet. Now only minutes from the pirate village, Desta knew that for some, this would be their last chance to catch their breaths. For others, it would be the last few breaths they would ever take. The two migrant leaders moved carefully ahead on their own to surveil the entrance to the pirate village. A hundred yards ahead, two pirates stood guard, rifles slung over their shoulders. Crawling forward on their stomachs for a better view, the two friends watched for a few moments then returned to their hidden army.

"My bowmen can take care of those guards and take their weapons," Desta said. "And then we must divide up, as planned."

"Yes, it is time to meet our destiny," agreed Kassab. "Hopefully it is a successful one, *Inshallah*."

Desta selected two archers who joined him at the head of the line. He made a conscious decision not to ask Lulu since she had agreed to continue guarding the two prisoners with her brother. After whispering instructions, the archers left noiselessly, careful not to break a twig or rustle a leaf. Minutes later, finding their targets standing close together, two arrows whizzed through the air. The guards were dead before they hit the ground. The archers dragged the bodies backwards into the jungle and hid them beneath palm branches and fern leaves. That added two more rifles to the migrant armory.

Minutes later Kassab, now armed with one of the captured rifles, shook Desta's hand as they prepared to split up their teams of fighters.

"All is ready," said Desta.

"Go with God," replied Kassab.

"You too," replied Desta. "Remember to wait for the ship's gunshots."

"And you remember not to kill those who surrender." The two men grinned at each other and embraced. "Good luck, my African friend," said Kassab.

"Good luck, my Arab friend," responded Desta, who immediately turned and motioned for his half of the migrant army to follow him due east toward the beach along the southern edge of the pirate village. Walking backwards, each migrant uncoiled their length of wire, wrapping it around low branches and shrubs, creating a deadly, knee-high fence, almost invisible to the naked eye. Still guarded by Ashé and Lulu, the two pirate captives were gagged with leaves and kept hidden in the jungle a few yards from where the two dead pirate guards lay concealed.

Mohammed Kassab led his half of the migrant army northward along the western edge of the pirate village. Uncoiling the barbed wire as they passed silently behind a number of thatched houses, each migrant focused on their task while keeping a watchful eye out for any movement. As planned, when they reached the northwestern corner of the village, Kassab gestured to Amman Boulas, who, along with Akila Samar, led half the fighters due east toward the beach as far as the wire would take them. The pirates were now boxed in by Desta's warriors to the south, by Mohammed's warriors to the west, and Amman and Akila's warriors to the north. When the wire had been strung out, both halves of the migrant army hunkered down to await Estrada's signal.

Kassab mumbled a prayer, "*'Allah, guard me from what is in front of me and behind me, from my left, and from my right, and from above me. I seek refuge in Your Greatness from being struck down from beneath me.'*"

* * * * *

Aboard the *Militobi*, Estrada and Fernandez peered through their binoculars as the old ship limped around the southeastern point and steamed northward, coming within view of pirate lookouts. One of Delgado's original Tenerife pirates, walking along the beach a half-mile from the village, stopped abruptly when he saw the freighter in the far distance, the bright sun making the ship unidentifiable. Shaken, he sprinted through the jungle and finally reached the village. He rang the ship's bell that served as an alarm. Moments later the pebbled walkways and paths swarmed with pirates scrambling for their weapons. Out of breath, the pirate scurried to Delgado's house but was stopped by the two female bodyguards posted at the door. Alerted by the commotion, Delgado emerged adjusting his shoulder whip.

"Commandant! Commandant! There's a ship in the lagoon." The pirate gestured repeatedly toward the sea.

"Get to the boats! Hurry! Don't wait for me!" Delgado snapped. Puzzled, he returned inside for his sidearm and wondered what the odds were for another ship finding this island so soon. As pirates raced to uncover their speedboats, Delgado shouted orders as the alarm bell continued to ring out its call to arms. "Hurry! Hurry up, you worthless...get to the boats!"

Anna Kruger and the captive women heard the bell ringing and the shouting erupting outside. Anxious at the loud noises and wild clamoring, the inside guard pulled open the door and exited, locking it behind her. Anna immediately rushed to the door and listened. Some of the captive women moaned in fear.

Anna snapped at them, "You *ladies* going to just sit there, or are you coming with me?" Several of the younger women, including all of those assaulted by the pirates, joined Anna and together they pushed against the locked door. "Come on! You can do it!" Anna shouted. The door burst open, and the captives poured out to find themselves totally unguarded. Startled, they watched as pirates ran toward the beach, some carrying rifles while others struggled to wrap sidearms around their waists. Anna pointed south toward the jungle. "This way!"

Estrada peered through his binoculars from the *Militobi's* bridge and spoke calmly to the Helmsman, "They see us, but they don't recognize us, not yet, anyway." Dr. Arun joined the First Officer who shouted into his walkie-talkie at his Navigator on the main deck. "Gabby? Prepare to fire the water cannon."

Developed in the late Nineteenth Century for use by fireboats, water cannons have the capacity of firing 1,350 gallons of water per minute. Used for riot control in Germany in the 1930s, the water cannon can shoot powerful and impenetrable streams of water that can sweep an enemy off its feet and flood smaller boats. The *Militobi* was equipped with four manually operated *Wasserwerter 9000s*, two on the port railing and two to starboard.

Gabby Fernandez pulled off the protective canvas tarp from one water cannon and switched it to its firing position. Crewmen did the same forward and on the starboard side. Armed with only the sniper's rifle, two captured rifles, a few handguns, and very little ammunition, crewmen took their positions and awaited their fate.

Still peering through his binoculars, Estrada called out to the Helmsman, "Hard to port!"

"Hard to port, aye, aye."

Estrada shouted a final message into his walkie-talkie, "Flank speed for one minute then all stop! Good luck to everyone!"

The first of the pirate's three speedboats, full of armed men and women, launched into the lagoon to the cheers of their buccaneer comrades standing on the sandy beach. The second boat started its outboard engine as the third pirate vessel was pushed into the water, waiting for late arriving gang members to jump aboard.

Anna Kruger and the captive women ran swiftly south along the pebbled path, scooping up rocks and pieces of wood as weapons. At the edge of the jungle Anna stopped and held up her hand, just barely noticing the twisted loops of barbed wire in time to avoid entanglement.

"Captain? Captain!" Lulu shouted from the jungle. Anna peered through the heavy green foliage and was overjoyed to see Lulu staring back at her. In Wolof, Lulu told her brother to continue watching the prisoners. Slinging her bow across her shoulders, she hopped over the barbed fencing and embraced Anna.

"Lulu? Lulu? Is it really you? I cannot believe it." Gunfire erupted in the distance far offshore. As if on cue, Desta and his warriors emerged en masse from their hidden positions, shocking the freed women at their number, stretching shoulder-to-shoulder nearly to the beach.

"Captain! I thought I lost you." Still hugging each other, Lulu looked up into Anna's eyes. "Oh, poor Miss Esha! I saw what they did to her." Saddened, Anna embraced the teen again.

"I know, dear. I am so sorry. She loved you."

Desta joined Lulu and Anna. "You are the Captain?"

"Captain, this is Desta," said Lulu. "He is leading us."

"What is the situation, sir?" Anna asked, surveying the village leader's machine gun.

"We have a small group of fighters here but only a few guns. There is another group at the far side of the village."

"Two small groups with just a few guns?"

"And there are many pirates."

"*Ja*, no kidding! Where is my crew?"

Desta pointed to the lagoon, and Kruger squinted into the sun as the roar of machine guns, rifles, and sidearms filled the air. He turned to his long line of warriors and raised his machine gun.

"For Chiké!" The warriors held their homemade weapons up to the heavens and repeated the boy's name as they charged ahead.

At the northwestern corner of the village, Mohammed Kassab held his rifle up to the sky and shouted, "*Allah akbar!*" The fighters held their weapons up to the heavens and repeated their leader's words as they followed him into battle.

Surprised, the pirates cheering the three speedboats on the beach turned to face the onslaught of migrant fighters attacking from the north and west. Sidearm fire immediately dropped many of those leading the charge. Spears and arrows flew in wide arcs, striking several of the pirates who ran for cover only to face Desta's screaming invaders attacking from the south. In the galley, pirate kitchen workers dropped everything and ran to find their weapons.

Frightened, Alonso Rivero hid among his pots and pans and prayed for his own safety. "Oh God! Oh God! Oh God! Not Alonso! Do not let this happen to Alonso! He means no harm to anyone!"

Joining the battle, Anna Kruger motioned for Lulu to stay close to her then barked orders at the freed women who huddled together just behind Desta's attackers. The women tightened their ranks and moved slowly around several thatched buildings, surprising three pirates and battering them to death with sticks and stones.

The *Militobi*, now under full-scale attack, fired their few rifles and handguns at the three pirate speedboats while Gabby Fernandez targeted his water cannon at the raiders. Long jet streams of water, bursting upon impact like artillery shells, knocked several pirates into the sea. Two *Militobi* crewmen were hit with machine gun fire. Dr. Arun scurried across the deck to aid the sailors, while dodging bullets himself. Three pirates grasped tightly to their speedboat's railing and ducked as yet another torrential burst from a water cannon slammed across their stern, knocking the outboard motor out of the water, its propellor spinning wildly. Jorge Estrada joined the crew on deck as the pirates drew closer. Dr. Arun pulled more wounded sailors to starboard and attended to them as best he could.

Ashore, Desta sprayed AK-47 fire across the beach as the battle raged in the bloody sands of the pirate village. Kassab's warriors continued to rain spears and arrows down upon them as the pirates scrambled to find cover. Hand-to-hand combatants grappled and toppled to the beach. Pinned to the ground by

Amman Boulas and another migrant fighter, one of the pirates immediately surrendered. Migrant fighters and pirates spent their final moments struggling for their lives covered in thick sand and dirt before dying. Attempting to escape the carnage, several pirates became ensnared in the barbed wire and were immediately stabbed or speared by Arab and African fighters, including Ada who scratched at the eyes of a burly pirate who fought with her to escape the death trap.

A group of pirates, now on the offensive, attacked migrant warriors to the north with rifle and sidearm fire, killing eight within a minute. Boulas motioned for his warriors, especially younger teenagers, to fall back behind the barbed wire barriers with Akila and some of the other Arab women and use the jungle for cover. His knee soaked in blood from a bullet wound, Mohammed Kassab said another short prayer and dropped his now empty weapon. Under heavy gunfire, he led his warriors in retreat back toward the jungle.

Many pirates became tangled in the razor-like wire coils and screeched in pain before being captured or killed. Out of ammunition, Desta used his machine gun as a club and was tackled to the ground by the female guard from the captive women's house. As she pulled a knife to strike the muscular African, Lulu's arrow thudded into her back killing her instantly. Lulu and Desta exchanged grim nods before rejoining the battle.

Split off from Desta's warriors, Anna and two other women, working efficiently as a team, disarmed a pirate and killed him with his own weapon. An African woman recognized one of her rapists trying to escape who became ensnared in barbed wire. He shouted for mercy as the woman beat him savagely with a length of bamboo. Racing to help, Anna removed the bloodied stick from her hand and hugged her, the pirate surrendering with his head bleeding profusely.

The pirates moved farther south, their firepower beginning to turn the battle their way. Anna led the women back toward the barbed wire fencing at the edge of the jungle. Within minutes she had linked up again with Desta and his fighters who were also retreating.

"Not looking good!" Anna shouted.

"Not too good, Captain," replied Desta. Anna noticed that the African leader no longer possessed his machine gun. "We must move back behind the wire and away from the beach. There is no protection here."

In the lagoon, pirates hurled long lines with grappling hooks up and over the *Militobi's* railing and began climbing toward the main deck. Gabby Fernandez suffered a rifle shot to the shoulder and fell backwards. Estrada immediately checked on him and the Spanish Navigator nodded bravely at his friend and gestured that he would survive. As Dr. Arun dragged Gabby starboard, Estrada climbed to the rail and grabbed the water cannon controls. He managed to smash two more pirates into the sea, their speedboat nearly swamped. Aft, rope-climbing pirates triggered the pneumatic motor dropping the long accommodation ladder down the port side. Pirates scrambled up the stairs, and the *Militobi's* crew members retreated toward the base of the bridge stairwell under heavy gunfire, water cannons abandoned and ammunition nearly gone.

From the jungle northwest of the pirate village, yelling and whooping roared like a thunderclap. Mohammed Kassab thought it was more pirates and steeled himself for an attack from the rear. He shouted a warning to his warriors who prepared themselves for death. The roaring grew louder as bushes, plants, and even dwarf trees were knocked to the ground. Jay Rawal led a huge contingent of Asian fighters through the forest. Six Asian scouts, just seconds ahead of the main force, used their spears to press down the coils of barbed wire, forming a wide avenue of attack. Running southeast through the center of the village, the horde of shrieking Asians hurled rocks propelled from homemade slingshots and slashed at the pirates with bamboo machetes, knives, and clubs.

Forcibly splintered into two groups, pirates scurrying north to escape the Asians ran directly into Arab warriors who counter-attacked with renewed vigor upon seeing the reinforcements. Pirates running south faced Desta's warriors and Anna's freed women, now taking cover behind the barbed wire fencing.

* * * * *

Commandant Delgado, handgun drawn and accompanied by two female bodyguards, emerged from his house where he had taken cover at the outset of the battle. Angry, he scanned the immediate area, shooting at the backs of Asian fighters running toward the beach.

"Where the hell is Lucia?" Delgado cried out.

His bodyguards shrugged, staying close beside their leader, and searched rapidly for an escape route. One pointed south along the main path.

"Commandant, this way!" Delgado shot wildly at more migrant fighters as the pirate trio edged their way toward the village's southern entrance.

The tidal wave of Asian combatants continued their fierce and deadly charge through the village center, linking their forces with the Africans and Arabs until finally all the pirates were either dead, wounded, or had surrendered. Migrant fighters from all three villages swarmed the beach in victory, shouting and yelling their triumph in numerous languages and dialects. Wandering through the massive crowd of joyous warriors, Desta spotted Mohammed Kassab and Jay Rawal. The former enemies embraced, jumping into each others' arms like long lost comrades.

"Were we too late?" Jay teased.

"Thanks be to God," shouted Mohammed Kassab in English. "Thanks be to God!"

"I am so very *happy* to see you!" Desta said to Jay. "I never believed I would ever say that! What happened?"

"Let us just say some of our elders are surprisingly progressive when it comes to interpreting the Quran and its lessons about protecting one's neighbors."

"And who reminded them of those holy words?" Kassab asked, grinning broadly.

"I have to say that it was my honor to remind them," retorted Jay.

At the edge of the jungle just behind the barbed wire fence, Ashé had moved the pirate prisoners closer so he could have a better view of the fighting. Peering through the foliage and trees he was excited to see the celebration beginning and the remaining pirates, now on their knees and tied with vines, surrendering. Many pleaded for their lives. Behind him, the scarred pirate struggled with his bindings. Lucia called out to Ashé through her now loosened gag.

"Cut me loose. Cut me loose!"

Ashé turned to face her just as the scarred pirate broke free, grabbed a coil of barbed wire in his bare hands, and looped it tightly around Lucia's neck. She shrieked in agony as he jammed his knee into the small of her back and strangled her to death before the paralyzed Senegalese teenager could move. Ashé stared in horror at the blood of the dead female pirate. Hands bleeding from the sharp barbs still held tightly between his fingers, the scarred pirate grinned at the youth and laid back, exhausted but satisfied at completing his savage revenge. In shock, Ashé picked up a heavy rock and slammed it repeatedly at the face of the scarred pirate. As if in a trance, he continued to hit the pirate until he was no longer moving. Blood splattered on his hands, arms, and face, Ashé realized what he had done and justified it in his own mind. *For Chiké*, he thought.

Sixty yards down the main path, Delgado and his two bodyguards moved quickly ahead, sensing that time was running out. Seeing more Asian and Arab fighters gathering together in the distance and his pirates surrendering, Delgado turned to the women and pushed them toward the enemy.

"I order you to stay and keep fighting!" His eyes crazed with fear, the frenzied pirate began slowly moving away from them. "Do you hear me? I order you to stay!" The bodyguards exchanged frantic looks. Knowing his escape routes north and south were cut off by the celebrating warriors, Delgado darted west between two houses and headed for the jungle.

Lulu, still armed with her bow, spotted Delgado stepping over the wire fence. She immediately sprinted after him but stopped abruptly as a blood-drenched Ashé emerged on the main path.

"What happened to you? Look at all the blood! Are you hurt?"

In Wolof her brother replied, "It's not mine. He killed her. I was just standing there, and he killed her and there was nothing I could do. He just took the wire and..."

Anna joined the siblings and was shocked at the blood covering Ashé. Lulu turned to Anna. "He's all right. We must go!"

Favoring his bad knee, Delgado hurried between tall breadfruit and palm trees to escape his pursuers. Lulu sprinted down the path with Anna and Ashé close behind. She hurtled over the wire at the very spot she saw Delgado enter the jungle and waited for Anna and her brother to catch up. Soon the trio found themselves in the trees and stopped to listen for the obese pirate. Thirty-five yards ahead, Delgado limped his way through the brush. Lulu gestured for the others to follow her.

Soaked in sweat from the tropical humidity, a winded Delgado hid briefly behind a thick banyan tree, gasping for air. Sensing her prey was not far ahead, Lulu signaled to her brother that she and Anna would take a different route and circle in front of the pirate. Ashé waited a few moments then carefully moved forward on his own. Minutes later he was first to locate his target, twenty-five yards away.

Drawing his knife, he called out in English, "Stop, stop right there!"

Panting for breath, Delgado turned to face his young pursuer, smiling when he realized it was just a teenaged boy covered in blood and probably wounded.

"So, you think you have defeated Delgado? You are wrong, my young pup." Confident that he was in no real danger, Delgado slowly drew out his sidearm and fired. Ashé slumped to the ground. Pleased, the pirate holstered his weapon but then stopped dead. Standing fifteen yards in front of him, tears streaming down her cheek, Lulu's bowstring was drawn fully back, an arrow pointing at his heart. Delgado snorted at her. "Well, well, it is the African..." Lulu fired her arrow at the precise moment Delgado reached for his pistol. It slammed into his shoulder, spinning him around, but did not knock him down. Delgado grinned at Lulu and reached again for his weapon. "Nobody can kill Commandant—"

"No!" shouted Anna Kruger who, flinging herself through the air, tackled the pirate to the ground, half the arrow breaking off from his shoulder. Delgado rolled on top of Anna, choking her with both hands. Frenzied, adrenaline pumping wildly throughout her body, Anna grabbed his whip, still wrapped around his broad shoulder, and pounded him savagely with its handle with little or no effect.

"Captain, it has come down to this," Delgado whispered, his nose nearly touching hers. His dead eyes reminded Anna of his pet snake. "Now it is either you or me." Gasping for breath under the weight of the corpulent pirate, Anna wrenched the broken arrow shaft from Delgado's shoulder. The pirate leader yelled in pain. Holding the bloody stub in her hand, she shoved its deadly point through his throat, killing him instantly.

"It's you!" Anna shouted.

Lulu rushed to the side of her brother. *So much blood*, she thought, searching for a wound. Anna hobbled weakly to her side, her back on fire once again and seeping blood.

"Ashé! Ashé! Are you hurt?" Lulu cried as she rapidly felt all over his body, looking in vain for a bullet wound.

Regaining consciousness, Ashé looked back at his sister. "No, I am...fine...I think."

"Were you shot?" Lulu demanded, wiping at her tears as her brother stood up. Ashé patted himself down thoroughly then broke into a smile, wiping blood off his hands with leaves.

"No, I do not think so."

"You are sure?" Anna asked.

Ashé nodded. Lulu smiled wryly at her brother. "You fainted, didn't you? I can tell. You fainted."

Insulted, Ashé brushed himself off. "I did not!"

Lulu headed back toward the village. She called out over her shoulder one last time at her brother, "You fainted. I knew it!"

* * * * *

Aboard the *Militobi* the battle raged on, now in favor of the pirates. The remaining ship's crew was pinned into a corner of the main deck beneath the bridge stairwell as the pirates fanned out to gain more favorable shooting angles. As the firefight continued, the *Militobi* crewmen, now completely out of ammunition, knew it was only a matter of time before they would be overwhelmed.

Gabby Fernandez, his arm in a makeshift sling, huddled next to Jorge Estrada. "I will try to reach the LRAD! It is our only chance now."

The Long Range Acoustic Device (LRAD) used pain-inducing sound beams to disorient and incapacitate its target. Higher than the tolerance level of the average human, its high-pitched whining noise was developed to quell rioters and to protect ships at sea. At over 149 decibels, the pulsating sound cannon was louder than a jet engine or gunshot.

"No, you are wounded, Gabby. I will go. Keep the men close together and cover your ears! Tell Dr. Arun!" Estrada climbed the bridge stairs as gunfire ricocheted all around him, pinging off the steel railings. He climbed another short ladder leading to the main mast and then up six more steps to the upper deck. The square-shaped LRAD, attached securely to the white painted railing, overlooked the main deck below. He punched the power switch but nothing happened.

"C'mon! C'mon!" Estrada cried. He slammed it repeatedly with his balled fist until it slowly hummed to life. A green light finally popped on the machine, and Estrada aimed the pulsating sound wave at the invaders.

In seconds, stunned pirates clutched at their ears and howled in excruciating pain. Immediately disabled by the wavering sound stream, many rolled in agony on the deck as *Militobi* crewmen watched in awe, still covering their own ears. Moments later, Fernandez signaled up to Estrada who switched the LRAD off and hurried back down to the main deck. Crewmen tied and herded the pirates together, several gesturing they had become deaf. Kneeling in surrender with their own weapons pointed at them, there was no doubt the pirates understood their reign of terror was over. Dr. Arun quickly examined all the wounded and lifeless bodies sprawled across the deck then checked on Gabby who was assisting his men secure the pirates.

"How's the arm, Mr. Fernandez?"

"Fine, *gracias*, doctor."

"Keep the sling on, okay?"

Fernandez nodded as Estrada joined them and playfully touched his friend's shoulder. Fernandez winced and Estrada grinned. "Gabby, the LRAD was the best investment this ship ever made...when it works. The effect on their hearing will wear off soon. Let's get these people to shore. I hope Anna is there and that she's all right."

* * * * *

Dead pirates floated face down in the lagoon while the luckier ones waded back to shore where migrant fighters waited to place them into custody on the beach. Dr. Arun, Fernandez, and several crewmen arrived on the first lifeboat. They walked to shore in knee-deep water where they were greeted by a relieved Anna Kruger.

"Dr. Arun! Mr. Fernandez! How are you? Dr. Arun, I'm so sorry about Esha."

"I know," he said. "Thank you."

Anna placed both her hands on the doctor's shoulders and looked him straight in the eyes. "Before she died, she told me to tell you how much she loved you and how she believed she was doing the right thing. She saved Lulu's life, you know."

"Thank you, Captain," said Dr. Arun. "I appreciate hearing that." Aside from dirt, blood, and sand in her hair, Anna Kruger appeared to be no worse for wear. "I'm glad you are all right too," the doctor said, giving her a quick scan for injuries. Splotches of dried blood dotted the back of her shirt. "Captain, what happened here?"

"I'll be fine, doctor. It is nothing."

As the second lifeboat arrived, Estrada jumped out into the water and immediately spotted Anna with Dr. Arun.

"Anna!"

"Jorge!" Anna grinned and ran to the husky Spaniard. They embraced. Estrada began to kiss her, but she stopped him with an embarrassed smile. "Jorge, please, not in front of the passengers!" Mortified, Estrada stepped back and resumed a more official role.

"Captain, Mr. Fernandez was wounded but the doctor patched him up. We lost four men, Ma'am. Five wounded. But it could have been much worse."

Anna nodded. "Mr. Estrada, your excellent strategy to split enemy forces was better than Bayern Munich's revolutionary formation that won the German Champions League in 2013! I am proud of you and the entire crew. I am sorry I was not with you."

"Thank you...Captain. You were missed. You were most definitely missed!"

Anna moved closer and lovingly touched Estrada's hand. "I missed you too, Jorge."

Walking past the couple to find the doctor, Fernandez shook his head in bemusement. "Officers!"

* * * * *

Later that day, Okeke Ka, Mohammed Kassab, and Jay Rawal rummaged through drawers and boxes inside Delgado's main house. Okeke was astonished to find the black snake in the glass case and a covered bucket of live mice. Curious, he sat down and tapped on the glass.

"What do we have here? Who are you, little one?" The snake hissed and the chubby African laughed and removed the glass. Unafraid, he snatched the snake behind its head and carried it outside along with the bucket. He walked behind the house to the edge of the jungle where the coils of barbed wire still fenced off the western side of the pirate village. Okeke dumped the mice who scrambled into the brush and then released the snake beneath a cherimoya tree.

"You are not so evil, little one," he said, watching it dart away. "God loves you. Good hunting!"

On the beach, the captured pirates sat tied together in the sand guarded by several of the freed captive women and some of the African, Asian, and Arab fighters. Several had head wounds bandaged with scarves. While the pirates were solemn and stared down into the sand, their futures uncertain, the fighters now joked and teased each other about the battle and how each had outdone the other to achieve victory. Lulu watched her brother wash off in the lagoon and throw away his bloodied shirt. They walked back together up the beach and perused the captive pirates. Lulu's eyes scanned the men and women and then abruptly turned to her brother in surprise.

"Someone is missing!"

"Who?"

"Come on!" Lulu ran down the main path, slinging her bow across her shoulders once again as Ashé raced to catch up.

"Who is missing?"

"Just follow me! Come on!"

Lulu led Ashé off the path, stopping at the galley's tin door. Bow and arrow at the ready, she kicked the door open and edged inside with Ashé five paces behind. Deathly quiet, boxes were overturned, foodstuffs scattered, and broken crockery was strewn everywhere.

Lulu drew her bowstring and called out in a sing-song voice that reminded Ashé of his grandfather, "Where are you Alonso? Where are you, you fat pirate?" As Lulu searched the large cooking area, Ashé moved closer to his sister for protection. "I said *show* yourself or this arrow will pierce your black heart."

In the corner, the balding head of Alonso Rivero appeared through a mountain of pots and pans. Cups, plates, and dishes slid off his body and shattered as he raised his hands.

"Miss Lulu! My little African princess! You have returned to Alonso. You are safe! I am so happy. I've missed you!"

"Let's go, you crazy cook." Lulu gestured with her arrow tip. Ashé backed away as the pirate scurried noisily through the galley toward the door, one eye on the arrow's sharp point.

"Oh, Miss Lulu! Please be careful! Be careful with that! You know Alonso always liked you. How is the Captain and Miss Esha?"

Lulu's face grew dead serious. "They killed her, Alonso. They killed Miss Esha."

Overcome by the news, Alonso began to weep. "Oh no, those idiots! Those bastards! Those stupid Isleños! How could they do such a thing? She was so nice to Alonso." Sobbing, the cook dropped to his knees. "I am so sorry, Miss Lulu. I am so sorry for what they did to Miss Esha. Please forgive me. Forgive me! Alonso is not like that. Alonso's heart is not black. Alonso would not hurt anybody."

Lulu and Ashé exchanged surprised looks. Ashé shrugged.

* * * * *

The next morning at the beach, Anna Kruger spoke with Desta, Jay, and Mohammed Kassab, whose knee was now wrapped in a clean bandage discovered with several other boxes of medical supplies hidden in Delgado's house. Estrada and Fernandez arrived back on the beach in the lifeboat. They slogged through the wet sand and stood before Anna Kruger.

"Captain, all prisoners are loaded into the cargo hold," reported Estrada. "Any remaining medicine and other supplies have been provided to Dr. Arun for distribution. No migrants have requested to board ship and come back with us."

"Very well, Jorge."

At that moment, Ashé and Lulu ran up to say goodbye and asked Jorge and Gabby to send a message to their parents in Senegal that they were alive and still awaiting an opportunity to get to France. Estrada assured them that he would personally see to it that their message was delivered. Lulu wrote down her family's contact information then hugged the two men and thanked them once again. Ashé shook hands with the two *Militobi* officers.

"Take care of yourself, Ashé," said Jorge. "Good luck with the fishing. The reef looks promising."

"Thanks," the teenager replied, a sheepish grin on his face.

"Take care," added Gabby. The two Serer ran off, but Lulu stopped to whisper something to a puzzled Desta as he walked up to join Gabby and Estrada to say goodbye.

"I know both of you will do your best to find a safe place for us."

"We will do our best," said Gabby, shaking the Head Man's hand. "Excuse me; the doctor is over there, and I have a question for him about my arm."

Estrada grinned at the African leader. "Desta, we will try and obtain asylum for all of you as soon as possible but you should know there's a lot of politics to deal with."

"I know," the Head Man said. "I know it will be difficult."

"And thanks for helping us rescue the Captain and the others."

"It is what family should do for family, right?" Estrada nodded, shaking Desta's hand.

"Be safe, my friend."

"I will; you too."

Anna Kruger motioned for Jorge to join her for a walk down the beach. Smiling, she took the Spaniard by the arm and led him away from the others. Jorge waited for Anna to speak first as they strolled along the sand, the wind blowing softly in the morning light.

"Jorge, I have to tell you something, and I know you will be surprised or perhaps even shocked, but I have decided it is for the best. I have been thinking about it for a while now."

"Of course, Captain. Tell me."

Anna grimaced and looked down at the sand. "I have been talking with these folks about me staying here on the island with them." Estrada stopped mid-step to stare directly at Anna. "I know you were not expecting this, but I have come to believe

290

that these migrants do not need a Commandant or a Captain to lead them but perhaps they could use someone like me. Someone to help out. Someone to provide a different perspective. Someone to work with the children. Someone to listen. I think I could be that person."

"But Anna!"

"I thought about this a lot when I was a captive with the other women. Many times I was afraid, but I could tell they were strong. Not all of them, of course, but many. Some were shy and unsure of themselves. I believe, with a little bit of coaching, they can make a difference on this island or in the real world, if that is where they want to go someday."

Estrada could tell that she was serious. "But, Anna I do not under—"

"Hear me out. This could be a place where no one will ever be turned away again because of some quota or some rule or because of the color of their skin."

"But you will be lonely. You will miss your friends."

"*Ja*, at first I will. But I have made many friends here. Like Lulu and Ashé and Dr. Arun and Mr. Okeke and so many others. I know I can help the young girls too. I could help them become productive individuals."

"But the ship?"

"*You* will be able to handle the ship, Jorge. You have proven yourself so many times in the past and again here the last few days. And you have always wanted to lead, to be a Captain."

"But Anna this was not the way I wanted to—"

"You can continue our work! Get back to Germany and refit the ship at Sea-Sweep then go out and rescue more people. Bring them here, if you possibly can! It is uncharted, remember? I will be right here waiting for you. Keep it our secret. A secret place where people can come who have nothing else to lose and nowhere to go. A safe place. Even if it is only a temporary solution."

Estrada could see the look in Anna's eyes was again one of determination. "I know when your mind is made up, Anna."

"You know me too well, Jorge."

"We will...well, *I'll* miss you."

"We will meet again, Jorge. I know it."

Captain Anna Kruger kissed and embraced her First Officer. Estrada saw that Gabby, Desta, Dr. Arun, and others on the beach were watching and grinning at them. He beamed at Anna.

"Please, Captain, not in front of the passengers!"

Gabby Fernandez turned to Dr. Arun and nodded over at the two lovers. "Just like *Casablanca*, no?" Dr. Arun had no idea what he meant.

* * * * *

Sitting in a circle around a fire that night in the old pirate village, the free people of Santa Inez Island celebrated their victory.

"And how will we start this new beginning of ours?" Desta asked the group awaiting dinner. "Estrada told me everything was now up to all of us. We can live any way we want."

"First, tear down those bamboo walls!" Mohammed Kassab exclaimed. "I am too old for such long brutal walks around the circumference of this island." Everyone laughed and held up their coconuts to toast the suggestion.

"We must bury the dead," said Lulu solemnly, and the others nodded in agreement. *I will lead Dr. Arun to Miss Esha tomorrow,* she thought.

"Attend to the wounded and sick." Dr. Arun added.

"Yes," agreed Desta. "All of those things are important and, with the help of our ancestors who I believe are still watching over us, we will be successful."

Sitting close beside Desta, Ada smiled and took his hand in her own. "I believe they do watch over us, as does Awa and our Chiké."

"And God watches over all of *them*," added Okeke.

Suddenly, everyone looked up in surprise as Alonso Rivero appeared, juggling several baskets of food in his arms. He placed one in front of each shocked guest. Desta scowled at the fat cook and made eye contact with Lulu.

"Sister? This is the surprise you were whispering about, today? You wanted *this* man to stay with us?" Afraid of the African village leader, Rivero slowly backed away, generating grins from Lulu and Ashé.

"Yes, this is our secret; our wonderful secret. Alonso *is* a very good cook!" Lulu said.

"And he is *not* like the others," added Ashé.

Alonso Rivero mouthed a *thank you* to Lulu before realizing that he forgot something.

"Oh, more coconuts! Alonso will be right back!" Desta continued to frown as Rivero hurried away, scolding himself, "Stupid! Stupid! Stupid! Alonso, you cannot be stupid for Lulu. She saved your worthless life!"

At sea, Estrada's walkie-talkie squawked to life. "Chief Engineer! As much speed as you can get out of her." Estrada turned to Gabby Fernandez, who was hovering over the chart table. "Navigator? Course set to Tenerife?"

"Aye, it is with the Helmsman...*Captain.*"

"Very well. How far are we from Tenerife?"

"Twelve hours give or take with the weather, Jorge."

"We need to get these pirates to the authorities, Gabby," said Estrada

"Aye, Captain," the Navigator responded. "You know we run the risk of entering Canary Island waters without proper registration or license."

"I know that," Estrada said, frowning.

"That's a year in jail, Captain," added the Helmsman.

Estrada clapped the Helmsman on the shoulder then did the same to Fernandez. "Gentlemen, this ship has prevented over six hundred lives from drowning or starving all over the Med in the past month. Maybe the politicians should *join* us on our next trip, instead of locking us up. What do you say?"

"Having a cargo hold full of pirates may help our credibility too," Fernandez added. Jorge and Gabby stepped outside and stood at the bridge railing. "Do you think we will ever return to Santa Inez Island, Jorge?"

"I hope we will, Gabby. It is a very special place, is it not?"

"It truly is. Do you think she will be all right?"

"You know the Captain. She is one head-strong lady. One day we will return. I can feel it. Can *you* feel it Gabby, or is this just *my* dream?"

"I believe we will return one day. And we must remember to bring her back some soccer balls."

The men laughed. Gabby shook hands with Jorge and returned to the bridge. The new Captain leaned over the railing and stared back in the direction of Santa Inez Island and smiled.

The *Militobi*, carrying its pirate cargo, headed due south for Tenerife, as a waning moon shone bright high above and a sea of stars twinkled in the night's sky.

CHAPTER 11

NEW HORIZONS

In the days following the departure of the *Militobi*, a renewed interest and excitement for attaining asylum spread throughout Santa Inez Island. Many villagers, especially teens and young adults, now placed their hopes with Jorge Estrada and Gabby Fernandez and their promise to advocate for new status. Yet, for many of the battle-scarred migrants, particularly those originally shipwrecked on the MV *Ralik-Ratak* more than two years earlier, new concerns and trepidations had also surfaced. What if someone wanted to stay on the island forever? Was it possible that they could be forced to leave?

Now free of pirate rules and bamboo fences, many migrants made their way across the island to join their fathers, mothers, aunts, uncles, husbands, wives, sons, and daughters who had participated in the life-changing battle. Abandoned pirate sheds, shelters, houses, huts, and shacks, once the sites of drunken brawls, card games, knife fights, and sexual assaults, now served as temporary housing for individuals and families wishing to change their living situations.

The pirate village was renamed New Horizons after a vote from a newly formed ad hoc committee consisting of Anna, Desta, Jay, Imam Ashraf, and Dr. Arun. They agreed to prioritize and complete the tasks most in need of attention around the village and across the island. One of the first ones was to gather and bury the bodies of the fallen. Many were still scattered throughout the area while others continued to wash ashore from the lagoon. It was decided that a mass grave containing the remains of all migrant warriors, no matter their origins, religions, or nationalities, would begin the island's healing process. Dead pirates would be buried together deep in the jungle in a remote location. The hope was that the jungle would rapidly grow over their final resting place, rendering it lost to future generations and ultimately forgotten by all.

A large migrant cemetery was dug just west of the village and served as the gravesite for Esha Rao, whose body was recovered by Dr. Arun under Lulu's guidance, the day following the departure of the *Militobi*. Okeke Ka eulogized Esha as a unique and distinguished healer who fought to alleviate human suffering. More than a hundred mourners attended the brief service. Okeke reminded the attendees of what they had experienced over the past few days and how Esha, while aboard ship, had aided and supported all passengers, no matter their home countries. Anna Kruger, tears welling, added that it was Esha's bravery that had saved Lulu on that fateful day and inspired her to remain on the island to continue the fight for all migrants. Okeke embraced Dr. Arun at the conclusion of the service then led mourners back to New Horizons for a funeral repast. The sky darkened and the wind strengthened. A light rain fell as if to remind the living that the island had now been cleansed of the evil that had once befallen it.

Remaining in New Horizons temporarily to join in discussions on what the future would hold for his people, Desta Kado organized small fishing parties for both men and women to help feed those who stayed. Malian women fashioned tall reed baskets, wide at the open bottom and narrow at the top, to fish for tilapia, crabs, and catfish. Standing side by side in the nearby stream, they would take one step forward, thrust their baskets together into the muddy bottom, and reach through the open top to grab their prizes with bare hands. Men whittled fishing poles from bamboo and made lines and hooks from the *agave* plant, twisting the tip of the thorny shrub into a thin fishing line. The agave is four times stronger than a similar line made of cotton. Its woody barbs made ideal hooks for snaring anadromous fish, like salmon and sea trout, who live in the ocean before breeding in freshwater rivers. Eels and lamprey, catadromous fish born in saltwater but living mainly in fresh or brackish water, were also easily caught by line or in bamboo fish traps.

Clay deposits were discovered along a large riverbank and soon villagers were digging out square blocks of it; removing stones and other organic materials from the blocks; mixing the clay in water; filtering it again by washing it through a cloth sieve; and, drying the clean clay in the sun for a day or two, sometimes longer. Mixed with water a second time, the clay was molded into varying shapes and sizes, often crude bowls or pots. Deep holes were dug near the river and shaped crockery was placed carefully inside so a wood fire could burn above it to solidify and glaze the shapes. While this technique was often effective, the greatest difficulty came during the hours-long cooling process that, depending on the size of the molding, could take up to thirty-six hours. Many times the result was cracked clay or the complete shattering of the vessel. Experimentation continued for many weeks, but soon oddly shaped cups, bowls, jars, and large vats were being used by migrants for everything from carrying water to storing fruits and vegetables.

In a remote section of land about a mile from the Asian village, a large field of cotton was found, and Indian and Bangladeshi women made drop spindles from bamboo and turned cotton balls into thread for making and repairing clothing. Under the direction of an elderly Indian women from Ranchi, bamboo leaves, avocado nuts, and other plants were boiled to make natural dyes and before long colorful head wraps and dresses of green, yellow, and red were spotted in the temple, mosque, and at the weekly prayer service of the Syrian Christians.

Anna Kruger rather enjoyed reconnecting with the sea and decided to make New Horizons her permanent home. She selected a petite house, about the size of two sheds, near the beach and joined a group of men who began rehabbing the three damaged pirate speedboats, all needing repair caused by the *Militobi's* water cannons. The larger *Luhrs Tournament 350* fishing boat lay in shallow water moored to a tree near gasoline drums sunk halfway into the sand. There were six and a half, fifty-five-gallon drums remaining. Anna offered to take the fishing boat out to assess its condition and asked Ashé and Hassan Alwan to join her.

Anna was delighted to take the helm at the boat's freestanding console. Within five minutes, she had pivoted the thirty-five-footer toward the pass in the reef at full speed and headed for open ocean. In choppy seas with a brisk easterly wind at her back, Anna felt truly alive again. The two anglers had immediately let out thick fishing lines with large double bamboo hooks as they searched the horizon for feeding birds, possible indicators of Blue Marlin and Giant Bluefin Tuna. Hassan first spotted the dark birds in the far distance and Anna raced toward them, still at full throttle. Seemingly hundreds of Cory's Shearwaters and three-pound Yellow Legged Gulls dove, one after the other, into the blue water chasing tinier fish who, in turn, were chased by the larger marlins and tunas. The fishing boat cruised right through the middle of the flock, scattering the noisy birds who squawked at the disruption to their feeding frenzy.

It took only a minute for Ashé to feel a jolt on his line and exclaim in English, "I have something!"

Anna cut the engine, and the young Senegalese teenager pulled at the heavy line. Screeching gulls, red rings of feathers circling their eyes, continued to plunge into the sea like a shower of hailstones.

"Pull him in, Ashé!" Hassan shouted above the noise, rechecking his own slack line. Grunting, the teen pulled hand-over-hand but made very little headway. Hassan cupped his eyes from the sunlight and peered in the fishing boat's wake. "I do not see anything yet!" Ten minutes later Ashé continued to struggle, his arms aching.

Finally, some forty-five yards aft, Anna could see something shiny flashing just below the surface. "I see it! I see it!"

"What is it?" Ashé cried, sweat pouring from his forehead and adrenaline pumping.

"It looks very big," said Hassan. "Very big! Do you need help?"

The teen shook his head and pulled until his arms quivered and he felt his fingers growing numb.

"Can you tell what it is, Hassan?" Ashé gasped. "A tuna? It must be a tuna. It is not a marlin or it would have jumped by now!"

Anna and Hassan, standing together, peered into the sea, but the birds' splashing and the sun's bright reflection made it impossible to identify the catch. Whatever it was, the large silvery fish was now only twenty yards astern. The Shearwaters continued to scream and flutter around the boat as Ashé, both arms now numb and tingling, kept steady tension on the line.

"Getting closer," exclaimed Hassan. "It is a big one!" Ashé prayed that he wouldn't lose the fish at the last moment as he had on too many previous fishing expeditions in Senegal.

"Can you hold it, Ashé?" Anna asked, her voice rising as the fish drew near.

"I can do it! I can do it!"

Anna urged him to stay strong. "Just a little bit longer, Ashé! Almost here!"

Leaning over the vinyl rubber railing, Hassan held a six-foot gaff in his hand and waited until the silver head of their prey hit the side of boat before hooking it under its chin and mouth.

"We have it, Ashé!" Tugging hard with both hands, Hassan pulled the long silvery fish into the boat.

"Look out!" Anna warned.

Ashé dropped his line and fell backwards as the sleek torpedo-shaped body slammed against the bulkhead, sharp teeth lunging at the teen's foot.

"Barracuda!" Anna yelled.

Hassan grasped the gaff. "Get back!"

Ashé jumped up the cockpit's steps. Hassan smashed the gaff repeatedly at the barracuda's head until it thrashed no more. He sank back against the railing and scanned the sleek fish.

"It is at least seventy pounds, Ashé. Biggest one I have ever seen!"

"Biggest one I have ever caught!"

Anna smiled at the new African and Arab friends. In their heart of hearts, they were just fishermen. Young men happy to do what they loved to do. She felt the familiar thrill of the sea's movement beneath the boat and smiled to herself. She had not felt that thrill in quite a while. No pirates; no hostages; no fighting. Just the salt sea air and that exquisite inner delight that comes when landing a big fish. This is what was missing, she realized. This was what she had longed for: that feeling of being at one with the sea.

That evening, Alonso Rivero slathered barracuda fillets in salt and marinated them in a concoction of onions, ginger, garlic, and lime juice. Grilled to perfection, he adorned them with pineapple slices and served them in plaited baskets. Anna smiled broadly as Hassan related the story of how Ashé landed the greatest fish he had ever seen. Lulu beamed at her brother. Ashé could not have been happier.

When he wasn't fishing, Ashé was also happy to assist Dr. Arun and Anna in organizing the health clinic in Commandant Delgado's large wooden house. It had ample space for tables and chairs to be rearranged into an office and examination room. Before he departed, Anna had directed Jorge to empty the ship's infirmary to provide Dr. Arun with bandages, blankets, sheets, a small microscope, and the remainder of medicines they had aboard. It was not enough for what was needed but it was a good start.

Dr. Arun developed a schedule and spent three days per month in each of the Western villages. Fearful of cholera, malaria, diabetes, and measles, especially in children and pregnant women, he conducted routine examinations with as many people as he could during each trip. He was astonished, however, to find virtually no symptoms. No runny noses, coughs, eye infections, fevers, or rashes in any of the villages. Okeke Ka said it was God's blessing that protected the island from disease. Desta Kado said it was their ancestors, still on the job. Luckily, the most serious medical problem Dr. Arun encountered was a broken arm suffered from a fall from a fifteen-foot coconut tree by a New Horizons teenager.

The first birth in New Horizons was an African baby boy, christened Chiké, by Reverend Okeke Ka. The pregnant woman and her husband had arrived at the new clinic a week before the anticipated event. Heartened by the successful birth and the seemingly rapid increase in the number of pregnant women, Dr.

Arun had recruited a Health Aide from each village and within three months had conducted basic training in first aid, CPR, the dressing of wounds, and in the handling of fractures, burns, and shock. The setting of the teenager's broken arm, caused by a fall while gathering coconuts, served as a real-time, practical demonstration during one of the training sessions. At graduation, each Health Aide was provided a basic supply of bandages, tape, two sheets, and two blankets, thereby establishing the first Santa Inez Island health care system.

Faced with the realization that asylum would still require a considerable wait on an island with really nothing to do, the creativity of bored young adults and teenagers was challenged to the extreme. Some found solace hunting, while others in fishing or growing a variety of fruits and vegetables. Some tried their hand at pottery making. Others joined groups to study the Quran or the Bible. Several joined a team of builders led by Amman Boulas, the Libyan carpenter. It seemed there was no shortage of rain catchments needing repair, pit latrines needing digging, and roofs needing fixing, especially after heavy rains or high winds. Requests were constant from all four villages for tables, shelving, and other furniture. Many Arab villagers wanted to add large courtyards to their existing homes for private worshipping by women and girls.

Boulas was glad to have more volunteer help and happy to teach interested young apprentices how to select wood and make tools: the basics of island carpentry. The Juniper tree was the primary source for hand tools. Using sharpened stones as wedges for splitting green branches and smaller saplings, Amman demonstrated to interested craftsmen how to make wooden mallets and hammers. His ever-expanding crew of builders and carpenters required thousands of yards of rope to meet the increasing demand for new construction throughout the island. Making rope required three teams of apprentices. After strands of coconut fiber were beaten, soaked in a river for several weeks, then laid in the sun to dry, the fibers were fed through the eye of a coconut shell while team members, standing on the other side, twisted and stretched it into a long, single strand. Each team then twisted their lengths together to form a three-strand rope, about a half-inch in diameter. This strong rope was used to lash bamboo poles and pandanus limbs to wooden frames and to tie together sections of walls, catchments, and roofs.

* * * * *

The romance between Desta Kado and Ada Niame had been, since the death of Ada's husband at the hands of the pirates almost a year earlier, a rather one-sided affair. Ada and Chiké, her son, had been virtually adopted by the village leader who had provided them with food and physical protection but seemingly did not reciprocate Ada's growing affection for him except through brief glances, an occasional touch, and a few kind words. After the great pirate battle, Desta returned to the African village only to become despondent and depressed but, on the positive side, more open about his growing feelings toward Ada. She spoke to him one night soon after making his usual rounds through the village.

"What is troubling you, Desta? You seem to be sad all the time now. It is not like you."

"It is just that things are changing very quickly with the pirates gone." Ada lounged on his floor mat, as comfortable in his home as she was in her own.

"Are you hungry?" Ada asked, but Desta shook his head. "Did I make you sad? Did I say something to make you sad?" He shook his head again.

"Of course not, Ada. You could never make me sad."

"I am very glad to hear that. Very glad. And, I too am happy the pirates are gone." Ada moved closer to the handsome Head Man and embraced him. "What is it then? You look troubled."

"Our village is different now, Ada. We are becoming a village of young children and the elderly who watch over them. So many have moved to New Horizons." His face registered frustration. Ada squeezed him tighter; the man for whom she prayed each night.

"It does feel like things are changing," Ada said. "Asylum may not be far away. You cannot blame the younger people for wanting to leave the island, can you?"

"No, you are right, Ada. How would you feel if your only future was to stay here in this village?"

"As long as I was here with you, I would not mind it."

Desta smiled and kissed her. "I feel the same, but some of the younger ones would feel differently. They would be angry. If I were their age, I would be angry too."

Over the next few weeks, Desta found himself in friendly debates late into the night with his close friend, Balla Mendy, who was eager to leave the island.

"But Desta, we have been here almost a year and a half," the Gambian complained. "And we still do not know when we will be accepted in the Canaries or anywhere else. Do you believe the rescue ship will help us, as they promised?"

"The Spanish officer, Estrada, will help us. I am sure of it. He is a good man."

"But what if he fails? What if we are never granted asylum anywhere?"

Desta frowned. "What do you think you will find in the Canaries anyway, Balla?"

"A place to call my own! A place where I can use my cell phone again. A place where I can go to the movies and my children can go to school."

"You have no children."

Balla took a long sip from a coconut and snorted. "A place to *find* a wife and have some then! I do not understand you. Did you not take the same journey that I have taken? Did we not come to this island on the same ship? Were we not told this would only be a temporary stay until the laws changed in the Canaries?"

Desta nodded. "Yes, we were told that by pirates who lied to us about everything."

"But it is hard to wait so long. It drives me crazy sometimes."

"You do know there are many others who have been here twice as long as we have."

"I know, but it is hard to believe they have not gone mad."

Desta shrugged. "Some have said they feel anxious at times about leaving, like you. But since the great battle, they do not even speak of it."

Balla was incredulous. "You mean they do not want to leave? Ever?" Desta shrugged. "And what about you, Desta? Do you not want to leave?"

The village leader considered the question. "It has bothered me before. I have asked myself, how can one live in a place with nowhere to go and nothing to do?"

"Exactly! And what was your answer?"

"I have come to believe that it does not matter where I live. Whether it is here on this island or in the Canaries or even back in Sierra Leone. It just does not matter to me anymore. I am finding peace in just living each day. I have a good woman who loves me. I have food. I have friends. I have ancestors that watch over me. I am at peace. But I know that you, and especially some of the younger ones, do not share my opinion."

Balla Mendy shook his head in disbelief.

* * * * *

The construction of Reverend Okeke Ka's chapel near the great waterfall was completed with the bamboo remnants of the pirate fence that once prohibited all villagers from the eastern half of the island. It was one of the first fences to be torn down following the battle with the pirates. The disassembled poles were stacked in large piles for future use and not burned, as suggested by Imam Ashraf as punishment for the evil their construction symbolized. Ironically, the chapel with its hope for eternal peace was erected not fifty yards from the site of Esha's murder.

The first prayer service was announced, and the island turnout was overwhelming. Entourages from all four villages arrived and camped out in the nearby clearing. While there were only a handful of Christians who actually entered the chapel for services, more than a hundred people sat just outside to listen to Okeke Ka who had become somewhat of an island personality, given his cheerful demeanor, inspirational nature, and his regular visits to all the other villages. There was no one on the island he had not befriended. Villagers had begun referring to him as *Reverend* Okeke. He had not objected.

Anna Kruger listened patiently from one of the six wooden pews carved by Amman Boulas and his crew of young carpenters. Three were placed on each side of the one-room chapel, divided by a single matted aisle down its center leading to a colorful, flower-decked altar. Okeke delivered his first sermon about friendship and the need to work and live together.

He began by quoting the Bible. " *'How good and pleasant it is when God's people live together in unity.'* " Anna glanced around the tiny place of worship and found there were eight Africans, four

Asians, and two Syrians. She wondered if regular prayer services like this were effective in reinforcing the camaraderie generated by the success of the pirate battle. *Could religion mend distrust and anger between the races or just intensify it? Could the comfort that religion brought to so many be reflected in new behaviors and a spirit of cooperation? Or, would the literal interpretation of the Bible and Quran by many village elders conflict with a generation of young people who wanted to live their lives differently?*

Following the service, Anna was greeted by Imam Ashraf, Mohammed Kassab, and several other Arabs who sat enjoying the beauty of the picturesque chapel framed by the enormous waterfall spilling down into clear blue pools. Akila Samar, one of the original passengers on the *Ralik-Ratak*, waited for Anna.

"Captain, the Imam and I are teaching school at our mosque. Would you be willing to speak to our students sometime? They have many questions."

Honored by the request, Anna immediately agreed. "Of course, but what would you like me to talk about?"

"They have asked where you came from? How you came to stay on this island, and..." she hesitated.

"Yes," Anna said. "Go on."

"And why you remained with us when you could have returned to your family? We hope you will also tell us about your life as a sea captain." It dawned upon Anna that Akila's request could be interpreted as sign that her decision to stay on the island was indeed the right one.

Akila Samar, a former elementary school teacher in Tripoli, was glad to have convinced Imam Ashraf that all the boys and girls in the Arab village should be taught together, although she acquiesced to his insistence that they be separated when studying religion. The schoolgirls who gathered at Akila's newly built home courtyard, completed in record time by her betrothed Amman Boulas and his crew, fascinated the young teacher. She found that they were much more advanced than the boys in many ways. Not only did they appear to be better readers, perhaps because of their parents' regular Quran study at home, but the boys just did not seem that interested in learning much of anything.

Akila also believed her girls quickly grasped the deeper meanings of the religious lessons they were being taught. For example, a lesson on the rights of Muslim women had resulted in a spirited discussion on their ability to marry the person of their choice, their right to divorce, and, personally important to Akila, their right to vote. The Libyan teacher soon believed this new generation of Arab women would be the strongest ever, and she was overjoyed that she could contribute to their development. It had taken her several weeks to subtly convince Imam Ashraf that Captain Kruger's appearance would contribute to his goal of increasing parental involvement and support for the school. She knew many adults would be quite interested in hearing Captain Kruger's story as much as her students. Akila was thrilled with Anna's immediate acceptance.

Anna's willingness to work with Akila Samar's young students fulfilled one of her own goals and was a key reason for choosing to stay on the island. She relished the opportunity to teach young girls and knew that it would also serve as a wake up call for Lulu, who was moping around lately without much to do. Anna quite enjoyed her private conversations with Lulu. Typically, after one of Alonso Rivera's delicious lunches, the two women would walk south along the beach past the speedboats undergoing repair. She was learning more and more about the Senegalese teen, including some information that totally astounded her. While she knew Lulu and Ashé were on their way to Paris, their tortuous journey through the Sahara was almost too shocking to believe. Not only had Lulu saved Ashé by nearly cutting the throats of two men, but they had barely avoided being captured and probably shot in Sebha, only one hundred miles from Tripoli. Lulu had told her the story.

"The *Yafars* nearly caught us just as our caravan arrived. A young Nigerien named Mashoul led us through the streets to escape the *technicals;* those are the trucks with machine guns on top of the cab. He said the *Yafars* wanted a Gaddafi-type military man to rule Libya again like their leader, Field Marshal Yafar."

"How did you escape?" Anna asked.

"We hid. Mashoul told us to meet him on the other side of town to pick up the truck caravan later. It was very scary, Anna. There were guns, and sirens, and flashing lights."

"But you found the caravan again."

"We were very lucky. I hope Mashoul was too. We never saw him again."

Down the beach in front of them, African, Arab, and Asian children tossed stones in the lagoon, laughing and playing together. As Anna watched them chase each other, fall in the sand, and then chase each other again, she was struck with an idea.

"Do you see those children?"

"They are so cute," Lulu smiled, watching them play.

"Do you know who they are?"

Lulu stared at her friend. "No, do you know them?"

"Why yes, those are *your* students playing down there, Lulu!"

"My what?"

"You have always wanted to be a teacher, and now is your chance. I will speak to their parents. You could use the galley as your classroom. It has the most space. What do you think? I am a kind of a teacher now so you can be too!"

Lulu was speechless and Anna laughed and clapped her on both shoulders. "I know! It is overwhelming. Aren't you excited?"

"What can I teach them? I have no idea what to do, Anna!"

"Remember what you told me once about your teacher back in Senegal? She said that teaching was the best way to help your country and your people. Well, this island is your country for the time being and these children are your people. Teach them English or French, or both! My grandfather used to tell me that first you needed an education and, second, you needed to be bilingual in English. It is time for you to step up to this challenge, young lady. It will be fun. I will help you. Akila will help you too!"

No one was more eager to assist Lulu set up her classroom than Alonso Rivera. He moved tables and benches and cleaned up around the galley to make room for the school children. He stood at the door each morning pleading with the children not to keep Lulu waiting. Accompanied by wary parents, Lulu welcomed eight students and grouped them by ages at different tables. A few older children could speak some English and a few more could speak some French, so she began a conversation with them that allowed her to assess their comprehension levels in both languages. For the first time in the village of New Horizons, school was in session.

After a week of lessons, Lulu had paired an older student with a younger one to sharpen accents and increase vocabulary. However, the word soon got out that there was a school in session and one morning Lulu had more than twenty students show up for her class. She continued to divide her students by age and ability. Older children met in the afternoons while the younger ones attended a short morning class. Alonso prepared snacks for all the students. The younger ones, with shorter attention spans, were often accompanied by a parent or an interested villager who would sit on one side of the room by the door to listen. Often Lulu became frustrated when someone would loudly whisper a word or phrase to help a child respond with a correct answer.

The older students were easier to manage. Anna Kruger often joined them and found herself engaged in stimulating

English conversations, especially about her childhood in Germany. Surrounded by teens asking questions about her travels to places like India and Pakistan, she was impressed that they also asked about difficulties she experienced working with crews from other cultures, like the Philippines, Spain, and Italy. Within a few months, parents began seeking out Lulu to ask for progress reports on their children, some even asked for grades. Lulu admitted to Anna how uneasy she felt about comparing one student to another, knowing their parents would discuss the evaluations with each other. Although Anna sympathized, she thought it very positive that parents were interested in their children's learning. While Lulu feared it could lead to unhappy parents blaming her for not really knowing how to teach, Anna believed Lulu was successfully facing the challenging task of becoming an effective teacher.

* * * * *

Raised a Christian in her native Swaziland, Ada Naime yearned to be officially married in the church. Some eight months following the great pirate battle, she finally persuaded Desta to request Okeke Ka to officiate their wedding at his new chapel near the waterfall. Amman Boulas and his team of carpenters volunteered to erect a temporary bamboo shelter with a palm leaf roof in the clearing. Okeke knew the wedding would be well attended and wanted to protect the invited guests, especially the elderly, from the hot sun or, God forbid, a heavy downpour. Using more of the bamboo from the dismantled old fence, the shelter was completed the evening before the big event. That night, Ada was *kidnapped* by her six closest friends, including

Lulu, to spend the evening together away from the men. They laughed and sang and told insulting jokes about married life and war stories about old boyfriends and current husbands.

Friends from the Asian village, including Jay Rawal, Mohamed Aboud, and many others, were invited to the island-wide celebration. Reverend Okeke walked miles to the Arab village himself to invite Imam Ashraf, Akila Samar, and his close friend Mohammed Kassab, who still favored his injured knee. Migrants from every island village gathered in the clearing by the waterfall on a bright and sunny Sunday—the wedding day of Desta and Ada. Guests from the Arab village brought three live goats as a gift to the newlyweds. The Asian village attendees, those not Muslims, brought two baked pigs as a contribution to the post-wedding feast. The very notion that Desta Kado, the African Head Man and hero of the great pirate battle, was marrying the wife of his late best friend, was the talk and the delight of every island inhabitant.

Ada's six friends began the traditional African wedding procession at noon by singing and dancing as they escorted the bride, wearing a long, red-dyed dress with tiny tribal shields painted down the front. As they made their way toward the chapel, they stopped suddenly and pretended that the groom was missing and nowhere to be found. Onlookers, especially the Arab and Asian guests sitting beneath the newly built shelter, were startled at first by the unexpected dramatics but eventually joined in the frivolity. Everyone laughed as the African guests pointed to different parts of the clearing to help in the search for the missing bridegroom. Desta sat on the ground beside his Best Man, Balla Mendy, at the nearest waterfall pool and was finally *found* by the women amid gales of laughter, teasing, and catcalls. Rising to their feet, all smiles, Desta and Balla were pushed and prodded by the women who continued their musical progression to the church.

The two men entered the chapel and joined Reverend Okeke at its tiny altar. Ashé, standing uneasily at the entrance and dressed in an oversized white shirt that Anna had lent him, awaited Ada and her female entourage. Her red gown shimmering in the midday sun, Ada was accompanied by her bridesmaids who entered the church still singing and dancing. Ada walked down the short center aisle carrying a bouquet of lavender and white marguerites with Ashé at her side. She dabbed at tears spilling from her dark brown eyes. Okeke Ka, standing proudly on the altar step, smiled at the gathering of his closest friends. Ada kissed and hugged Ashé, who gave the bride away. Desta shook his hand.

The chubby Ghanaian officiant read from the Bible in English, "'*Love is patient, love is kind. It does not envy, it does not boast, it is not proud. It does not dishonor others, it is not self-seeking, it is not easily angered, it keeps no record of wrongs.*'"

Desta surprised an unsuspecting Ada with a ring that had been given to him by one of the wives of a village elder who had kept it secreted away for going on three years.

"Ada, I know that Awa and Chiké are watching over us at this moment," Desta said, placing the ring on her finger. "I know that they have joined with our ancestors to watch over us always."

Weeping gently, Ada nodded as she whispered, "Yes, I know they are. I know they are." She lifted her ring finger to her lips and kissed it.

The wedding feast was expertly prepared by the women of the African village. Alonso Rivera inhaled the aroma of roasted pig and fried fish and examined the side dishes of potatoes, onions, carrots, fried bananas, breadfruit slices, and mounds of other fruits and vegetables before pronouncing the feast perfect in every way. The African villagers had come to know Ada as the most helpful and loyal a friend they could have or ever imagine. Any woman who had lost both her husband and child on this uncharted island so far from home, yet remained so positive and caring, was a woman who earned the respect of the entire island. Dr. Arun congratulated the couple as did a long line of visitors from all four of the island's villages.

Jay Rawal took the groom aside as Ada was carted away by her girlfriends who gawked over her wedding ring.

"Ada will make you a wonderful wife, my African friend."

"I have no doubt of that."

"But will *you* make her a wonderful husband? That is what we do not know."

Desta grinned. "I will do my best, my trouble-making Pakistani friend."

"You are always welcome in our village, Desta. Let us go hunting for rabbit soon. I know the best places."

"You mean you know the best places in the *Arab* and *African* sectors?"

Now it was Jay's turn to grin. "There are no *sectors* anymore, Head Man, but yes, that is *exactly* what I mean!" Both men laughed and embraced each other. Anna stepped forward and shook the groom's hand.

"My congratulations, Desta; I hope you and Ada will be very happy." Anna appeared noticeably distracted.

"Thank you, Captain."

"Please, call me Anna."

"Is everything all right with you, Anna?"

"*Ja*, of course; weddings always make me a little sad."

"Are you happy that you remained with us on the island? Has it been what you were looking for? Hoping for?"

Anna paused before answering. "Working with the young students has been wonderful as has helping Dr. Arun. Perhaps I am just a bit homesick."

"I missed my relatives and friends for a long time after we came here, even with my own people all around me. You have no one, but all of us are happy you are here."

Anna was appreciative of his comment. "Then I am happy too."

* * * * *

One of the remaining island priorities was to find the MV *Yap Islander.* Lucia Santos had admitted months earlier that the ship remained hidden somewhere on the island. Was she lying? After all, she was under duress with *crazy ants* swirling over her stomach at the time. But why would she lie about it? Rumors about the whereabouts of the smuggler's ship flew across the island and into the hearts and minds of nearly every teenager aching to leave Santa Inez. Elderly gossipers imagined the ship had been sunk offshore by Commandant Delgado when he realized the battle was lost. Island youths, who dreamed of sailing it to freedom, imagined that it was somewhere near the old pirate village, just waiting to start engines and set sail. But where could it really be and what happened to it?

Anna Kruger cajoled Desta and Jay Rawal into joining her to form a search party. Mohammed Kassab begged off, now under Dr. Arun's orders to rest his ailing knee. Ashé and Lulu volunteered to accompany the exploration team on its hunt for the missing freighter; the old smuggler's ship that had brought Desta, Jay, and Awa Niame's family to the island almost two years earlier. Desta led the group through the jungle north from New Horizons, past the cemetery, and followed several overgrown paths for almost two hours before emerging onto the rocky shoreline.

"Let's follow the beach for a while," suggested Anna. "Delgado never knew when the Spanish authorities might show up. He would want to make a quick escape. If there *is* a ship, it cannot be too much farther." They walked less than a half-mile before reaching a hidden cove, protected from the sea by large banyan and cherimoya trees. By sheer luck, Ashé spotted mooring lines drooping between two sturdy dracaena trees. The ship appeared untouched with wide palm leaves now brushing the side of its rusting hull.

"They did a good job of hiding her," Anna said, leaping up to grab one of the lines and pulling herself hand-over-hand to the ship's railing. "We did not spot her when we first came around this side of the island. We must have sailed right past this inlet looking for a break in the reef."

The others followed Anna's lead and soon the group was searching the late Captain Hassan Al Bourké's ship, the two-hundred-foot *Yap Islander*. Anna immediately headed below decks, brushing through several spiders' webs to the engine room. The musty chamber was damp and lifeless. Groping in the dark, she located the main oil, cooling, and fuel systems. There was plenty of diesel left, but she knew it would have to be hand-pumped to ever get the emergency generator running. The stand-alone battery packs, still in their casings, were stowed exactly where they should have been on a vertical supply rack. Anna realized the ship's batteries would also need hand-cranking to get lights, air compressors, and cooling pumps working again. She sighed and wished her *Militobi* Chief Engineer was with her. He could start a cold ship in an hour.

Exploring the bridge, Jay Rawal found that the radio and sonar could be made operational when, and if, power was ever restored. Desta and the two teenagers searched crew cabins both forward and aft and found a plethora of useful supplies including twin-sized bunks, pillows, sheets, blankets, plastic buckets, tables, and various sizes of coat hooks and towel rods. In the Captain's cabin, Desta discovered a small refrigerator, a sofa, a shower curtain, towels, and a carton of toilet paper.

Most of the cabins had tiny sinks with mirrors attached to their bulkheads. Lulu stopped before one and gasped, aghast at her reflection. *I can't look like this,* she thought, and began to sob just as Anna Kruger entered the dimly lit compartment.

"Oh, Lulu. What is it, dear? Are you all right?" Anna hugged her.

"I am such a mess!" Lulu moaned.

Anna chuckled gently and held the teenager close, pausing for a moment to glance at herself in the mirror.

"My dear, you are *not* a mess." Anna moved closer to the mirror and grimaced. "I know what a mess is. *This* is a mess!"

Lulu grinned. "You are not a mess, Captain."

"Ha! I am what you call a very big mess. And I am not your Captain any longer."

"You will always be my Captain, Captain." They both laughed at the ridiculous statement.

"Yes, I will always be your Captain-Captain," Anna repeated, and they both laughed again.

Ashé stopped in the passageway outside the cabin. Plastic buckets hung from each arm while he balanced a teetering stack of sheets and towels piled high atop his head.

"Lulu! Help me!"

Lulu dried her eyes on her sleeve and sneered at the mirror as she left. "I am *not* a mess!"

Over the next few days, the group made its way to the *Yap Islander* several more times to retrieve various items anyone deemed worthy of saving, carrying them back to be sorted and stored in empty New Horizons huts. Lulu and Ashé, exhausted from carrying heavy boxes of tools and clothing through the jungle, sprawled on the swept floor of the health clinic to watch Dr. Arun inventory medical supplies and refold his new sheets, towels, and pillowcases.

"Dr. Arun?" Ashé asked from a prone and relaxed position on the floor. "Do you ever think about leaving this island? I mean, since we found the ship I've been thinking about it."

The Pakistani stopped for a moment and shook his head. "No, my work is here now with the people of this island. And, my Esha is here too." Anna entered, overhearing his comment, and turned to the two teenagers.

"What about you two? Ever think about leaving?"

"I never thought about it until we found the *Yap Islander*," said Ashé. "I thought that maybe we could get it running and leave on it someday. But there is still nowhere for us to go, is there?"

Anna shrugged. "Not at this time, I'm afraid. Hopefully it won't be too much longer."

"Someday I want to get back home," Ashé exclaimed. "Home to Senegal. Home to my family. Home to my delta!"

"Nothing wrong with that," added Dr. Arun, fluffing up new pillows.

"But we will have to make do here until we have the chance to find asylum," Lulu opined. "But it won't be forever, will it?"

"Not forever," said Anna.

"We have the right to live in peace, don't we?" Lulu asked, that determined tone in her voice reappearing. "It's not asking *too* much, is it?"

Anna shook her head. "No, it is not."

"There must be a country that will eventually accept us," Lulu said. "But I know many of the older people want to stay here. They should be allowed to do that too, if they want."

"I agree," said Dr. Arun. "I plan to stay."

"No one should be *prevented* from finding a safe place to live, right?" Lulu asked.

"I believe that," agreed Anna.

"Well, we can wait awhile longer but not forever," said Lulu, using that determined voice again.

"We can be as happy or as unhappy as we want to be on this island," offered Dr. Arun. "Until things change and there are more options, I choose to be happy."

Anna pondered his statement. "I like the way you put that, doctor. I choose to be happy too."

"Me too," the teenagers said together.

CHAPTER 12

AFTERMATH

After turning the captured pirates over to the authorities in Tenerife without penalty or fine and with the heartfelt thanks of the local police as well as the *undying gratitude* of the *Guardia Civil,* Jorge Estrada had immediately contacted Sea-Sweep officials in Germany. He concocted a story about Captain Anna Kruger volunteering to stay with the six hundred *Militobi* migrants to help acclimate them to their new homes. Thinking he meant they had been smuggled into the Canary Islands, Sea-Sweep officials recognized the illegality of releasing so many undocumented migrants in a country with a ban on accepting asylum-seekers and, therefore, said no more about her disappearance.

Jorge Estrada sent a registered letter to Senegal alerting the Gaye family that their children were safe but was vague in identifying their exact location. He wrote they were still awaiting asylum and his organization was working fervently to help them resolve their immigration status. Jorge and Gabby Fernandez continued to lobby Sea-Sweep officials to strengthen their efforts to petition for the asylum of all the migrant passengers who had been rescued by the *Militobi.* They also requested asylum for hundreds of others from such ships as the *Ralik-Ratak* and the *Yap Islander.* According to immigration officials, this was a rather bizarre request since those two ships were reported lost at sea years earlier.

The *Militobi* remained in the Port of Santa Cruz de Tenerife for a month undergoing Sea-Sweep sanctioned minor repairs and the recruiting of four new seamen for the return voyage to Germany. The ship arrived back in Regensburg without delay and spent the next four months in dry dock before heading out to sea once more. Jorge Estrada, now the ship's official Captain, made sure that water cannons and the LRAD were operating effectively before they departed. Several sniper rifles and numerous boxes of ammunition were now locked safely in separate bridge closets. Over the next three months the *Militobi* made numerous rescues, rendezvousing with crowded rafts off the coasts of Egypt and Libya.

Extremely anxious about Anna and the rest of the migrants on Santa Inez Island, Estrada and the crew of the *Militobi* remained on the lookout for an excuse to divert their ship to the Atlantic. Their chance came a month later at a mid-sea transferring of eighty African and Arab migrants rescued by a non-profit group operating out of Libya. Although the mission was to sail the migrants to a detention center in Lampedusa, Italy, Captain Estrada and Navigator Fernandez agreed that an option should be presented to the passengers for a safer destination with zero chance of detention and ultimate deportation: Santa Inez Island. Of course, the alternative to stay with the ship and take their chances at the southern Italian migrant camp was also offered. The passengers decided that another week at sea to explore the first option sounded better, and the *Militobi* followed the same course it had taken nearly eighteen months earlier.

Loaded with extra food, gas drums, diesel fuel, and a bag of soccer balls kept for months in a locker for safekeeping, the week-long trip found fair weather and calm seas. After an anxious nighttime passage through the Straits of Gibraltar, once again eluding the Spanish Maritime Rescue Service, Santa Inez Island appeared on the horizon the morning of the seventh day at sea. Gabby Fernandez navigated the ship through the reef's eastern pass where the rusted hulk of the *Ralik-Ratak* still lay splayed over the sharp coral at the lagoon's entrance.

Walking along the beach early that morning, Ashé Gaye spotted the newly painted white and blue ship with bright red crosses now prominently featured across both the port and starboard sides. As the ship entered the azure-blue lagoon, he raced to the old pirate's bell, ringing it repeatedly. As more and more villagers ran to the beach, Ashé sprinted to Anna's house.

"A ship! A ship, Anna!"

As the beach filled with onlookers, Anna Kruger watched as six men rapidly cleared the giant palm leaves protecting the three repaired speedboats from the sun. Outboard engines were started and each boat sped off to meet the rescue ship.

Jorge Estrada stepped outside the bridge and peered expectantly toward the island with his binoculars. The refurbished ship dropped anchor where, seemingly so long ago, it had rigged for battle with Commandant Delgado's pirate horde.

Her heart racing, Anna Kruger ran to the beach, shading her eyes from the morning sunlight. She immediately recognized its superstructure. It was the *Militobi!* Standing ankle deep a few steps into the warm water, she reflected on the time she had spent on the island. She had befriended many, guided Lulu into the classroom, facilitated Ashé's return to fishing, taught at several village schools, found the *Yap Islander*, and provided support to Dr. Arun's efforts at the clinic. Of course, there was always more to do. There were always greater contributions to make. And, while she knew the next year or so would be a challenge for everyone on the island, she believed this was the place she was meant to be. It was the fulfillment of her grandfather's wish—and now her own.

THE END

ANOTHER FREE BONUS!

Do you want to read even more about Ashé and Lulu's desert trek?

Download "A Dangerous Journey Through the Sahara."

Available for FREE here:
https://braddude.com/findingeden/deletedscenes

OTHER BOOKS BY BRAD DUDE

Quick! I Need to be a Leader in 30 Days!

40 Tips for Figuring Out Your Boss!

Keeping Our Teens Safe on the Road Should Be: No Accident!

The Great Shadow's 5 Christmas Secrets!

Successfully Applying the Basic Elements of Temperament: At Home!

What Makes You Tick and What Ticks You Off

(www.braddude.com)

www.ingramcontent.com/pod-product-compliance
Lightning Source LLC
Chambersburg PA
CBHW072203130726
47910CB00011B/1799